EMPRESSES

of

SEVENTH AVENUE

EMPRESSES

of

SEVENTH AVENUE

World War II, New York City,
and the
Birth of American Fashion

Nancy MacDonell

ST. MARTIN'S PRESS

NEW YORK

First published in the United States by St. Martin's Press, an imprint of St. Martin's Publishing Group

EMPRESSES OF SEVENTH AVENUE. Copyright © 2024 by Nancy MacDonell Robertson. All rights reserved. Printed in the United States of America. For information, address St. Martin's Publishing Group, 120 Broadway, New York, NY 10271.

www.stmartins.com

Designed by Omar Chapa

Endpaper images by Louise Dahl-Wolfe © Center for Creative Photography, Arizona Board of Regents

The Library of Congress Cataloging-in-Publication Data is available upon request.

ISBN 978-1-250-28873-8 (hardcover)
ISBN 978-1-250-28874-5 (ebook)

Our books may be purchased in bulk for promotional, educational, or business use. Please contact your local bookseller or the Macmillan Corporate and Premium Sales Department at 1-800-221-7945, extension 5442, or by email at MacmillanSpecialMarkets@macmillan.com.

First Edition: 2024

10 9 8 7 6 5 4 3 2 1

For Francesca

CONTENTS

EMPRESSES

of

SEVENTH AVENUE

INTRODUCTION

Before World War II, the American fashion industry was built on the conviction that the French were the only possible arbiters of style, with centuries of savoir faire to back up their claim. The clothes that were produced by American manufacturers, sold in American stores, promoted by American tastemakers, and covered in the American press were rarely the work of American designers, who spent most of their professional lives imitating or simply copying the output of their Parisian colleagues. When they ventured to express original ideas, these were all too often deemed unworthy, uninteresting, and unwanted. The result was that American designers were relegated to second-class status. And because the name of the manufacturer or the store, not the designer, appeared on the label, they often toiled in anonymity.

Elizabeth Hawes was different. Though she was Paris-trained, the American designer refused to follow Parisian dictates at her successful fashion house in New York. By the 1930s, she was a household name, and American fashion's first real star. She detailed her dim view of the practice of copying French design in a best-selling book, *Fashion Is Spinach*, in 1938. The American fashion industry, in Hawes's view, was continually trying to sell women what they didn't want or need—i.e., spinach—while brightly pretending it was something else. The culprit was their obsession with Paris, or what she termed "the French Legend": the widespread belief that all beautiful clothes were made by French couturiers and all women wanted those clothes.[1] Hawes, like a handful of other American designers, had her own made-to-order business; she was, in essence, a couturier herself. Her unusual fame and success emboldened her to state publicly that it was time to put a stake through the French Legend's heart.

It made no sense, Hawes pointed out, that just because the Marquise de X wore a particular dress to the races at Auteuil that a typist in Brooklyn should wear the same style to Coney Island; women who ordered their wardrobes from haute couture houses led completely different lives, with completely different needs, from women who shopped for ready-to-wear on a budget. But American fashion executives of the era insisted on conflating these two groups of women. In the 1930s, just as they had for decades, the couturiers of Paris held American taste in a silken vise grip.

Then the Nazis invaded Paris, and everything changed.

Fashion is not a natural codicil to war. But World War II, and specifically the fall of Paris, had a profound effect on the American fashion industry. When the Nazis marched into the French capital, the flow of ideas that had for so long been considered vital to American fashion stopped as abruptly as if a spigot had been turned. American designers were suddenly faced with the necessity of completing their fall collections without any input from Paris, a situation they had never encountered before. The manufacturers and retailers who employed them quaked at gambling on designs that lacked the preapproval of one of the great Paris couturiers. In Manhattan's Garment District, people asked themselves if American women, who had been trained to think of Paris as fashion's version of the *Good Housekeeping* Seal of Approval, would buy anything at all come September.

Despite its status as a powerhouse of garment production, New York City had nothing approaching the cachet of Paris when it came to determining style. To some, Hawes included, the war was an opportunity to rectify what they perceived as a wrong—New York, they argued, was just as qualified to be a fashion capital as Paris. Others felt that without Paris, New York was just a manufacturing hub, all factory and no flair. The summer of 1940 forced the issue to a head.

Those who saw American designers as flunkies best suited to adapting the work of their French betters were forced to comply with their more optimistic peers. But the more interesting story is that American fashion did not just survive the war; it thrived beyond even Elizabeth Hawes's considerable imagination. By 1945, there was genuine debate over which city, Paris or New York, would be the future capital of fashion. In four years, New York had gained the artistry and confidence to challenge the city that had dominated style since the seventeenth century.

This incredible shift, in both capability and perception, was made possible due to the efforts of a group of remarkable women.

They were journalists, retailers, advertising executives, publicists, and, of course, the designers who created the clothes that came to define the unfussy ease of American fashion. Many had come of professional age in the fertile period between the World Wars, when, for the first time in history, large numbers of women were able to build careers and lead independent lives. This progress benefited white women, but women of color saw far fewer gains. There were successful Black made-to-order designers working in the United States during this period, like Zelda Wynn Valdes, who created clothes for Harlem's elite, and Ann Lowe, who would go on to make Jacqueline Kennedy's wedding dress. But there were very few women or men of color working in the ready-to-wear industry. Although it was not officially segregated, as the American Armed Forces of the time were, the fashion industry of the 1930s and '40s was almost entirely white. By 1973, when American designers and Parisian couturiers met for the Battle of Versailles, that had begun to change. Despite these gains, there are still very few people of color in leadership positions in fashion.

When Paris fell, the women of Seventh Avenue redoubled their efforts on behalf of American fashion. All the energy and skill that had gone into publicizing the Parisian couturiers was now turned to glamorizing designers who worked much closer to home. Edna Woolman Chase, the editor in chief of *Vogue* and a lover of haute couture, became a proponent of Seventh Avenue. At *Harper's Bazaar*, Chase's archrival, Carmel Snow, collaborated with two of the greatest creative talents in the business, Diana Vreeland, who was then her fashion editor, and the photographer Louise Dahl-Wolfe, to create sumptuous, color-saturated images of American clothes in American landscapes. Eleanor Lambert, fashion's first superstar publicist, dreamed up New York Fashion Week, the Coty American Fashion Critics' Awards (which were succeeded by the CFDA Fashion Awards), and the International Best-Dressed List, all of which showcased American design. Lois Long of *The New Yorker* paid American designers the highest compliment possible for a critic: She held them to the same high standard she had applied to their Parisian counterparts. Virginia Pope, the fashion editor of *The New York Times*, launched *Fashions of the Times*, a biannual fashion show–cum–Broadway musical that ran to sold-out crowds until her retirement in 1952, when it was downsized into the paper's fashion magazine.

None of these efforts would have meant anything without the

design talent to back up the hype. As it happened, these were boom times for women designers, especially for that most American of genres, casual wear, or what was then known as sportswear. Of the many women who excelled at designing this type of clothing, Claire McCardell was a virtuoso. Fashion editors raved about her unstructured bathing suits, wool jersey leggings, and hooded suits, describing them as "futuristic" and "revolutionary." Dahl-Wolfe, who shot her clothes time and time again and became a close friend, said it was impossible to take a bad picture of a McCardell design. Even today, designers continue to consult her deceptively simple garments for inspiration.

By the time the war ended, "the American Look" was synonymous around the world with the fresh, youthful style associated with designers like McCardell. The American Girl, typified by the model-turned-actress Lauren Bacall, was the French Girl of her day, lauded for her long-legged athleticism, shiny hair, and good grooming. While haute couture would make a resounding comeback in 1947 with Christian Dior's New Look, New York had already staked its claim to be the world's leading producer of stylish and affordable ready-to-wear. The type of clothes that American designers proved to be masters of turned out to be the clothes that everyone, everywhere, wanted: wearable, comfortable, practical yet imaginative. It was, as in the words of Jessica Daves, Chase's successor at *Vogue*, a "ready-made miracle."[2]

As the war years receded and the inevitability of American dominance in fashion began to seem preordained—manifest destiny in denim and sneakers—the names of the women who worked so hard to put that concept in motion faded. Long, a sparkling prose stylist whose editor credited her with inventing fashion criticism, is forgotten. McCardell, the creator of American sportswear, without whom it's difficult to imagine the careers of Calvin Klein or Donna Karan or Marc Jacobs, is unknown outside the industry. Lambert, whose service to American fashion spanned an action-packed eight decades, has no name recognition. Even Hawes, who was so ahead of her time that she got married in jeans in 1937 and suggested, in 1938, that men might want to try wearing skirts, has disappeared from public view. Although it was Lambert who was known as "the Empress of Seventh Avenue," a moniker that recognized both her outsize contributions to the industry and its mid-century headquarters, the honorific applies to all of these women. When others couldn't see past the safety of the way things had always been done, they had the vision to know where fashion was going.

These women deserve credit for building the billion-dollar industry that employs millions of people around the globe, and which shapes the way every one of us gets dressed each day. Long before second-wave feminism, they insisted on having careers. Some were gigantic talents; many others led poignant personal lives. All shared a common belief: that fashion could be both beautiful and democratic. In their insistence on this truth, the women who lifted American design onto the international stage were revealing their ideals. Their resilience changed how we all think about the clothes we wear. It's time to tell their stories.

1

Such Clothes Have Never Been Made in America Before

Edna Woolman Chase and Carmel Snow

Vogue's role in the first few months of the war was a gratifying if complex one . . . We were the liaison between Paris and New York. The most cogent questions from the Paris office were: How does the wind blow on Seventh Avenue? Are the wholesalers profiting by the war to push American design?

—EDNA WOOLMAN CHASE[1]

I was no more willing to concede the permanent fall of Paris than General de Gaulle.

—CARMEL SNOW[2]

New York, January 13, 1940
The morning was chilly and overcast, with a promise of rain before the day was done. The ice-cold waters of the Hudson, lapping up against the hull of the SS *Washington*, docked at Pier 59 on

Manhattan's West Side, were the same discouraging gray as the sky. Passengers filing onto the ship turned up their collars against the wind that gusted skirts above knees and threatened to send hats pinwheeling into the river. As they waited to show their tickets, they could not help but notice the ship's new wartime insignia. High above the waterline, on both the port and starboard sides and large enough to be visible even in poor conditions at sea, were painted her name; the name of the shipping company that owned her, United States Lines; and two enormous American flags. It was a precaution meant to prevent attacks on civilian vessels. No ship wanted to meet the same fate as the *Athenia*, a British passenger liner that had been torpedoed and sunk by a German U-boat in September, just two days after the outbreak of the war, with a loss of 125 lives, many of them children.[3] By unmistakably labeling the *Washington* a civilian ship, United States Lines hoped to keep her and her passengers safe.

The risk involved in crossing the Atlantic, combined with wartime restrictions on travel to belligerent countries, meant that although the *Washington* had been built to carry more than 1,100 passengers, only 167 were boarding that day for the crossing to Genoa. One group that was not to be deterred, however, were the American retailers and journalists who bought and reported on Paris fashion. They were bound for the spring 1940 collections, which were proceeding despite the fact that France was at war. Neither Hitler's submarines nor his armies could dissuade them from making the pilgrimage, even if it meant traveling via a neutral Italian city and continuing their journey by train.

In previous years, the American fashion contingent had made the Atlantic crossing so frequently, some as often as seven times a year, that their preferred boat, the French liner *Normandie*, had been nicknamed the Seventh Avenue Express, a reference to what was then the very center of the American fashion industry, a square mile of midtown Manhattan where more than five thousand firms designed and produced almost all the nation's clothes.[4] The war, however, had raised concerns about how the French Legend would continue to work its charm. World War I had registered as barely a blip to the fashion world, with almost no interruption in the haute couture schedule or the export of French clothes; like migratory birds, American buyers crossed the Atlantic twice a year throughout that conflict, running the gauntlet of German submarines and mines each time.[5] So far, Paris had again been spared. But if that was to change, the fashion industries of both the United States and France would be radically altered. To those who worried about the continued good health of the Paris couture, the fate of the *Normandie* presented a troubling metaphor. On this winter morning, Seventh Avenue's favorite boat was docked forty blocks uptown, at Pier 88. At the outbreak of the war, the $50 million liner had been in New York Harbor; rather than bring her back to her home port, where she could fall into German hands, the French Line had opted to leave her there[6] (she would later be scrapped after being damaged by fire while being converted to an American troop ship).[7] Her opulent Art Deco interiors, which had once hosted celebrities like Cary Grant and Marlene Dietrich, were silent and dark.

Fashion was one of France's chief industries, both culturally prestigious and, with an annual turnover of 25 billion francs, of vital economic importance.[8] But the presence of international buyers and press, coupled with the ability to export the couturiers' designs, was critical to its well-being. If the war made this impossible, the economic fallout would be instantaneous, as it had been when the onset of the Great Depression had curtailed spending from North and South America and dozens of couture houses had closed. When France found itself at war in September 1939, the government instituted an immediate mobilization. Trenches were dug in Paris's Tuileries Garden, and able-bodied men, including many couturiers, were instructed to report for duty.

Vogue's Paris editor, Bettina Wilson (who would become Bettina Ballard when she married for the second time, in 1947, to an architect named William F. R. Ballard), reported that within a week, the city had emptied of men: "You couldn't find a doctor, a dentist, a lawyer, a butcher—it was a mass male exit."[9] But as the Phoney War—or *drôle de guerre*, the nine-month lull in military action that followed the defeat of Poland in September 1939—dragged on, the French government, conscious of the economic importance of their work and the many jobs that relied on the success of their collections, gave the couturiers leave to return to their studios to design the spring 1940 collections. To woo the Americans and ease the inconvenience of the voyage, the couturiers' association, the Chambre Syndicale de la Couture Parisienne, had paid for a special train to transport them from Genoa to Paris. Traveling on the *Washington* were officials from the French embassy, ready to deploy their professional charm to ensure that the orders from New York continued to flow. For their part, the Americans boarding the ship that morning did so with the feeling that they were coming to the aid of their French colleagues; many had even packed food and other small luxuries to distribute when they arrived in Paris.

The bulk of the fashion deputation was made up of buyers and designers. Chief among them was Carmel Snow, the Irish-born editor in chief of *Harper's Bazaar* and one of the two most powerful women in American fashion journalism. At fifty-two, she was a veteran of transatlantic crossings. A petite woman with an uptilted nose, her white curls tinted anything from a pale blue to a startling violet, Snow was always ready for adventure. Mercurial, charming, and tough, "Bossy," as she was known by her staff, more or less affectionately, would never let an inconvenience like a war keep her from Paris, whose couturiers she revered.

Not making the crossing was Edna Woolman Chase, the sixty-two-year-old editor in chief of *Vogue*. Like Snow, Chase was small, and she also went gray early. Her favorite fashion period was the late nineteenth century, and she had a way of making everything she wore vaguely reminiscent of that era's trailing draperies and general fussiness. There were many reasons Chase might not have wanted to cross the North Atlantic in January, including the war, the weather, and the sciatica in her shoulder.[10] But what might have tipped the balance in favor of remaining in New York was the knowledge that she'd be stuck on a boat with Carmel Snow for four days. The two women couldn't abide each other. Snow had once been *Vogue*'s fashion editor, hired in 1921 with the expectation that she would be promoted to the top job when Chase retired. But a decade after Snow joined *Vogue*, Chase was as firmly dug in as ever. She resented Snow's charm and popularity and found constant fault with her work. For her part, Snow felt professionally stifled and chafed at Chase's heavy-handed management style and endless sniping. By 1932, she'd had enough. Although Snow had declared that she would never defect to the competition, when William Randolph Hearst offered her a job at *Harper's Bazaar* that she knew would shortly lead to the magazine's editorship, she seized the opportunity.[11]

Chase was livid when she heard of Snow's decision. The women's accounts vary, but both agree that Snow broke the news to Chase in her hospital room, where Snow was recovering from the birth of her third daughter. Chase insisted their talk was decorous;[12] Snow described it as a harangue that involved multiple staff members ranged around her bedside, decrying her treachery.[13] The relationship between the two magazines, which had always had a Hatfield-and-McCoy quality, sank to its nadir. Employees of Condé Nast Publications, *Vogue*'s parent company, were instructed to never speak to Snow again, a sentiment they took to heart. In 1957, shortly before Snow's retirement and almost a quarter century after she left *Vogue*, an editor there was asked to assess Snow's considerable contribution to fashion. Her reply was indicative of a grudge that had lost none of its freshness: "To discuss fashion in relation to Mrs. Snow is like writing the history of the United States from the viewpoint of Benedict Arnold."[14]

Snow was right to trust her instincts. Chase did not retire from *Vogue* until 1952—fifty-seven years after her first day at the magazine in 1895, as an eighteen-year-old assistant in the circulation department. She became editor in chief in 1914, and by 1940 had been in her job long enough to be considered an institution.[15] At the office, she exuded as much warmth as one; in private, she could be affectionate and spontaneous, and had a close relationship with her only child, the actress Ilka Chase. Her public persona, however, was brusque, and her editors knew her to be a master of the devastating comment.

Chase's magazine reached more subscribers than the *Bazaar*, as everyone called it, and boasted more ads, which was partly a function of its publication schedule—*Vogue* then came out every two weeks, while *Bazaar* was a monthly publication, supplemented with an extra issue in each of the fashion-news-heavy months of March and September. *Vogue*'s publisher, Condé Nast, was a bon vivant who loved lavish interiors. Consequently, *Vogue*'s editors worked in a considerably more chichi setting than *Bazaar*'s did. The reception area was lined with faux leather–bound books and staffed by an expensively dressed young heiress who sat behind a Chinese Chippendale desk and directed visitors to wait in a glassed-in conservatory. *Bazaar*, Snow thought when she arrived, looked like the office of a small-town newspaper, a reflection of its publisher, William Randolph Hearst, who'd begun his career in daily journalism. When Ray Milland, one of the stars of the 1944 film *Lady in the Dark*, about a fashion editor undergoing psychoanalysis, stopped by to soak up the atmosphere, he thought he was in the wrong place.[16]

But *Vogue* concerned itself solely with the very wealthy; it was stuck in the exclusive milieu that Diana Vreeland, who had appeared in its pages numerous times as a debutante, described in her memoir: When she was young, she said, very few people had ever even "breathed the pantry air" of the type of woman who wore dresses that appeared in *Vogue*.[17] *Bazaar*'s readership was equally well-heeled, but the magazine's editors saw to it that they were kept informed about everything from literature to public works. It was an editorial policy summed up in Snow's remark about whom she created the magazine for: well-dressed women with well-dressed minds. Even a *Vogue* loyalist like Bettina Wilson acknowledged that her boss's vision wasn't as adventurous as Snow's, confessing that she envied "a certain fashion conviction and personal daring in *Harper's Bazaar*."[18] When Chase did manage to replicate some of *Bazaar*'s allure, the victory could be sour. In the mid-1930s, when she lured away one of Snow's prize illustrators with an exclusive *Vogue* contract, Snow consoled herself by reflecting that Chase couldn't stand his work.[19]

Between them, Chase and Snow determined what was fashionable for a considerable swath of American women. Although their magazines were mainly read by an affluent, white readership, they exerted their authority in myriad other ways. Simply by giving their approval to specific fashions, they directly influenced what was manufactured and sold. Outside of editing their magazines, they gave radio addresses and speeches to women's clubs and industry groups, further promoting their ideas about what it meant to exercise good taste. They had the ears of the couturiers, the manufacturers, and the retailers. And soon, they would liaise with government officials, too.

Once the *Washington* slipped out into the Narrows of New York Harbor, the atmosphere relaxed. The wartime camaraderie meant that even traditional enemies got along. *Vogue* cozied up to *Bazaar*, Bergdorf Goodman palled around with Henri Bendel, and everyone stayed up late for the after-dinner dancing. Even the Atlantic weather was unusually warm, fading to winter drabness only when the ship entered Mediterranean waters.[20]

The train journey from Genoa to Paris, so thoughtfully arranged by the Chambre Syndicale, was an altogether different experience. The train was crowded with soldiers, and to pack in as many passengers as possible, the sleeping cars had been replaced with more seating. The temperature had dropped precipitously, and there was neither heat nor light on the train. Nor was there any food or water. And the mountain of luggage that the *Washington*'s fashionable passengers deemed necessary for an expedition to Europe had been piled in the corridors, which meant access to the toilets was blocked. At the French border, everyone had to stand in the Alpine snow to have their passports checked (Snow, a self-described "goddess" when it came to bodily functions who, she claimed, never felt the cold, rarely experienced hunger, and drank little except for alcohol, conceded that the journey was uncomfortable for her fellow travelers).[21] When they finally reached the Gare de Lyon twenty-four miserable hours later, the Americans found Paris dusted with snow and in the grip of a frigid winter. But the welcome from the French was so warm that any discomfort was, if not forgotten, certainly mitigated. The French called the visitors *les hirondelles*—the swallows—optimistically equating their presence with the first sign of spring.[22]

Despite the nightly blackouts, Paris had lost none of its panache.

The tins of sardines and fruit that the visitors brought turned out to be superfluous; dining was as sumptuous as ever, even if it was now necessary to pack a gas mask when dining at Maxim's, the famous restaurant in the rue Royale. The military authorities had even decreed that the city's nightclubs, which had been ordered to close early at the onset of the war, be kept open until midnight so that the visitors could be properly entertained.[23] But taxis were nonexistent, heating fuel was scarce, and the cold penetrated even the warmest coats. On a visit to Guillaume, the most fashionable hairdresser in Paris, Snow noted women huddled under the dryers, reluctant to relinquish their warmth.[24] However, these inconveniences were considered secondary to the main event: the clothes.

Fashion in the 1930s had had a perverse, schizophrenic quality. Severe suits and knowing evening gowns coexisted with deranged, Surrealist-inspired oddities, a combination that is often described as "hard chic." Elsa Schiaparelli, the aristocratic Italian-born couturier who collaborated with artists such as Salvador Dalí and Jean Cocteau, excelled at using the latter as a foil for the former, a talent that made her one of the most successful couturiers of the era. Although she could neither sketch nor sew, "Schiap," as she was known to her intimates, possessed a provocative aesthetic that was perfectly in step with the times. The dark-haired, dark-eyed designer even had her own personal Surrealist emblem: a spray of moles on her left cheek in the shape of Ursa Major.[25] Only the most confident ordered Schiaparelli's wilder experiments, like the hat that looked like an upside-down high-heeled shoe or the evening dress printed with a ripped-flesh motif, but her meticulous tailoring earned her a devoted following.

The advent of the war, however, had a sobering effect on the output of the haute couture. Both *Vogue* and *Bazaar* applauded the lack of eccentricity and exaggeration in the "fresh" and "feminine" spring 1940 collections.[26] Narrow skirts, which were considered especially attractive when worn with the bloused jackets proposed by the English-born couturier Edward Molyneux, were the biggest news. Comfortable shoes with low heels and big pockets for carrying essentials, created in response to the new need, for Parisians at least, to walk everywhere, got a nod of approval, as did the sooty gleam of jet appliqué on evening dresses, hats, and suit collars.

For the staffs of *Vogue* and *Bazaar*, the two main couture collections, shown in February and August, were the busiest, most stressful, and most enjoyable times of the year, comparable to elections for political reporters or coups d'état for foreign correspondents. Along with attending the showings by the various couturiers, they had to select and photograph the choicest picks from the collections for their magazines. Since everyone wanted the same clothes, this involved considerable cajolery and subterfuge. Shoots often started late, after the buyers had left the couture houses, and could last all night. Once the photos were taken, it was vital that they be dispatched as quickly as possible to New York to make the print deadline for the magazine.

Snow, who reveled in her time in Paris, preferred to see proofs from the previous night's shoots early in the morning. She always took a suite at the Hôtel Westminster, which she pronounced in the French fashion, *vest-main-stair*. Clad in the lace nightgown and pearls in which she'd slept—bolt upright, with the lights on— she'd begin her day at dawn, making phone calls, dictating cables to secretaries, and receiving editors and photographers from her bed, like a queen at her levée.[27] The photographer would come in with proofs, which Snow would examine with a huge magnifying glass, quickly making her choices. The photographer would then rush the print to the retoucher. After the retouching was done, the final print was made, fixed, washed, dried, and captioned before being rushed to the Gare Saint-Lazare, where it would be put on a train bound for Cherbourg or Le Havre and then a ship headed to New York, a journey of about four days. At any point, this system could break down, and the photo would miss the deadline.[28]

To Snow, this kind of exhilaration was meat and drink—almost literally, as she rarely ate anything while she was in Paris, surviving on a diet of vitamin B shots, martinis, and patisseries.[29] She even left the bathroom door open when she bathed, so as not to miss a minute of the action.[30] Paris, she believed firmly, would always be the center of fashion. This was one of the few points on which Snow and Chase agreed.

Despite the cold and the many small deprivations, the spring 1940 collections were a huge success. The American love affair with the haute couture was as fervent as ever and was now fed by an intense admiration for the way the French carried on in the face of the Nazi threat. In return, the French were grateful for both the concern the Americans expressed for their plight and their large orders. Everyone promised they'd see each other soon and wished one another *bon courage*. Paris, Snow observed, was still so completely Paris that it seemed impossible that it could change. The Americans boarded the train for Genoa confident they'd be back for the fall collections in August.

But on May 10, German tanks and paratroopers invaded France by circumventing the Maginot Line, constructed in the 1930s to prevent just such a catastrophe, instead approaching from the north, via the Low Countries. In the process, one million French officers and soldiers were taken prisoner, and millions more of their compatriots were displaced from their homes.[31] The uprooted headed south, away from the advancing German army, in a protracted, chaotic, and terrifying flight known as *l'Exode*. The Phoney War had come to an abrupt end. There was no question of boarding a ship to attend fashion shows now.

Snow began frantically cabling Louise "Louie" Macy, her Paris editor, to come back to the United States *immediately*. Macy refused. Instead, she sent the French staff home to their families and ran the office herself. When she wasn't working, she delivered food and medical supplies to the endless flow of refugees that were streaming into Paris. On one single morning in May, Macy reported that more than three thousand refugees arrived at the Gare de l'Est, many on trains that had been bombed.[32] As the Germans advanced ever closer to Paris, Macy finally gave in to Snow's entreaties. She sailed from Genoa on the SS *Manhattan*, the sister ship of the *Washington*, in early June, with Schiaparelli's nineteen-year-old daughter, who was universally known by her nickname, Gogo, in tow.[33] The *Manhattan* carried three times her usual capacity on that voyage: 3,300 people, who slept on cots that were set up in every available space.[34]

Bettina Wilson, to her everlasting chagrin, was in California visiting her family when France was attacked. After months of writing about chic attire for air-raid shelters and the disappearance of frivolous hats, a mainstay of prewar fashion, she longed to test her mettle by reporting real news. To assuage her disappointment, she joined the Red Cross (true to her *Vogue* roots, she had her uniforms tailored at Garfinkel's, the Washington, DC, department store, before she left and ordered matching blouses from the designer Clare Potter to wear with them).[35] She was back in New York on June 11 when the manager of the Paris office sent her one last cable before he headed for Bordeaux with *Vogue*'s financial records and all the liquid cash of Les Publications Condé Nast piled in his car: "Burying your silver between two trees in the forest of Yvelines."[36] More than any other news that reached her from France, it conveyed to her the despair and hysteria of war.[37]

When the *Manhattan* steamed into New York Harbor on June 10, the disembarking passengers also included Alice Perkins, the Paris fashion editor of *Women's Wear Daily*, better known as *WWD*, the newspaper that was required reading for everyone in the fashion industry. Perkins's account of her final week in Paris appeared the following day. She described visiting Lucien Lelong, the president of the Chambre Syndicale and the man who had arranged for the Americans to travel from Genoa just a few months earlier. His business, "like every other dressmaking house in Paris," was still open on the afternoon Perkins left.[38] Lelong had spoken cheerfully of future plans, she said, and sent messages to his many friends in New York. But what had really impressed Perkins was the value that Parisians placed on the messages sent to them by their American friends, whether they were letters of sympathy or packets of coffee. "In every case it was the thought which prompted the message rather than its contents which counted; the thought that they were not forgotten over here seemed to give them immense comfort," she wrote.[39]

Although occasional couture orders were still being placed, retail business was slow. Department stores, however, were doing a brisk business in mothballs, rope, trunks, and boxes, for those packing up houses or planning to leave the capital, as well as camp beds and cushions for the refugees who were being housed in railway stations and public halls until they could be routed farther south. She ended with a description of a dogfight between French and German planes over the house of a colleague who lived north of Paris, on the main road to Germany, that had taken place just days before she left the city.[40]

But the day before Perkins's article appeared, with its uneasy blend of near-normal and ominous, the French government abandoned Paris. Four days later, on June 14, 1940, the Nazis marched into the French capital. They were to remain for four years.

The fall of Paris stunned the world. It was the ninth European capital to come under the boot heel of the Nazis, but because of its paramount importance to Western culture, its loss was interpreted as a uniquely devastating blow. To the American fashion industry, with its deep-rooted personal and business ties to the city, Paris's disappearance into the Axis maw was almost incomprehensible. Those, like Snow and Chase, who were old enough to remember World War I, when the possibility that Paris might be captured by the Germans was a continual worry, now had their worst fears come true.

The same day that German troops marched down the Champs-Élysées, *WWD* rushed a story onto its front page about the calamity. Several industry figures were quoted, all of whom sounded as though they were staring into the abyss. One confessed herself too "emotionally upset" to "crystallize" any coherent views.[41] Another, one of the last American buyers to leave the city after the mid-season collections in April, reassured *WWD*'s readers that even if the haute couture could not continue to function by moving its operations to the unoccupied south of France (as was generally hoped would occur), there was no reason to panic—after all, there were enough recent French designs in the US to provide at least six months' worth of inspiration for American firms. He spoke for many in the industry when he added, "The American trade realizes more than ever today how much it needs Paris."[42]

Although Elisabeth Kübler-Ross would not name the five stages of grief for several decades, American fashion executives exhibited all of them—denial, anger, bargaining, depression, and, finally, acceptance—as the terrible news from Europe unfolded. As late as May 14, *after* the invasion of France, *WWD*'s Paris bureau chief was reporting that the couturiers were considering skipping the mid-season collections, but that they would, of course, show their

fall collections as usual in August.[43] The swastika was already flying from the Eiffel Tower when the Countess Illinska (who, despite
her Edith Wharton–ish name, was the director of made-to-order
fashion at Bonwit Teller) declared that she would travel to see the
couture showings anywhere they were held.[44] Whether from a persistent belief that American design talent was not of the same cali-
ber as the Paris variety—"You would have thought, the way some
of the girls went on, that we were about to be reduced to wearing
Mother Hubbards,"[45] said Lois Long, *The New Yorker*'s fashion
critic, referring to a high-necked, long-sleeved, tent-like dress of
the nineteenth century—or from the paralysis that can set in after
a traumatic event, a significant proportion of the American fashion
industry remained too shell-shocked to grasp that it would very
soon become necessary to move forward without the help of their
French colleagues.

An editorial that appeared on the front page of *WWD* on Monday, June 17, laid out in stark terms the necessity of putting aside, at
least for the time being, the dream of Paris and focusing on American leadership. "Fashion has no nationality," it argued. "Here and
now, this season, today, we must develop our own industries and
beware of any sort of confusion which might arise from wrong
thinking on the part of executives and leaders. We must build confidence, develop leadership, accept the authority of our greatest
producers, our best qualified retailers and our gifted designers."[46]

The writer was Winifred J. Ovitte, the paper's New York fashion editor. Her tone was respectful but firm. She acknowledged
both the sorrow that every "friend of France" in the United States
felt for the terrible events of the past month and the enormous debt
that American fashion owed to Paris—but she refused to believe
that American fashion could not thrive on its own.

For American fashion to succeed, two things had to happen: The industry had to rally around its designers and focus on producing clothes without input from the French, and the public had to be convinced that American designs were just as valid—just as desirable—as anything that originated in a couturier's studio.

Unlike the Parisian haute couture, American fashion had no governing body. But most women who worked in the industry, including Chase, Snow, Dorothy Shaver, and Claire McCardell, belonged to the Fashion Group—men were excluded from membership for several decades—which was founded in 1930 with the aim of promoting American fashion and women's roles within it. Its monthly luncheons, which always included one or two speakers, served as town halls for whatever was on the minds of its members. When they gathered at the Biltmore Hotel on Madison Avenue on July 11, 1940, there was only one thing everyone wanted to talk about: how the American industry could move forward without Paris. Although the Fashion Group did not coordinate the response to the crisis, the meetings that it hosted throughout the war served as forums for education and discussion. When members emerged into the sunshine that July afternoon, one thing was clear: Convincing American women that designs that originated in their own country were as legitimate as anything that came from Paris would require a sustained campaign—one that combined the efforts of a cross section of professionals, from journalists and publicists to retailers and manufacturers.

The first collections that American designers would be solely responsible for would appear in stores around Labor Day. Guiding the public through the new silhouettes and colors would be the twin bibles of American fashion: *Vogue* and *Harper's Bazaar*. For Chase and Snow, these issues would be unlike anything they had ever edited before. The September issues were traditionally the most important of the year. This was when fashion's big-ticket items—wool suits, fur coats, the most formal evening gowns—would appear, and the magazines were consequently heavy with both content and advertisements. This year, for the first time in either *Vogue* or *Bazaar*'s history, not a single haute couture design would be shown, a momentous change for publications that had made the worship of Paris fashion the cornerstone of their editorial policy.

The first inkling most American women would have had that something had gone awry in the way their clothes were designed came in late summer. In its August 26 issue, *Life* magazine published a story about the clothes that would begin arriving in stores the following month. Instead of spending August in Paris nosing around for inspiration, the magazine explained, American designers had been closeted in their studios, designing their fall collections *without any input from France*. Although all the designers featured appear quite calm (even Countess Illinska, who is shown draping a satin evening dress), the article suggests that they are "hysterical" over their newly independent status, demanding, Chicken Little–style, "What shall we do, who will inspire us, who will lead us now that Paris is no more?"[47] That was not at all the tone taken by Chase and Snow, whose September issues came out a week later. They elected to treat the situation with gravitas. Using the sort of hushed and reverent language that might have been used to announce the death of a beloved elder statesman—which, in a sense, they were—they wrote of their love for Paris fashion and of the need to face the future calmly and with conviction. "We publish this record of the New York autumn openings with pride in the achievements of our American designers and with full acknowledgement of our debt to France. We have learned from the greatest masters in the world," ran Snow's introduction to the fall portfolio in the September 1 issue of *Bazaar*. She ended, grandly: "Such clothes have never been made in America before."[48] The message appeared across a red, white, and blue collage of a model in an American-designed and -made evening dress, standing like a colossus over Seventh Avenue.

Vogue, while less imaginative in its layout, was just as stirring in its language. "American talent has risen to the occasion with all its native resourcefulness and skilled dress-making technique. The years of Paris dominance and Paris tradition cannot help but have their influence," Chase wrote. "But aroused is a new eagerness, a reaching to achieve—if for any prolonged period importations are cut off—clothes with the definite and recognizable quality of America." [49]

The message from both women was one of reassurance. It was their business as editors in chief to retain both readers and consumers of fashion, and they did that very cannily, by evoking both the quality of Paris and the promise of America.

They didn't have to equivocate. The clothes American designers turned out in the fall of 1940 were trim and slender, with an artlessness that suggested real-life uses. The evening clothes were celebratory but not untouchable-looking. And there were flourishes that showed that the French weren't the only ones who knew how to work with materials: fur peplums on strictly tailored wool suits, touches of velvet and leopard on coats and day wear, gold lamé blouses paired with spreading black velvet evening skirts. If the American fashion industry had been holding its breath, it could now exhale. Even the no-nonsense Long applauded the September 1940 collections. Although she thought they included, "naturally, some horrors," which she felt was to be expected from a first solo effort, especially one produced under such enormous pressure, she professed herself satisfied overall, concluding, "The designers can drop those jitters now, like good girls and boys. They should be very proud of themselves." [50]

Long's cool-eyed assessments aside, the language used by *Vogue* and *Bazaar* to describe American design was calculated to appeal to patriotic pride. For as long as the American industry had existed, it had labored in the shadow of Paris, an eager kid sister looking up to an elegant, self-assured swan of an older sibling. The September 1940 collections were a coming-out party for American designers.

One of the industry's strongest allies in the effort to build support for American design was New York City mayor Fiorello La Guardia. With his perpetually rumpled suits and disheveled hair, the mayor was no one's idea of an elegant man. But he understood the importance of the fashion industry to the city he governed. As a young lawyer, he had represented New York City's garment workers in a landmark case to win better wages and more humane hours. And his adored first wife, who had died of tuberculosis just months after the couple lost their infant daughter to the same disease, had been a dress designer.[51]

Even before Paris had succumbed to the Nazis, La Guardia had begun searching for ways to strengthen what was already one of the city's most important industries. In March 1940, he had addressed the Fashion Group, telling them, unprompted, that New York was the center of the fashion world and that the time was coming when people would copy its designs.[52] A few months later, he urged manufacturers to be more considerate of their designers and encouraged them to work with union leaders to keep jobs in the city.[53] And in August, he summoned twelve fashion editors, including Winifred Ovitte and Alice Perkins of *WWD* and Virginia Pope of *The New York Times*, to his office to share their views on how the industry worked. Give New York two years without Paris, he bragged, and American designers would be able to compete with anyone in the world.[54]

Ovitte's *WWD* editorial calling for unity represented not only the idealistic view that American fashion was as worthwhile as its French counterpart but a very practical one: the continued viability of an industry that took in $12 billion in annual revenue.[55] The success of the fall collections was both an enormous relief and a turning point in the way American design was perceived: In two weeks, American designers had received more acclaim than in the previous two decades.[56] The couturier Main Bocher, the rare American to achieve success in Paris—first eliding his name to the more French-sounding Mainbocher—was now back in New York after fleeing from the Nazis, and was heartened by what he saw. "American designers have before them a golden path," he told *WWD*.[57] An idea was forming that not only would American fashion survive the disconnect from Paris, but it might even benefit from the enforced independence. The mayor's suggestion that New York was the center of the fashion world was now spoken of openly and with pride.

Even before New York began to exhibit signs of this cocky new self-assurance, the couturiers were sufficiently concerned about losing their status in the United States, their biggest export market, to dispatch an emissary to the city. It fell to Elsa Schiaparelli, who had already been booked for an American lecture tour when war broke out, to defend the haute couture. After conferring with Lucien Lelong, she made her way laboriously to Lisbon, the crossroads of wartime Europe, where she bought a ticket for a Clipper flight to New York. In mid-July, after numerous delays due to engine trouble, she stepped off the plane at LaGuardia Field. On the lapel of her jacket, she had pinned a large brooch in the shape of a bird. When a reporter questioned her about it, Schiaparelli replied, "It is a phoenix, a bird which after being burned, rises again from the ashes and grows in full beauty. It is the symbol of France."[58] Although she was taking some license with Gallic symbolism, she had made her point: France, and haute couture, were not to be written off.

In September, Schiaparelli began her three-month coast-to-coast lecture tour, entitled "Clothes Make the Woman," of the United States and Canada. She had arrived in New York toting $70,000 worth of jewelry and four suitcases, the most she could bring with her on the Clipper, which imposed a strict weight limit—both passengers and their baggage were put on scales before takeoff. Following by boat was a wardrobe that Schiaparelli had designed with the intention of having it copied by five specially selected American manufacturers, a foray into ready-to-wear that she undertook to raise funds for unemployed Parisian dressmakers. The clothes never arrived in New York, however—the ship they were on was sunk by a German U-boat. Bonwit Teller offered to remake the couture pieces that the manufacturers were to copy, but Schiaparelli was dissatisfied with the results. This was the unpromising backdrop against which she began her tour.[59] After a trial run at Bonwit Teller in Philadelphia, she arrived at Lord & Taylor in Manhattan on September 24, where she was greeted by a crowd of 1,500 people eager to hear what the famous Parisian couturier had to say.

Eight decades later, her outrage is still palpable. New York, Schiaparelli told her listeners in no uncertain terms, would never supplant Paris as the capital of fashion. "Your press is making a veritable campaign on this subject, a campaign which is not justified by facts. And your buyers who know Paris, who know all the ins and outs of the dress business, will agree when I say that it is not possible for New York or any other city to take the place of Paris."[60] The reasons, she continued, were myriad: Paris had a centuries-long tradition of nurturing elegance and was populated with craftspeople who happily spent endless time and money in pursuit of perfection. Americans, meanwhile, focused on quantity over quality, practicality over style. They considered fashion frivolous, she complained. It is the women of a country who determine its standard of elegance, Schiaparelli declared. Lingering in the air around this remark was the suggestion that perhaps American women simply could not live up to this delicate expectation.

Two days later, Schiaparelli received New York's official reply.

The occasion was La Guardia's appearance at the New York Advertising Club, where he was to become the first recipient of its Man of the Month Award. But from the moment he stepped up to the podium and announced that the title of his speech was "Making New York the Fashion Center of the World," it was clear that the event was really a coming-out party for this brash new initiative. The mayor then bowed to the fashion journalists who were present, including Chase and Pope.[61] "The girls of the fashion press"—"girl" in the 1940s being used to refer to every female from newborn through to centenarian—"know more about their jobs than political writers know about politics," he said.[62] It was an acknowledgment of the August meeting, and a tacit admission that the women of the fashion press had influenced what he was about to say. But La Guardia gave it his own spin.

As far as fashion went, he said, Europe was dead. The future belonged to New York. Because of its mass-production capabilities, New York City had more well-dressed women than in all the countries of Europe combined. As it should—a pretty dress, in the mayor's opinion, was something every American woman deserved, no matter her size or budget.[63] Recognition of New York City as the fashion center of the world would give the city both the prestige that was its due and access to market opportunities that would bring it even greater wealth, he continued. Moreover, attaining this prestige was not at odds with creating as much individuality in dress as the greatest number of women could enjoy. In other words: Think again, Elsa Schiaparelli.

When La Guardia spoke of New York as the fashion center of the world, he was making a claim that had no basis in reality. It was a piece of Big Apple bravado from the city's biggest cheerleader. But like the women who sat with him on that September day, he grasped the possibilities of what the city's fashion industry could achieve. In the fall of 1940, New York had everything it needed to become a fashion capital. The only thing holding it back was the French Legend.

2

The Birth of the French Legend

Paris and New York

There is, we hope, no such thing as American design.
                                    —*Vogue*, NOVEMBER 1, 1914

On June 15, 1940, the day after the world learned that Paris had succumbed to the Nazis, *The New York Times* published an extraordinary lament. It began, "The first thought of many millions of people must have been one of gratitude that Paris was spared physical destruction."[1]

Appearing amid sober analyses about the crisis of leadership in the French command, the advance of the Nazis as far as Romilly-sur-Seine and Saint-Dizier, and the three-day festival ordered by Hitler in Germany to celebrate the city's capture, this brief, emotional piece lovingly catalogued the myriad contributions Paris had made to Western civilization. The city of Voltaire, Rousseau, and Molière, of Notre Dame, the Louvre, and Les Deux Magots, was "where the creative imagination of modern man burned at its freest and brightest," the writer insisted. *This* city, with its blocks of harmonious buildings, tree-lined avenues, and graceful bridges, would never be understood by Hitler and his followers, nor would it ever be theirs: "They may park their machines of war in the Place de la Concorde. They may parade the Champs Elysées. But the Elysian Fields of Paris, as of civilization itself, they cannot traverse or conquer."

It is an indication of the universal acceptance of Paris's perch at the apex of European culture that the *Times* would run this extravagant panegyric alongside its war reporting. The fall of other European cities, while devastating for their inhabitants, had not been marked with elegies in the American press. Paris, however, was special. It was, as the *Times* assumed its readers would agree, where modern life at its most refined was invented, and most ably practiced.

But while the *Times* correspondent rhapsodized about high culture, he ignored a vital point: the French Legend. In the public imagination, Paris equaled fashion, and had done since the seventeenth century. Parisians created fashion; everyone everywhere else followed it. This was popularly believed to be the result of some mystical combination of genetic happenstance (i.e., the French were just better at fashion than anyone else) and geographic luck, a circular argument that held that Paris was where all the best designers and craftspeople were because the best designers and craftspeople were in Paris and thus it had ever been.

But the French Legend was not a fluke, nor did it arise out of a lack of originality on the part of American designers. It was carefully plotted and methodically implemented, and it was rooted in the ambitions of one man: Louis XIV. The Sun King molded France into a global luxury brand.

At the start of his reign, in 1643, this was far from obvious. The last few decades of the sixteenth century had been disrupted by religious wars in France, and by the time these conflicts ended in 1598, Paris was run-down and shabby, a place where citizens had to take care to avoid the packs of wolves that roamed the streets at night.[2] But this was not the France of Louis's imagination. He envisioned his country as a great mercantile power and himself the most illustrious monarch of the age. The best way to persuade everyone else of the rightness of his thinking, he concluded, was to dominate the market that would soon prove to be the most consequential in the world, the luxury trade. It was a resolution that changed French history. But Louis was a big-picture sovereign, focused on image-building exercises like amassing the largest collection of diamonds ever owned by a European royal, an ambition that leapfrogged the French crown jewels from mediocre to the most valuable in the Western world.[3] To transform France into the ultimate arbiter of style, he needed a partner who could focus on the mechanics of world domination.

He found that partner in the man he named his First Minister, Jean-Baptiste Colbert, a native of Rheims who rose from relatively humble origins to become one of the most consequential civil servants in French history. Colbert understood his role in the king's plan perfectly. Luxury, he is alleged to have said, would be to France what the gold mines of Peru were to Spain: the source of limitless riches. Where Louis was mercurial and glamorous, Colbert, twenty years his senior, was methodical and practical. The king dictated, and Colbert delivered. Beginning in 1661, the combined talents of these two men reshaped France into an economy built on the merits of excellent taste.

France was not the first country to enjoy a reputation for defining fashion—that is, clothing that changes for the sake of change.

During the Renaissance, the Italian city-states set the standard in dress and the decorative arts. In fact, Italian taste was the basis of French Renaissance style: From the silks Louis wore to the gardens in which he strolled, he was surrounded by Italian ideas. But within a few years of the king's partnership with Colbert, it was France, not Italy, to whom the world looked for aesthetic guidance. Their positioning of France as a leader of fashion was so successful that it has endured for centuries, crossed socioeconomic and geographic barriers, adapted to the demands of successive generations, and become so ubiquitous that the machinery that put it into motion has long since ceased to be thought of. The reason seems obvious today: The French recognized that promotion and marketing are everything.[4] Louis XIV and Colbert left nothing to chance. And in making France synonymous with fashion, they created the conditions upon which the modern industry rests. The concept of seasonal collections, the use of sex to sell products, the vital role of celebrity, the delicate balance of inspiration and aspiration, all can be traced to seventeenth-century France.

There were several elements necessary for this gambit to work. The first was Louis himself, who provided the inspiration. Because he was France—*"L'état, c'est moi"*—whatever he decreed to be fashionable was identified as French. The second was Colbert, an early practitioner of protectionist economic policies. Colbert worked closely with France's business leaders, making sure that every detail of the economy, from trade regulations and import duties to the operation of state-sponsored luxury goods workshops, was oriented to enhance and promote the glory of the French crown. Silk weavers, for example, were mandated to regularly introduce new colors and patterns, which ensured that fashion was renewed on a seasonal basis. In short, whatever Louis wanted, Colbert ensured that (a) it could be made in France to the highest specifications possible and (b) as many people as possible would also want to buy it for themselves. In this way, Colbert established the essential link between fashion and aspiration.

The third element in the construction of France's image as the world's leader in luxury were the artisans and inventors who produced everything that Louis considered vital to lead a cultured life, from shoes to dinner services. Under the close management of the king and his First Minister, France embarked on a period of stunning creativity. Excellence in any one of these fields would have been noteworthy; to have dominated them all is extraordinary.[5] Fashion became so much a part of the upper-class French mindset that it even permeated the new literary genre of the fairy tale. In Charles Perrault's "Sleeping Beauty," when the prince awakens the princess who has been in an enchanted slumber for one hundred years, he is struck by her beauty—and then wonders why she is dressed like his grandmother.[6] Perrault, it's worth noting, was not just a writer but a civil servant—who reported directly to Colbert.

Perrault's boss spared no resources in attaining his goals, a tactic that was particularly true of his decision to take over the mirror industry. In the mid-1660s, everyone agreed that the Venetians made the world's best mirrors. They were true luxury items, extravagantly priced and difficult to come by. They were also quite small. The largest mirror in France, owned by Colbert's predecessor, Nicolas Fouquet, and considered splendidly gigantic, was twenty-four inches square. Anyone who wanted to see themselves in their entirety would have to purchase several, and likely bankrupt themselves in the process. Louis, naturally, loved mirrors, and was spending the equivalent of $1 million a year importing them. To correct the imbalance in the royal spreadsheet, Colbert decided that it would be far more expedient to knock the Venetians out of the game and move the industry to France.[7]

He enlisted the French ambassador to Venice to persuade some of the top mirror makers in the city to emigrate. This plan had serious challenges. The Venetians treated the details of mirror making as state secrets, and any artisan who was caught engaging in industrial espionage faced harsh consequences. Should they flee abroad, their families would be taken prisoner. If they refused to return to Venice, assassins would be sent to murder them. And if they did return to Venice, they were executed.[8] Unperturbed, Colbert charged ahead. With the help of the French ambassador and some hefty bribes, he smuggled several master mirror makers out of Venice and set them to work in the brand-new Royal Mirror Manufactory in Paris. By the end of the century, the French had surpassed their onetime rival's accomplishments with their ability to make larger mirrors than ever dreamed possible.[9] Louis made these giant new mirrors a necessity in every well-appointed home by creating the Hall of Mirrors at Versailles.

But what really interested the king was fashion. His role as an absolute monarch obligated him to be more splendidly arrayed than anyone in his orbit. Louis took this idea even further than his predecessors, requiring that those around him keep up with their (almost) equally resplendent toilette, while never forgetting that they dressed for his pleasure. An admirer of women's shoulders and décolletage, he ordered that court dresses display both. When two elderly ladies appeared in church one cold winter morning muffled to the neck, he roundly chastised them for their disobedience. Louis expected his style commands, no matter how inconvenient or uncomfortable, to be followed to the letter.

At Versailles—the mega-palace to which he moved his court in 1682, and where all French nobles were required to spend part of the year—to be fashionable was mandatory. Wearing clothes that displeased the king was not just embarrassing, but a mark of failure. Remaining on the right side of Louis's fashion barometer took considerable effort on the part of his courtiers. Restraint was anathema to the king, who demanded constant novelty and ever-increasing leaps of extravagance to pique his jaded eye. The Duc de Saint-Simon, an indefatigable diarist, described how, at a party one evening in 1697, Louis took, "great pleasure in examining everyone's outfits. The air of contentment with which he savored the profusion of materials and the brilliant inventiveness was evident, as was the satisfaction with which he praised . . . the most superb and ingeniously designed outfits."[10] The occasion at which Saint-Simon made this observation, a celebration of the wedding of Louis's oldest grandson, was one of the most awe-inspiring of the era, and the competition to catch the king's eye was so intense that two duchesses were said to have kidnapped their favorite dressmaker, so as to be assured of denying her services to any rivals. "There was no way to restrain oneself in the midst of so much madness," bemoaned Saint-Simon, noting that he and his wife spent 20,000 livres on their clothes for the evening. Although it's very difficult to accurately translate the value of seventeenth-century French currency into a modern equivalent, the historian Joan DeJean estimates that this sum came to about $1 million—for a single occasion.[11]

Expenditures like this kept the aristocracy continually short of cash, and perhaps too distracted by the endless round of costume changes to mount any real challenge to Louis's authority—a convenient consequence of his realpolitik approach to fashion. The French court's total devotion to image also made it the most glittering in Europe, and its members were certainly what we would now call influencers. Thanks to their example, everyone aspired to wear French fashion, which was just as the king wanted it. As

Saint-Simon shrewdly discerned, conspicuous consumption was to Louis a "political maxim."[12]

For centuries, European countries had strictly curtailed the production of luxury clothing through the guild system. If you wanted to legally make clothes for the wealthy and titled, you had first to be admitted to one of the appropriate guilds—tailors, boot makers, and hatters all had their own—which strictly regulated the number of members they admitted. One way of controlling membership was to deny admittance to women. In theory, this meant that only men could legally make clothes. In practice, this law was continually flouted. Female dressmakers existed, but they operated clandestinely, working for lower wages, taking on less prestigious jobs, and having fewer recourses if a client didn't pay her bills—for if they pursued legal action, they sometimes received a beating by the police instead of their fee.[13] Understandably, they desired the same recognition that their male colleagues enjoyed.

After years of lobbying on the part of the dressmakers, Louis XIV officially recognized their existence in 1675 and declared that they were henceforth allowed to form guilds. Although he couched this new law in terms of feminine modesty and morality, it was more likely that he wanted a well-regulated, revenue-producing fashion system—once women had guilds, they were subject to taxation.[14] Under Louis's edict, guilds were established for both *couturières*, or seamstresses, who sewed dresses, and *marchandes de modes*, or fashion merchants, who sold accessories.

Almost straightaway, the *couturières* put their stamp on fashion. They were prohibited from making Louis's favorite style, the *robe de cour*, or court dress, a technically challenging, rigidly boned, and wildly uncomfortable gown that remained the preserve of male tailors. But they were permitted to produce the loose-fitting *robe de chambre*, also known as a *manteau* (not to be confused with the modern French term for "coat") or, as it became known in English, a mantua.[15] Given the choice, and now having the opportunity to easily order them from legal *couturière* establishments, women vastly preferred this less restrictive, relatively inexpensive dress, and the style exploded in popularity. As one observer noted in 1678, "Almost no one today wears anything but a *manteau*."[16]

The mantua was one of the first truly international fashion trends. Prior to the seventeenth century, high fashion equaled court fashion. But every court in Europe interpreted fashion differently. So while the reigns of, for example, Elizabeth I of England and Philip II of Spain overlapped, the fashions of their courts did not. The mantua, however, was worn by women from all walks of life. Although we might not consider it comfortable by modern standards—it was still worn with a corset—the mantua was the seventeenth-century version of casual clothing, with many variations that allowed for personalization. Some looked like belted dresses, while others resembled a loose coat worn over a skirt and bodice. It evolved over the decades, eventually becoming the back-pleated *robe à la française*, or French-style dress, that is familiar from countless eighteenth-century portraits, but it remained more forgiving than the constrictive *robe de cour*.[17] Moreover, the mantua's rise coincided with the emergence of three early forms of fashion reporting: the fashion doll, the fashion illustration, and the first fashion magazines.

Fashion dolls were small, jointed wooden figures that were dressed and coiffed in scaled-down versions of the latest fashions. At first, they circulated privately, between family members or friends. Madame de Sévigné, one of the towering figures of seventeenth-century French literature, posted them to her daughter, stuck on her husband's estates in faraway Provence, so she wouldn't look like a hick when she came to court.[18] By the late seventeenth century, however, these dolls began to be dispatched abroad to spread the message of French chic. At first, they were sent to London and other easily accessible cities, where the appearance of a new doll was reported in the newspapers as though a visiting dignitary had arrived. But soon, these dolls were making the voyage across the Atlantic. In Boston and New York City, aspiring fashionistas paid to see them; if they wanted to take them home for closer inspection, the fee was tripled.[19]

But as successful as fashion dolls were, they reached only a small audience. The fashion illustration, however, could be printed an infinite number of times and was easily distributed. The earliest, which date from the 1670s, showed a solitary figure against a plain background. The focus was solely on the woman wearing the clothes, like a fashion photograph shot on seamless paper. Soon, artists began to include background and context, portraying not just the clothes of a wealthy woman but also her luxuriously appointed home. She might be depicted making up at her dressing table or lounging on the sofa, her feet propped up, suggestive scenarios that provided a glimpse into a private world of extreme privilege. Some even portrayed noblewomen out and about, without the face-covering masks they normally wore in public. This was an especially racy subgenre.[20] The fashion-plus-lifestyle illustrations were more like ad campaigns, promoting not just clothes but also the furnishings and pastimes of fashionable society.

At first, the figure lolling on the cushions or playing with her small dog was identified merely as "a woman of quality."[21] But eventually, just as in modern ad campaigns, fashion illustration began to portray celebrities, in the form of the ladies of the French court. They were not portraits from life. It's unlikely the artists ever saw the women they were drawing and, in any case, a true representation wasn't necessary; only their intimates knew what these women looked like. But to specify that a particular fashionista was Madame la Princesse de Rohan or Madame la Duchesse de Bourgoyne added to the appeal of an illustration by making it more real. And of course, mesdames profited from the public recognition of their elegance.

The growing popularity of these illustrations soon demanded their own magazines, notably *Le Mercure Galant* (*The Gallant Mercury*), whose editor, Jean Donneau de Visé, might be described as the world's first fashion reporter. He launched his magazine in 1672, and by 1677 had been given a royal privilege.[22] Donneau de Visé was an unabashed supporter of French primogeniture in fashion. "Nothing pleases more than the fashions born in France, and . . . everything made there has a certain air that foreigners cannot give to their works," he smugly noted.[23] Although his magazine was printed in Paris and discussed the tastes of the aristocracy, Donneau de Visé, like any competent lifestyle journalist, knew that his readers were not the people he wrote about, but those who dreamed of living like them. He described the elegant world of the aristocracy so that it could be decoded by women whose lives were far less glamorous. He not only gave his audience minute details of dresses and accessories but also told them from which Parisian *couturières* and *marchandes de modes* they could buy them.[24] To keep this flow of information manageable, Donneau de Visé further codified the concept of fashion seasons that had been introduced by Colbert, explaining in January 1678 that from that point onward, he would publish as much information about the current fashion as he could glean at the start of each season. This reinforced the idea, still current today, that different clothes were required for different times of the year.[25]

These three promotional tools—fashion dolls, fashion illustra-

tions, and fashion magazines—spread the gospel of French chic far
beyond the borders of France. An approximation of this chic could
be had at home, of course. But the allure of Paris, and the idea of
partaking in true French taste, made it a top tourist destination, in
no small part because the city itself was so stylish. Louis XIV, with
his insistence on elegance in all things, had transformed his capital into the premier city in Europe. He laid out handsome squares
and gardens, inaugurated the first public transportation system in
Europe, and, despite less-than-ideal conditions for their survival,
stocked the Seine with swans. Instead of traveling to Paris to appreciate the past, as they did in Rome, which had previously been the
most visited European city, tourists came to experience the thrill
of the new. They shopped for the latest fashions, booked appoint-
ments with celebrity hairdressers, and drank coffee in smart cafés.
They were advised about all these activities by their guidebooks,
which listed the names and addresses of *couturières, marchandes
de mode*, hairdressers, shoemakers, and tailors as well as trendy
eateries and other places at which to exhibit one's new finery.
"Everywhere you look, you see boutiques," marveled one book,
underscoring how different Paris was from other places.[26] It was
emerging as the city in which fashion was a way of life, with shopping and display its main attractions.

By the late 1770s Paris had a population of about six hundred
thousand and was home to an estimated three thousand *couturières*.[27] But as important as the *couturières* were to Paris's reputation as a fashion capital, what really drove fashion, and separated
the woman of style from her merely well-turned-out counterpart,
was the way in which a dress was accessorized—the job of the *marchandes de modes*.

Unlike the dressmakers or tailors, the expertise of the *marchandes
de mode* was not the construction of clothing. What they sold was

more elusive. Although the term is often translated as "milliner," a better analogy is that of the modern-day stylist. *Marchandes de mode* helped their clients achieve flair and distinction—qualities of paramount importance in fashion-obsessed Paris—with the clever use of accessories. Lace, ribbons, fans, hair ornaments, hats, and other small trinkets were their stock in trade. In an era when the fashionable silhouette changed very slowly, these small details were what indicated whether an ensemble was au courant or behind the times. The most famous *marchande de modes* was Rose Bertin, aka Marie Antoinette's Minister of Fashion.[28]

The fourteen-year-old Austrian princess Marie Antoinette had arrived in France in 1770 to marry the dauphin, the future Louis XVI. She had ash-blond hair, blue eyes, a slender figure, and a luminous complexion—all details that had been confirmed by Louis XV, who would not agree to the match until he was reassured that the prospective bride's looks would be a credit to his court.[29] In preparation for her life at Versailles, Marie Antoinette had practiced the correct way to move under the tutelage of a French dance master. Women at the French court did not walk, he told her; they glided, as though on wheels.[30] Still, nothing could have prepared her for the importance of style in this strange new environment. The first intimation came when her entourage reached the Franco-Austrian border. There, in what was surely an excruciating ordeal for a teenage girl, she was publicly stripped naked by French courtiers and dressed from the skin out in French clothes—the only kind permissible at Versailles. She tried to hug the Comtesse de Noailles, a prickly stickler for etiquette, but was harshly rebuffed; to touch a royal personage was a mortifying faux pas. Even her little dog, Mops, was taken from her and sent back to Austria, where his muddy paws would not mar her new finery.[31]

By the time the young queen met Bertin in the spring of 1774, not long after her husband's coronation, she had already demonstrated her impatience with the protocols of fashion. She rode in men's breeches, and she refused to wear the constrictive whalebone corset known as the *grand corps*, a major breach of etiquette that provoked malicious gossip at Versailles.[32] But she had not yet grown into her role as the living expression of French fashion. For that, she needed Bertin's assistance.

Bertin had at that point been in business for about six months and was already making a name for herself among the women of the French court. Her boutique, Le Grand Mogol, was located on the rue Saint-Honoré near the Palais Royal.[33] Named to suggest the riches of a maharajah's palace, Le Grand Mogol boasted large, tantalizingly arrayed and continually updated display windows (another Parisian innovation) with which to entice passersby.[34] Liveried footmen ushered clients inside, which was decorated like the salon of a private house, albeit with the addition of piles of fabrics, arrangements of ribbons and lace, and mannequins dressed in Bertin's handiwork. Bertin presided over her empire from a chaise longue, from which she dispensed advice and disparagements. Although neither wellborn nor personally elegant—she was pudgy, with the ruddy complexion of a countrywoman—Bertin was supremely confident. She was "full of her own importance" and treated "princesses as equals," huffed one aristocratic patron, but her creations were "original" and "of rare perception," which made the ordeal of dealing with her bearable.[35] Bertin cowed her wealthy clients into accepting her creations, playing on their insecurities as they racked up enormous bills.

The fashion trend that endeared Bertin to her most illustrious client was the *pouf*, a radical new hairstyle that was devised by Bertin in collaboration with a celebrity hairstylist named Monsieur Léonard. This teased and powdered confection, one of the most instantly recognizable fashion quirks of the Ancien Régime, was quickly adopted at Versailles. Sometimes reaching heights of three feet, the *pouf* was the setting for tiny scenes, complete with miniature people, flora, fauna, even entire sailing ships, that messaged political events, personal milestones, or whatever storyline the wearer and her *coiffeur* dreamed up. It was a hairstyle-cum-meme, and because it was left in place for days, it required elaborate modifications to sleeping and travel arrangements. Marie Antoinette was enchanted with the *pouf* and seized on it as an ideal vehicle with which to increase her public standing. It became her signature look, and the élan with which she carried it off established her as the most fashionable woman in France. Soon, the queen and Bertin were collaborating on a constant stream of innovations, which were recorded in hundreds of fashion illustrations depicting the young royal. The result was that Marie Antoinette set trends for not just her fellow aristocrats, but women of all classes.

Although it was not unreasonable for a French queen to be preoccupied with fashion, Marie Antoinette, isolated and lonely at a court that looked on her with suspicion for her Austrian birth, lost her equilibrium, and eventually her head. She looked on fashion not as an indulgence but as her "principal occupation," reported her duplicitous maid, and seemed set on "introducing a new fashion almost every day."[36] It wasn't long before Marie Antoinette was deemed flighty and self-centered, and her popularity plummeted. Her household spending reached outrageous heights, and both her mother, via a nonstop stream of letters, and her husband implored her to curtail her shopping habits. By the time she did, it was too late. In her subjects' eyes, she was "Madame Déficit."

Even after the royal family was arrested in 1792, Bertin's deliveries to Marie Antoinette continued. The queen was wearing an ensemble Bertin had created for her the day she was transferred to the Conciergerie, the prison from which she would be taken to her execution, which occurred in October 1793, about nine months after her husband met the same fate.[37] For her rendezvous with the guillotine, however, she dressed not as an aristocrat but in the humble jacket and petticoat of a woman of the people, both pure white. Marie Antoinette was conscious of the power of style to her last breath.

But not even the revolution, which forced many *couturières* and *marchandes de modes* out of business or into exile, dampened Paris's fashion enthusiasm for long. After the Reign of Terror ended with the death of Robespierre in July 1794, the negative political implications of being expensively dressed—i.e., an appointment with Madame Guillotine—relaxed. The monarchy had been overthrown, but France's status as the center of fashion remained intact.

One thing did change, however: The revolutionary government abolished the guild system, which meant that both women and men could make women's clothes. Although many *couturières* continued to flourish, they now faced competition from male couturiers like Louis Hippolyte Leroy, a former hairdresser who become the preferred dressmaker of the Empress Joséphine, the first wife of Napoléon I.[38] But the man credited with inventing the modern couture house was not French at all—he was an Englishman. Charles Frederick Worth was born in Lincolnshire in 1825, apprenticed at a dry goods shop, a sort of proto–department store, as a young boy, and landed in Paris at the age of twenty with five pounds in his pocket. He spoke very little French and knew no one. But these proved to be minor inconveniences. Within a few years, he was working as a salesman at one of the most prestigious dry goods shops in the city, Gagelin-Opigez. By the early 1850s, he'd been promoted to dress designer, and at the Exposition Universelle of 1855, Worth's employer was awarded a gold medal for his work.

Two years after that, Worth left to go into business with a partner, Otto Bobergh.[39] His timing couldn't have been better.

In 1851, Louis-Napoléon Bonaparte, a nephew of Napoléon I and the first elected president of France, staged a coup d'état and declared himself Napoléon III, Emperor of the French, a career move that was confirmed in a plebiscite the following year. Although not personally very impressive—Karl Marx, who was admittedly not impartial, described him as a "grotesque mediocrity"—Napoléon III presided over the Second Empire (1852–1870), a period of intense economic growth and technological advancement.[40] Like Louis XIV, he had a grand vision for France and was determined to turn Paris into his showplace. To achieve this, he appointed Georges-Eugène Haussmann prefect of the Seine and gave him carte blanche to initiate a series of modernizing public works that did away with the city's decaying medieval infrastructure and reinvigorated the economy.

Haussmann sliced up Paris with little regard for its less fortunate inhabitants. Entire neighborhoods were cleared away to make room for the broad avenues, arranged like the spokes of a wheel, that facilitated commerce (and were more difficult to erect anti-government barricades along than the narrow, twisting streets they replaced). The Paris he created, with its uniform blocks of apartment buildings, well-ordered public parks, and state-of-the-art sewage system—the latter a major tourist attraction—was intended for the prosperous middle classes and the elite.[41] Napoléon III's Paris is, more or less, the city that we know today.

With the return of imperial rule, France once again had a court and all the functions and receptions associated with it. Its buoyant economy, meanwhile, attracted wealthy pleasure-seekers from all over Europe and North America. The combination meant innumerable opportunities for display. It was the era of the cage crinoline, a steel wire structure that held women's skirts out to enormous widths and provided endless fodder for caricaturists. Its deceptive solidity has been described as a metaphor for the Second Empire—showy but ultimately empty. To Worth, it was a blank canvas.

Although he did not invent the cage crinoline, which was already in fashion when he launched his business, Worth had a genius for devising graceful trimmings for its voluminous expanse. One trick was to layer fine silk net over heavy satin, which gave the illusion of gauzy weightlessness, like the wearer was floating on a billowing cloud.[42] One of his early clients, Princess Pauline Metternich, called the dresses he made for her "nothing less than masterpieces."[43] In early 1860, she wore a Worth dress of white tulle and silver lamé trimmed with daisies to a ball at the Tuileries Palace, where it was noticed by her good friend, the Empress Eugénie.

Eugénie de Montijo was a Spanish aristocrat who had married Napoléon III in 1853. She had auburn hair and plump, sloping shoulders, like the contours of a champagne bottle, which were then considered the feminine ideal. Although Eugénie dressed simply in private, she understood the power of fashion. A foreigner married to the French monarch, she modeled herself, completely unironically, on Marie Antoinette, whose execution had made her a royalist martyr and erased the Austrian identity that had been so troublesome in her lifetime. In 1854, Eugénie commissioned a portrait by Franz Winterhalter in which she wore an eighteenth-century-style dress and powdered white wig that approximated the *pouf*. By symbolically donning the clothes of France's most fashionable queen, Eugénie recast herself as a leader of French fashion and reinforced her commitment to her adopted country. It was a brilliant marketing maneuver.

When she was on display, which was often, the empress was

expected to uphold the French reputation for impeccable taste. Princess Metternich's elegant Worth gown made the other women at the ball look ostentatious and gaudy, "a mass of lace, feathers, ribbon, fringe and frills."[44] Intrigued, Eugénie demanded an introduction to the designer of her friend's dress. Worth presented himself at the palace the following morning, and Eugénie placed her first order before he left. It was to be one of the most successful partnerships in fashion history.

With the empress's patronage, the success of the House of Worth was assured. Worth became Eugénie's main couturier, responsible for creating the lion's share of her wardrobe. This was no small undertaking: When engaged in her public duties, the empress changed her dress multiple times a day. For major events, like the inauguration of the Suez Canal in the autumn of 1869, she pulled out all the stops, ordering one hundred gowns. Eugénie never appeared in the same ensemble twice, nor did she condone parsimony or questionable taste in the women who frequented the court. When a dress worn by the wife of an American banker did not meet her standards, Eugénie withdrew the woman's standing invitation to attend the weekly evening receptions at the Tuileries Palace.[45]

The underlying reason for this staggering expenditure was, as always, the support of the French fashion industry and the ongoing promotion of Paris as the center of the fashionable world, with the added caveat of confirming the Bonaparte dynasty as its rightful rulers. The dissemination of French style that had begun under Louis XIV gained momentum in the mid-nineteenth century, when technological advances made illustrated newspapers and magazines much cheaper to print. In the new age of mass media, the empress was the face of Paris fashion and one of the most recognizable women in the world. Images of her at the races, attending the opera, hosting state balls, riding in her carriage, and sailing down the Suez Canal on the imperial yacht were transmitted to newspapers and magazines around the globe. Her photo was displayed in the windows of the new department stores to establish their fashion credentials. Publications like *Godey's Lady's Book*, the leading American women's magazine of the middle years of the nineteenth century, followed Eugénie's every move, reporting on fads like empress blue, reputed to be her favorite color, and hairstyles *à l'impératrice*.[46]

Worth was the ideal designer for this moment. He was able to mold the cloying aesthetics of the nineteenth century into dresses that exuded charm while making clear their exorbitant cost. Although Worth was in his grave by the time Thorstein Veblen published *The Theory of the Leisure Class* in 1899, his passages about women wearing expensive dresses as signs of their husbands' wealth captured the essence of the Worth aesthetic of beauty in the service of display. He could harmoniously combine a dozen different fabrics, all costly, in one bodice, and managed to make even the most lavish embellishments look airy. His prices were sky-high, and his client list was drawn from *Debrett's Peerage* and the *Almanach de Gotha*, the stud books of the European aristocracies, as well as the Four Hundred members of American society who fit into the ballroom of the snobbish Caroline Schermerhorn Astor's faux French château on Fifth Avenue.

Worth was indispensable in crafting Eugénie's image. She referred to him as a tyrant; although she was the empress and he was a commoner, it was she who acquiesced when they disagreed on points of style. When Worth decided that it was time for the crinoline to go, Eugénie became his partner in relegating it to the dustbin of fashion. Together, they shaped Eugénie into a paragon of elegance. She remained a client even after the Second Empire collapsed in 1870 and she and her family went into exile in England.

For the rest of his life, Worth acknowledged his debt to her with an annual bouquet of violets, Eugénie's favorite flower, tied with mauve ribbon embroidered with the Worth name in gold.[47]

Worth's authoritarian manner was part of the persona he constructed for himself. His son, Jean, said his father recognized only two authorities: the emperor and God.[48] Unlike the dressmakers of the past, Worth did not collaborate with his clients; he dictated to them. When a customer dared to voice an opinion of which he disapproved, he would order her from the premises, with the disdainful suggestion that she patronize some lesser establishment.[49] He viewed himself as an artist, and from the 1870s onward he dressed as though he were playing one on stage, in a velvet beret and fur-trimmed cloak that made him look like Rembrandt, if Rembrandt had sported a large walrus mustache. It was Worth who originated the idea that a designer was a creative genius—temperamental, perhaps; inspired, certainly—a template that's still in use.

But while Worth wished to be perceived as an artist, it was his business instincts as much as his aesthetic sense that made him a towering figure in fashion history. The Maison Worth combined the intimacy of the private dressmaker's salon with the variety of a dry goods store, to create an entirely new, and completely opulent, shopping experience. Like most dressmakers' shops, it was located on the upper floors of a building on a residential street. Upstairs were a series of salons, each with its own unique decor, where Worth displayed the fabrics he stocked and sold, something dressmakers did not typically do. These included a room dedicated to black and white silks, another for colored silks, and one known as the *salon de lumière*, which simulated a candlelit ballroom and gave clients the opportunity to try on an evening dress in the exact conditions in which it would be worn. In the showroom itself, models were available to try on dresses for any customer who wished to see a design on a live body. A few of Worth's finished gowns were always on display, to be admired like works of art, prior to being delivered to their owners.

His designs often referenced the dress of centuries past, of which Worth was a connoisseur. He owned a collection of historic fashion plates, and since his apprenticeship in London had studied historic portraits for inspiration. But his production and distribution practices were thoroughly modern. Using efficient cutting techniques and sewing machines, his twelve hundred employees could make five thousand dresses a year, a figure that dwarfed that of a typical dressmaking establishment.[50] He was the first designer to sew a label bearing his name into his clothes and was a pioneer of the practice of selling designs for reproduction, initially by provincial and foreign dressmakers and eventually to the workshops of the department stores that were replacing the old dry goods emporiums in the middle years of the nineteenth century.

The structure of Worth's *maison de couture* became the standard by which other couturiers organized their businesses. And these soon proliferated. By the 1860s, when he and his original partner went their separate ways, Worth's competitors included Pingat and Félix; by the time he died and his business passed to his two sons in 1895, these had been joined by Jeanne Paquin, Jacques-Antoine Doucet, Callot Soeurs, and Redfern. All practiced the art of haute couture as it exists today: A seasonal collection was designed, using the finest fabrics and the handiwork of specialized craftspeople such as embroiderers, lace makers, button makers, and *plumassiers*, or feather workers. Clients selected the garments they wanted to order, which were shown to them on house models, and three fittings were scheduled to establish a perfect fit. The client might request a small change, but the overall design remained as its designer intended. Close relationships developed between clients and their saleswomen, who ensured that everything an haute couture customer purchased fit her lifestyle perfectly.

For American women, even the wealthiest of whom might experience social anxiety when interacting with their supposedly more cultured European counterparts, a dress from Worth was an assurance of money well spent, a badge of good taste that could pass without question in any situation. In return, Worth loved his American clients, whom he said had the faces, the figures, and the all-important francs to wear his designs. Edith Wharton, who was one of the most sharp-eyed chroniclers of this milieu, made Worth the designer of May Archer's wedding dress in *The Age of Innocence*, a novel that contains a telling observation on how focused American women were on wearing the right thing. May's husband, Newland Archer, is "struck by the religious reverence of even the most unworldly American women for the social advantages of dress."

> "It's their armor," he thought, "their defense against the unknown, and their defiance of it." And he understood for the first time the earnestness with which May, who was incapable of tying a ribbon in her hair to charm him, had gone through the solemn rite of selecting and ordering her extensive wardrobe.[51]

So many Worth dresses were ordered by Gilded Age Americans that today they fill the collections of American museums. One of the most spectacular is the one Worth made for Alva Vanderbilt to wear at what was perhaps the most lavish party ever thrown in New York, the 1883 costume ball that was her successful bid to elevate the upstart Vanderbilts into the upper echelons of society. Determined to literally outshine everyone else there, Vanderbilt went as "Electric Light." Inside her dress, which was made of yellow satin embroidered with silver tinsel thunderbolts, was concealed a battery pack for the torch she carried. In the photograph taken to commemorate the ball, she holds it aloft like a self-satisfied Statue of Liberty. Her guests, meanwhile, were costumed as European aristocrats, some with real gemstones studding their attire, just like Louis XIV's courtiers.[52]

Extravagance was not always the American way. In the years after the Declaration of Independence and subsequent revolution, it was considered patriotic to dress plainly. But as the United States prospered, its citizens developed a taste for grandeur. The business opportunities produced by the combination of the Industrial Revolution and the Civil War created a dazzling number of millionaires, and families who had accumulated huge fortunes set about building houses that resembled English castles and Italian palazzos and filling them with European art and furniture.[53] When it came to choosing their clothes, they were similarly Eurocentric: The men dressed in Savile Row, while the women made a beeline for the rue de la Paix, the center of the French luxury trade.

Only the wealthiest were able to travel to Paris to order their clothes, but the influence of its designers was pervasive in American cities like New York. In the early nineteenth century, dressmakers and their wealthy customers collected porcelain figurines that arrived biannually from Paris garbed in the latest styles, descendants of the original fashion dolls. By the 1830s, middle-class women could peruse colored prints (mass-produced prints were previously black-and-white) of Paris fashions in *Godey's Lady's Book*.[54] Within two decades, they could not only study such prints but have the editorial assurance that they were entirely up to date: "Our arrangements give us time to engrave the most approved French fashions and lay them before our readers at the same time they appear in Paris," boasted one New York editor in 1854.[55] The new department stores like A. T. Stewart and Lord & Taylor proudly displayed Paris dresses in their windows. Stars of the European stage like the French actress Elisabeth Félix, known professionally as Rachel, who crossed the Atlantic with forty-two trunks of Paris dresses in 1855, were scrutinized for their style.[56] And even dressmakers with unambiguously un-French names like O'Donovan styled themselves "Madame."[57]

What Americans were really getting when they shopped at Lord & Taylor or brought their fashion magazines to their dressmakers for inspiration was an American interpretation of a French design. This often meant that any overt raciness was toned down, as when Sarah Josepha Hale, the editor of *Godey's Lady's Book,* had artists redraw Paris fashion plates with higher necklines. But French origins carried enormous weight in a country that had no long-standing fashion tradition of its own. And beginning in the late 1890s, when buyers for American ready-to-wear manufacturers began importing haute couture to license for production, it was possible to buy line-for-line copies.[58] Even for those who would never wear one, the idea of a "Paris dress" had become an ideal. Many of these purported Paris dresses were fakes, but this did little to quash the desire to own one.[59] The relationship between French fashion and American consumers was so important that the designer for one early twentieth-century New York retailer declared that Paris was nothing less than "American made."[60] One facilitator of this alliance was a young Carmel Snow, who was then working for her mother's custom-dress salon. Annie White would take Snow and her sister Christine with her to Paris, where each girl was assigned a part of a dress to memorize so that it could be copied. Snow scrutinized bodices, her sister skirts.[61]

There were, however, dissenters to the French Legend, and

their objections had a nationalistic flavor. Edward Bok, the editor of the Philadelphia-based *Ladies' Home Journal*, was a leader of the "American Fashions for American Women" movement, which was also the title of an editorial he wrote for the September 1909 issue. This was not Bok's first crusade: He'd previously allied his magazine with the muckraking journalists at *Collier's* to take on the patent-medicine industry, an effort that resulted in the passage of the 1906 Pure Food and Drug Act. Emboldened by this success, Bok turned his attention to other social causes, which is how he came to announce in his 1909 editorial that the *Journal* was launching an American-only fashion department.[62] Over the next few years, Bok stoked patriotic sentiment by extolling the virtues of American women and contrasting them favorably with their French sisters. When it proved difficult to find enough American fashions to feature, he tried shaming the country's designers into action, publishing a piece titled "Are the Only Clever Women in the World in Paris?" in January 1910.[63]

Bok's middle-class readers responded with enthusiastic letters of support, and orders for paper patterns of the styles shown in the *Journal*'s pages surged (cynics suggested that was the impetus for Bok's pro-American stance). In 1912, he took his campaign to *The New York Times*, via a letter to the editor that laid out the case for American fashion, which Bok explained would be far better for American women than the "freakish" styles coming out of Paris—a reference to the revolutionary designs of Paul Poiret, who rejected the pastel, ultrafeminine look of the Edwardian era for a vividly hued, Ballets Russes–tinged Orientalism that seemed dangerously modern.[64] To Bok and his followers, the more outré ideas of Paris designers, like the *jupe-culotte*, or divided skirt, were a threat to the purity of American womanhood. Americans, they maintained, should be clothed in fashions that reflected republican ideals like self-sufficiency and thrift, not the effete and decadent designs of French Svengalis. Moreover, were there not moral and practical obligations to support the nation's economy?[65]

The editors of the *Times* agreed with Bok's pro-American stance and followed up his letter with a series of editorials that lampooned Paris fashion and praised native design. This effort culminated in December 1912 with the announcement of an "American fashions" design contest, to be chaired by Bok.[66] The difficulty of separating American fashion from the French variety was immediately apparent: Thousands of submissions were received, pretty much all interpretations of prevailing Paris trends. Nevertheless, nine winners—representatives of "American genius"—were announced by the *Times* in February 1913.[67] Among them was Ethel Traphagen, who won in the evening dress category for a design inspired by James McNeill Whistler's painting *Nocturne: Blue and Gold—Old Battersea Bridge*. She went on to found the Traphagen School in New York 1923, which trained American designers for sixty-eight years.[68]

By the time the winners were announced, the American Fashions campaign was national news, supported and publicized by newspapers across the country. Critics pointed out that it wasn't possible to take the place of Paris because the United States lacked the infrastructure to support a completely independent fashion industry—very few of the country's fabric mills produced silk, for one thing, and it was the most common fabric used in expensive women's clothing. But the biggest hurdle faced by the American Fashion movement was the unwillingness of American women to give up Paris, the city they had been trained to look to for decades. It was just too enormous a change to contemplate. As Edna Woolman Chase, then the newly installed editor in chief of *Vogue*, told *WWD*, "Revolutions do not occur in fashion."[69] How wrong she turned out to be.

In August of 1914, World War I began, and the output of the haute couture houses was—temporarily, as it turned out—lessened. American retailers panicked, as did the American fashion press, which covered Paris almost exclusively; without it, they wouldn't have much to illustrate or write about. *Vogue*'s solution was to host an American fashion show, which would give designers publicity and the press fodder. In the 1890s, *Vogue* had hosted fashion exhibitions using dolls; Chase's innovation was to instead use live models, the daughters of the city's wealthiest families. She persuaded leading retailers and dressmakers to provide the fashions, roped socialites into participating, and announced that the proceeds would go to help women and children affected by the war in Europe. Lest anyone think that *Vogue* was abandoning Paris, Chase clarified her position in the November 1 issue, which was published just days before the Fashion Fête—note the French name—opened at the Ritz-Carlton. Although it was a "coming of age" for American fashion, an opening of "the door of opportunity for our dressmakers," *Vogue* explained, there was no question of cutting loose from the apron strings of Paris—in fact, "heaven grant us till our old age the sanity to follow in her footsteps!" Of the designers whose work would be modeled, the magazine stressed, "American fashions for American women is no part of their platform." The very idea of American fashion, *Vogue* continued, was "too awful to contemplate."[70]

The Fashion Fête went off without a hitch, and the reviews were positive. *Harper's Bazaar*, ticked off by the accolades its rival had received, spread the rumor that *Vogue* was deserting Paris and suggested that the couturiers' only true friend in New York was *Bazaar*. Chase was furious and had to promise a French Fashion Fête for the following year to soothe the couturiers' ruffled feathers.[71]

In any case, the spotlight did not shine on American design for long. Shortly after the Fashion Fête, the Paris couture houses resumed normal production, and the flow of dresses across the Atlantic continued. By the 1920s, one of the most economically meteoric decades in the country's history, Americans, chiefly in the form of department store and wholesale buyers, were the best customers of Parisian haute couture. The import and adaptation of French design was a smoothly functioning machine, able to siphon up Paris models at one end and spit out American facsimiles at the other, at prices that ranged from thousands of dollars to two or three. It seemed like this system could go on forever, enriching both sides, giving American women affordable (whatever that meant to them) versions of the best clothes in the world. The door of opportunity that *Vogue* had alluded to in 1914 seemed permanently wedged shut.

And then an American came back from Paris and kicked it in.

3

She's Barred from France!

Elizabeth Hawes

The beauty of the French clothing business is that for decades nobody ever questioned its God-like quality. The build-up has been so perfect, so subtle and so unceasing that a legend is still accepted as reality by nearly the whole world.

—ELIZABETH HAWES[1]

It took a near-death experience for Elizabeth Hawes to decide she was done with Paris. It was August of 1928, and she was sitting in the garden of a friend's family's house in the countryside near Poitiers, recovering from a botched tonsillectomy during which she'd almost bled to death.[2] For two weeks, she basked in the sun and reflected. She'd been in France for three years and had achieved what she set out to accomplish. She'd learned to differentiate between what the French caricaturist Sem had called *"le vrai et le faux chic."*[3] She had acquired fluency in the art of designing and making beautiful clothes to order. She'd studied the habits of the *beau monde*, or fashionable world. And in the process, she'd discovered that her cherished vision of Paris fashion was a lie. She had seen the inner workings of the French Legend, and she judged it to be a complete fraud. In fact, the whole idea now nauseated her. She no longer wanted to be a couturier in Paris.

Instead, Hawes resolved to dress American women, making them clothes with their needs and lifestyles in mind. It was time to go back to New York. It was time to tear the French Legend down. Less than a month later, she was on her way home.[4]

Becoming American fashion's foremost iconoclast had not been part of Hawes's plan when she arrived in France in 1925, a sheltered twenty-two-year-old from an upper-middle-class family in Ridgewood, New Jersey. She had sailed from New York on the eighth of July, traveling student third class on the RMS *Berengaria*, a Cunard liner named for the wife of Richard the Lionheart.[5] She had a degree in economics from Vassar; $300; two freelance jobs reporting on fashion trends, one for a department store and another for her hometown paper; and a diamond that had belonged to her grandmother to pawn in case she ran out of money. Her traveling companion was a college friend, Evelyn Johnson, who was going to Paris for the conventional reason wealthy young women did: She was ordering her trousseau.

It was Hawes's first crossing, and it was a good one. After a senior year that included advanced French classes, designing for a Poughkeepsie boutique, and doing alterations for better-off classmates (the source of the $300), she was ready to enjoy herself; as she later recalled, she learned to drink on that voyage.[6] The six-day journey had the added bonus of intrigue: In the early-morning hours before the *Berengaria* sailed, one of her would-be passengers, twenty-eight-year-old Helen, Baroness Vernuehlen of Java in the

Dutch East Indies, after complaining of feeling faint, had plunged to her death from the window of her seventh-story suite at the Ritz-Carlton, shattering the glass roof of the hotel's Japanese Garden and landing on the front page of *The New York Times*.[7] It was a story straight out of Agatha Christie. Thrillingly for Hawes and her fellow passengers, a companion who had been present in the Texas-born baroness's hotel room when the fall had occurred was nevertheless aboard the ship, still occupying the cabin the two were to have shared. This proximity to notoriety was in some ways a portent of things to come—Hawes would soon become involved in rather shady undertakings.

The *Berengaria* docked at Cherbourg on the fourteenth of July, Bastille Day, when everything was either closed or operating at reduced capacity. The train to Paris, which normally took five hours, stretched to fourteen. Hawes barely noticed. "I felt as if I'd gotten home after all those years," she said.[8]

The Paris she arrived in was at the height of its interwar glamour, what *The New Yorker*'s columnist Janet Flanner called "the capital of hedonism of all Europe."[9] Josephine Baker, who made her entrance in *La Revue Nègre* wearing a single flamingo feather—the banana skirt came later—was performing to delirious crowds.[10] Surrealism was enchanting and perplexing the art world. Scott and Zelda Fitzgerald, Ernest Hemingway, John Dos Passos, and Djuna Barnes were all there, drinking and writing on the Left Bank. On the Right Bank, the wealthy congregated at the Ritz Bar, where Hawes exercised her newfound capacity for liquor with double alexanders, discovering only later that "double" was not part of the drink's name.[11] Yet for all its modernity, Paris remained very much a nineteenth-century capital. "Its charm lay in its being in no way international—not as yet," remembered Flanner.[12]

Within days of her arrival, Hawes visited her first haute couture house. She watched as her friend ordered dresses, suits, and evening gowns, "quite terrified at finally being right in the middle of all that chic."[13] After a month, Johnson went home, and Hawes started her first job, which had been arranged by Johnson's mother via her dressmaker. It was not until Hawes reported for work that she realized she'd been hired by a criminal enterprise. She'd been sent to a copy house, a small dressmaking establishment that illegally manufactured and sold copies—today we'd call them dupes—of the dresses created in the important *maisons de couture*. In the 1920s, such businesses flourished in Paris. They existed on the margins of the city's fashion industry, down side streets and up dingy flights of stairs. The good ones, like the firm that hired Hawes—the pseud-onym she used for it was Doret—turned out copies that were vir-tually indistinguishable from the originals. Monsieur and Madame Doret, the owners, liked to boast that they never copied a dress without first laying hands on the real thing—truly an example of honor among thieves.[14] A genuinely good copy, which was pretty much identical to the real thing, down to the material, buttons, embroidery, and trim, sold for about half the price of an original, hence the proliferation of fashion counterfeiters and their steady stream of clients.

Although larceny had not been part of Hawes's fantasy Paris experience, the copy house supplied an excellent introduction to high fashion. Doret had no need of a designer, for obvious reasons, but it employed a crack production team of patternmakers, cutters, fitters, and seamstresses. It provided the opportunity to examine real haute couture dresses up close. And, as Hawes quickly learned, it showed her that the workings of the fashion industry had noth-ing in common with the economic theory she'd studied at Vassar.

First, there was the matter of acquiring the dresses that were to be copied. Sometimes, she was surprised to learn, they were simply purchased from a legitimate haute couture house. This was one of the things Hawes had been hired to do. As a young and unknown American, she could go to a couture house and pose as a tourist eager to bring home a Paris original. If the dress in question was sufficiently *jeune fille*, she ordered it for herself, going for the requisite three fittings and acting the part of the wide-eyed American girl excited at the prospect of owning an honest-to-goodness Paris frock. If the style was more mature, she pretended to order it for her mother, supplying a false set of measurements for what she assured the vendeuse would be a delighted dowager back home in New Jersey/Iowa/Illinois or some equally exotic-sounding locale.[15] But one could only pose as an ingenue a limited number of times before the saleswomen caught on, so this method was used sparingly.

The bulk of the originals arrived at the Maison Doret by other, equally perfidious means. A model for one of the couture houses might "borrow" a gown for a few hours, for example, scurrying into Doret with it and shifting nervously from foot to foot while Hawes sketched it—another of her responsibilities— and the patternmakers swiftly took its measurements before pocketing her fee and the dress and disappearing back out the door. The *petites mains*, or seamstresses, who worked in the couture houses were on the take, too, smuggling muslin patterns out under their clothing and selling them further down the fashion food chain. Thrifty haute couture customers might lend their originals to the Dorets in exchange for a reduced price on the copies with which they padded out their wardrobes. Another source was the mistress of the manager of one of the famous couture houses. She presumably got her clothes for free but picked up extra cash by renting them to the copy houses. Madame Doret did not approve of this particular source, not on moral grounds but because the lady's dresses were shopped around to every copy house in town, thus eliminating any cachet the House of Doret might claim.[16] Ditto the muslins hawked by the *petites mains*, who were woefully underpaid and always eager to supplement their meager incomes.

Far more satisfactory was the arrangement the Dorets had with a resident buyer for an American manufacturer in Paris, whom Hawes referred to only as "Madame Ellis." An American who had lived abroad for years, Ellis was in some ways a glorified version of the girl-on-the-scene whom Hawes played for her hometown paper and the provincial department store. Beautifully groomed and gowned, she frequented the haunts of the upper class, the better to know exactly what well-dressed Parisiennes were wearing. When the fashion shows rolled around, she used this knowledge to help her visiting colleagues choose the styles that most closely aligned with this narrow definition of chic. These dresses were then bought by the manufacturer and shipped back to the United States to be bowdlerized for mass production. But like seemingly everyone in fashion, Ellis was not above earning a few extra francs. The dresses sometimes made a brief stop chez Doret before being loaded onto a train and then a fast boat to New York. It was on one such detour that Hawes first made a more meaningful acquaintance with her compatriot.

Hawes owned a roomy beaver coat, which she was instructed to wear to work that day. Upon arriving at the office, she was put into a taxi and dispatched to Ellis's office. Ellis was there alone, a large pile of Chanel boxes at her elbow. As soon as Hawes was inside and the door was closed, she began emptying the boxes and shaking the contents free of their tissue paper. Out came eight Chanel dresses. "Put them under your coat and get back here as fast as you can," she ordered (the skimpy styles of the time made this relatively easy).[17] The frocks stashed, Hawes taxied back to Doret at top speed. There, the usual measuring and sketching was done.

Madame Doret took notes on the belts and buttons and clipped snippets of materials from the seams. As they worked, Hawes realized that even copyists had their professional pride: Between the cutting and the measuring, the Doret team made comments like "How Chanel has the nerve to deliver clothes made this way! Look, it's all cut off the grain. The inside seams aren't even finished."[18] When they were done, they had all the information they needed to make dresses so closely resembling their originals that Coco herself would have had trouble telling them apart. Moreover, the Doret customers would get their fake Chanels before the American customers received their authentic Chanels.

The dresses transcribed down to the last detail, they went back under Hawes's coat. She climbed into another taxi and returned to the waiting, and no doubt skittish, Ellis. The dresses were repacked, the tissue paper rearranged, and the boxes resumed their journey to New York.[19] The French Legend continued to hum.

For Hawes, still in thrall to the novelty and drama of her new job, the whole thing had been a lark. For Ellis, it was an opening. She began to size Hawes up with a speculative eye. Here was a fellow American who had shown herself to be a willing partner in her enterprise with the Dorets. Perhaps she would be inclined to involve herself on a more permanent basis. Ellis approached Hawes with an offer: Would she like a job as a sketcher?[20]

Ellis worked on the same system as all the other buyers of expensive Parisian couture dresses that were copied for the American market: She bought what she had to, paying the fee demanded by the couturier for the privilege of copying his or her dress for large-scale production. Everything else, she stole. This was accomplished by bringing with her to the four annual fashion showings—major ones in August and February, mid-season ones in November and April—a person who was ostensibly a junior buyer. In fact, this

person was a sketcher, recognizable to anyone in the know by his
or (usually) her youth and lack of fashionable attire. It was illegal
to bring a sketcher to a fashion show, but all the buyers tried to get
away with having one there because if a sketcher could provide an
accurate drawing of a dress—a blueprint, really—the buyer could
bypass the fee. A well-regarded couture house might charge $200
for a dress. Added to this was the duty that had to be paid to cus-
toms officials to bring the dress into the United States, plus the
traveling expenses of the buyers. Hawes estimated that it cost about
$400—1926 dollars—to legally copy one dress.[21] This was why every
buyer strove to avoid paying the fee.

At a small house, where a buyer might buy one dress and
steal six, the sketchers could ply their trade openly—the money
the house earned from the one order was worth it. But at one of
the larger, more established houses, a sketcher didn't dare do any
sketching or even take extensive notes at a show. The exception
was Patou, where drinks were served and a festive, if not downright
raffish, atmosphere was encouraged. More often, once a buyer gave
the sketcher the signal that a dress was of interest—usually a nudge
in the ribs—the sketcher would commit its particulars to memory.
These dresses, which everyone was interested in, were known as
Fords, after the car that was ubiquitous on American roads.[22] The
sketches had to be detailed enough to supply a drawing that would
be used as the basis for a mass-produced copy of the couture original, so to merely remember that a dress was black and had a belt
and a ruffled collar would not suffice. More likely, a sketcher might
take a note or two and then silently repeat an extensive litany of
details such as "black wool crepe with four six-inch pleats on the
left hip, patent leather belt with snail buckle, square neck quite high
with pleated ruffle on it"—doing this however many times she was

nudged—until she was safely back in her room and could put pencil to paper.[23]

If a sketcher was good at her job, she could churn out about fifteen sketches per show, for which the going rate in the 1920s was $1.50 each.[24] By the time the last model walked out—most designers of the era showed two or three hundred ensembles in a fashion show, far more than their modern counterparts—she was holding a lot of information in her head. She lived in continual fear of the gimlet-eyed vendeuses, who kept a constant lookout for any pen they thought might be moving more than the couple of strokes it took to indicate that a particular number had caught one's eye. If they spotted such a flurry of activity, they simply leaned over the offender's shoulder and yanked the program out of her hands, blowing her junior buyer cover. From then on, the offender was banned. But with a bit of practice and a photographic memory, being a sketcher was a lucrative, if nerve-racking way to make a living.

When Ellis approached Hawes, she had been at the Maison Doret for about six months. She had learned how to recognize the styles of the various French designers through copying and selling their clothes, and, courtesy of Monsieur Doret, she had acquired a reasonably fluent, if slangy French. She was luxuriating in the freedom of her new life, but she felt that she had not yet achieved her goal of learning how beautiful clothes were conceived. Ellis's offer would give her access to all the great Paris couture houses—the forward-looking trimness of Chanel, the breathtaking construction techniques of Vionnet, the *sportif* insouciance of Patou—where she could drink in their wonders for herself.

And then there was the question of money. Although the Dorets were friendly and hospitable and paid her a perfectly reasonable rate, and Hawes enjoyed the jolly midday meals that

Monsieur Doret, the only man on the premises, presided over like a paterfamilias, her salary was insufficient for her American standard of living, which no amount of appreciation for France could alter. She rented a two-room apartment with central heat and running water—luxuries for a French working girl, necessities for her—for which she paid the lion's share of her income. The rest went to pay for food. Even with her earnings from the department store and the newspaper, to which she had added a gig writing fashion dispatches for *The New Yorker* (nom de plume: Parisite), she was constantly broke. As a sketcher, she could easily earn $450 for three weeks of work, and even more once she was established.[25]

And so, in February 1926, Hawes became a sketcher for Ellis's firm, which she called Weinstock and Co., another pseudonym, and described as one of the largest and best expensive dress manufacturers in New York. She convinced herself it was an excellent idea, suppressing any misgivings she had about what was essentially wholesale theft, and telling herself that she was supporting her education in fashion. The first season went quite well. She learned that the two biggest shows were Patou and Chanel, both of whom showed in the second week. Patou was a gala affair, with the guests packed to the rafters in a huge salon on the rue Saint-Florentin. As everyone sat jammed shoulder to shoulder on tiny gilt chairs, their voices soaring, the champagne circulated and the cigarette smoke slowly filled the room. When the models came out, holding the card displaying the number of their dress at hip level (hence the habit of referring to particular styles as "numbers"), there was no need for the nudge in the ribs. Jean Patou was a showman and knew exactly how to display his Fords: He sent them out six at a go, perfectly alike in line and cut but in a rainbow of colors. This, mesdames et messieurs, he announced, is a Ford—feast your eyes and place your orders! When a Ford appeared, the buyers all leaned forward and strained to get the model's attention. "Mamsel! Your number. Come over here, Mamsel."[26] They exchanged furtive whispers with their colleagues about the competition: Bergdorf's took that number. Lord & Taylor took that number. Hattie Carnegie took that number. Weinstock took that number. No one wanted to miss out on a Ford that was in high demand. How could they please their customers if they didn't provide exactly what everyone else offered? The pandemonium was such that Hawes, seated in the back row, could take all the notes she liked. Weinstock might buy eight of Patou's Fords, but the collection yielded at least thirty, so she made extensive use of the large programs Monsieur Patou thoughtfully supplied.

Chanel was a different story. Just getting in required resolve and dedication. Gabrielle "Coco" Chanel's *maison* on the rue Cambon had only two small salons, and she restricted her guest list accordingly.[27] She could afford to; since opening her first shop in 1910, she had been heralded as a visionary for the streamlined modernity of her designs—what Paul Poiret, whom she toppled from the top of the haute couture pyramid, called *misère de luxe.*[28] Her innovations, from her co-opting of jersey, previously relegated to the manufacture of men's underwear, to her promotion of the little black dress, made her one of the most imitated designers of the era. Only those who placed large orders were permitted to see her fashion shows. Weinstock, which bought as many as ten dresses every season, made the cut. But that didn't mean that getting in was easy. Like everyone else, the Weinstock contingent had to fight their way through the baying crowd gathered outside 31 rue Cambon, all screaming that they deserved a seat. By the time they emerged onto the house's famed mirrored staircase, their coats had been pulled half off their bodies and their hats were askew.[29]

Once seated, Hawes didn't dare move her pen more than a millimeter or two—not that she had room for much more. The tiny slip of paper provided by Chanel left little room for any meaningful jotting; it was as meager as her skirts, which were said to be the shortest in Paris.[30] Amazonian saleswomen were posted everywhere, keen to catch anyone who dared to steal from Mademoiselle. Their icy glares were trained on meek little sketchers and established buyers alike; no one was spared at the House of Chanel. Hawes saw her job here as a contest of wills between herself and the model. The model's job was to show the dress as quickly as possible, escaping backstage before any sketcher could get too close a look at it. Hawes's job was to master the dress's cut before the model disappeared. By her second season at Chanel, she had become proficient enough, she reported, that "I could have designed you as pretty a Chanel as the master herself."[31]

During her second season, Hawes's Faustian bargain with the buyers began to unravel. The Weinstock delegation, with Hawes in tow, had returned to Chanel for their postshow appointment. One buyer remained with Hawes in the fitting room, holding up dresses for her to sketch, her body braced against the door to keep out nosy saleswomen, while the other two remained outside. Hawes heard a saleswoman on the other side of the door, speaking loudly to be heard above the general din, ask her assistant, for the love of heaven, to track down number 234, which was urgently needed by a client.[32] Hawes knew that the two Weinstock employees who were loitering in the showroom would be on the trail of number 234 like bloodhounds, as would every other buyer on the premises. No one wanted to go home and be asked why they hadn't obtained Chanel's best dress of the season. But the Weinstock faction was especially intrepid. Almost every time a cry went up for a sample, it was being held in front of Hawes. That season, she was able to sketch almost the entire collection.[33]

But as they were preparing to leave, Hawes began to seriously reconsider her life of crime. No longer content with absconding with sketches, the buyers had begun to pilfer the actual clothes. One was stuffing fabric samples into her mink pockets. Another tore the fringe off a slew of dresses to have it copied in New York. A third, brazenly, filched a belt from yet another dress.[34] Hawes was aghast (although not as aghast as the House of Chanel, which allowed no belts into the fitting rooms the following season). She had never felt much respect for the buyers she worked with, but the flagrancy of their purloining disgusted her. She signed up for one last season with Weinstock, again reasoning that the money was hard to resist, but she deliberately made bad sketches. When she was recognized and turned away from one of the smaller couture houses—ironically, a copy house that had gone legit—she told them they were quite right. Design, she decided, should be paid for.[35]

She spent the next two years working various fashion jobs, including as a stylist for Macy's. Today, that suggests helping customers put together a look, but in the 1920s, stylists were a form of retail insurance, hired to prevent buyers from buying anything in bad—i.e., un-Parisian—taste.[36] Hawes realized the futility of this when a jewelry line she thought awful turned out to sell spectacularly. When she persuaded Macy's to buy some of the trompe l'oeil sweaters with which Elsa Schiaparelli launched herself onto the fashion scene, they didn't know what to do with them, and the clever knits languished.[37] She left Macy's and took a similar position with Lord & Taylor, but the average American woman continued to resist undiluted Parisian chic. Fed up with buyers from the United States, Hawes went to work as a designer for a couturier named Nicole Groult, the sister of Paul Poiret, who had disparaged the clothes of Coco Chanel. After a few weeks there, Hawes made some bright suggestions as to how Groult could improve her business. Her employer pointed to her elbow and said, "I have diamond bracelets up to here. Would I be any happier if I had them to my shoulder?"[38] Just as American women might struggle to embrace the most avant-garde of Paris fashion, modern American methods were not for the haute couture.

Shortly thereafter, Hawes had her tonsils out and experienced her epiphany. She had accomplished what she set out to do; she knew how to be a couturier. But she was certain that she no longer wanted to be a couturier in Paris. The only woman Paris couturiers understood, the only woman they designed for, was the chic woman. To be chic, Hawes now knew, required unswerving devotion to wearing the correct clothes, at the correct time, in the correct place, with the correct accessories, alongside the correct people. It demanded unlimited funds, a household staff, a lady's maid to maintain one's clothes, and freedom from quotidian concerns like work. Being chic took all day, every day. Very few women, perhaps several hundred, met this definition.[39] This small group was photographed and written about ceaselessly—they were the ambassadors of the French Legend. It was for these women, and only these women, Hawes realized, that the couturiers of Paris designed; they had no interest in or knowledge of the lives of other women. But Hawes had no interest in dressing chic women. They bored her to tears.

Moreover, she did not think a fashion system that rested on a few hundred women wearing the clothes of a select few Paris couturiers had much life left in it. American manufacturers and department stores, she had come to understand, knew perfectly well that the French Legend was hollow. But they used it anyway because it was an excellent marketing tool. American women had been schooled to believe that the French Legend was, despite its absurdity, undeniable fact. The buyers from Macy's and Lord & Taylor she had tried to steer toward the cutting edge of Parisian fashion knew that it was not what their clients really craved. American merchants didn't want the Paris ideal; they merely wanted its imprimatur.

But Americans had become so good at aping Paris that they were undermining the very system on which they relied. In 1928, American women could buy a dress from the House of Chanel in Paris for about $200. They could buy the exact same dress in New York from a luxury made-to-order retailer like Hattie Carnegie or Bergdorf Goodman for $250. For less than $60, they could get a ready-to-wear version of the Chanel from a department store like Lord & Taylor. And for prices that ranged from $10 to $20, they could buy yet another ready-to-wear copy of the same dress, albeit in lower-quality fabrics. How much longer, Hawes wondered, could businesses like Hattie Carnegie continue to charge more than $200 for a dress that could be had for substantially less?[40]

In her three years in Paris, she had been thoroughly indoctrinated in the principles of good design, and she knew that the buyers and designers who had been making the biannual trek to see the haute couture collections, some for more than a decade, had been similarly well educated—they knew precisely what was worth stealing, and why. The only thing stopping them from designing their own collections was the continued power of the French Legend. What American women needed, Hawes reasoned, were their own couturiers. They needed someone to create their own legend.

American couturiers—designers who created original, made-to-order collections with no input from Paris—did exist in the late

1920s, but they were rare. Hawes was familiar with only one, Jessie Franklin Turner, who was known for her tea gowns, diaphanous garments that started out as intimate attire and were transformed by her artistry into ultrafeminine evening dresses that referenced European folk costumes and Middle Eastern fables.[41] There was also Valentina, a Russian émigré who used one name professionally, and would become known for her timeless, rather severe designs and her one-liners, delivered in an accent that gave everything she said the aura of a pronouncement. "Meenk is for football," she retorted to a customer who demurred when the designer suggested she buy a sable coat, explaining that she already had a mink one.[42] Like Hawes, both these women ignored the dictates of Paris to pursue their own design edicts.

When Hawes arrived back in New York in September 1928, she assumed she would get a job with a department store or established made-to-order house. It was only after she realized that American firms expected their designers to uphold the French Legend that she went into business for herself, with another Vassar connection, a wealthy debutante named Rosemary Harden, as her partner. Harden's father supplied a line of credit, and the two women rented a space on East 56th Street, around the corner from Bonwit Teller. Hawes-Harden opened in December 1928, and instantly attracted a clientele—proof, in Hawes's mind, that women were eager for clothes that weren't merely Paris imitations. Even the dress that was considered the most outlandish in that first collection, a number called "1929, Perhaps; 1930, Surely" found a home. Unlike the prevailing tubular style that skimmed the knees and relocated the waist to hip level—the "flapper dress" that is sartorial shorthand for the Jazz Age—"1929" had a floor-length hem and a waistline positioned just below the bust. Hawes, whose eye had been trained to register the smallest shifts in fashion, was certain that longer hemlines and higher waistlines were imminent. She also knew that American buyers tended to gravitate toward the newer version of what they'd seen the season before, which meant her audience had no idea of these developments; to them, "1929" just looked weird and wrong. But when Patou dropped his hemlines and raised his waists the following year, American women followed suit like everyone else.

The launch of Hawes-Harden was not without hiccups: Neither woman knew anything about running a business; the stock market crashed less than a year after it opened, putting a damper on customers' appetite for expensive clothes; and Rosemary Harden subsequently left the partnership, selling her shares to Hawes for one dollar, in 1930. But despite these challenges, Hawes Inc., as the firm was now called, flourished. In 1933, Hawes moved to larger premises, taking over an entire townhouse at 21 East 67th Street. She ripped out the curlicued "Louis something" decor and remade it in her stripped-down modernist aesthetic, with bare floors and venetian blinds. The painters' union went on strike just ten days before the September opening, leaving her with bare plaster walls. She went ahead anyway and lined up a row of dressmaker dummies with placards reading "Contractors are unfair to union labor" to greet her guests.[43] Her next-door neighbor, Jessie Franklin Turner, bristled. She thought Hawes uncouth and her employees low class.[44] Eventually, Turner moved back to Park Avenue, which she considered more suitable for her clients' needs, leaving East 67th Street to her rival.

Hawes's customers loved the informal atmosphere of her salon. Most were nonconformists in some way; they wrote, they had advanced degrees, they collected modern art, they advocated for women's rights. One, Jane Kendall Mason, a wealthy socialite who posed for *Vogue* in a striped silk evening gown Hawes made for her,[45] dedicated herself to scandalizing her neighbors in Havana and energetic extramarital affairs (Ernest Hemingway, one lover, called her the most uninhibited woman he had ever met).[46] Another Hawes client was Katharine Hepburn, although their relationship skidded to a halt in 1934, after Hawes refused to make a sequined dress for the actress, arguing that it wouldn't suit her (an assessment that seems right on the money).[47]

Sequins, along with ruffles, tulle, and frippery of any kind, were not part of Hawes's design vocabulary. She was a modernist who believed that her success as a designer depended on intuiting what her clients wanted to wear before they realized it themselves. She designed clothes that were comfortable and flattering, stylish rather than fashionable. She liked mitered stripes, full skirts, bias cuts, and pockets and buttons that functioned, and she liked them whether they were in fashion or not. One day in the late 1930s, when skirts were narrow, hats were de rigueur, and makeup was an essential component of a woman's public face, she was observed strolling up Fifth Avenue in a full skirt, hatless, her lips their natural color. People stopped in their tracks and stared at this alien apparition. "A dinosaur could not have made a more startling sight," a friend remembered.[48] When Hawes reached Bergdorf Goodman, Mr. Goodman, the founder of the store, spotted her through the window. He was visibly apoplectic, sputtering, "That woman is crazy!"[49] Hawes pushed the boundaries of acceptable dress even further at her second wedding, to the filmmaker Joseph Losey, for which she wore jeans. The justice of the peace was so discomfited by her attire that he referred to her as a man.[50]

Hawes's ease with the unconventional was nurtured by her mother, Henrietta Houston Hawes, Vassar class of 1891, who taught all four of her children to follow their instincts.[51] Sam, as her offspring called her, invested her small inheritance in the stock market and local real estate, then used the money she earned to send Hawes and her two sisters to her alma mater (their brother went to Princeton).[52] She got involved in Ridgewood affairs, becoming so integral to the town's housing development that the local plumbers' union made her an honorary member, giving her the distinction of being New Jersey's first female plumber.[53] When her son joined the navy, Henrietta taught herself Morse code so she could communicate with him. An early and enthusiastic supporter of Montessori education, she encouraged her children to pursue creative projects.[54] For her second-born daughter, this meant launching a dress business before she started high school. Most important, Henrietta showed her children that to be different was laudable, and that it required both strength and conviction. When Hawes told her she was moving to Paris to learn how to be a couturier, her mother's only response was "How long are you going to stay?"[55]

While at Vassar, Hawes had embraced leftist politics, writing her senior thesis on the British Labour politician Ramsay MacDonald. Her interest in socialist economics led her to accept an offer from Soviet officials in 1935 to put on a fashion show in Moscow. A trip to the Soviet Union was unremarkable for the left-leaning intelligentsia of the era—Schiaparelli went and came back raving enthusiastically about the imperial family's apartments and complaining about Soviet dreariness like used soap in her hotel room— but was looked on with suspicion by the majority of Americans, as well as most of her clients.[56] Hawes gave an interview to *The New York Times* when she came back, telling a reporter that she'd been politely received and that Soviet women wore nail polish and got permanent waves and were interested in fashion. But she understood the potentially dangerous implications of appearing to support Communism. When, a few years later, her book publisher promoted her as having been offered a job as a designer with the

Soviet Dress Trust, she immediately sent an angry letter denying it
and demanding that the blurb be removed from the dust jacket for
the book's second printing.[57]

It was a rare instance of Hawes shying away from controversy.
Decades before fashion embraced gender fluidity, she questioned
why men were content to be imprisoned in "the masculine strait-
jackets of our Western civilization."[58] Why shouldn't men wear
skirts, she wondered, or bright colors? In 1937, she held a fashion
show that included her ideas on what men could wear, if they dared:
a lime-green belted tunic paired with elastic-waisted silk trousers; a
flowing robe inspired by Arab dress; plum silk trousers with a strap
around the instep. The clothes were modeled by her friends, most of
whom worked in creative fields, like the dancer Paul Taylor and the
writer and gourmand Lucius Beebe, who had to be dragged onto
the runway after last-minute cold feet.[59] If anyone would be open to
fresh ideas in menswear, she reasoned, it would be this progressive
group. Instead, she was startled at the pushback she got from them. It
inspired her to write her second book, *Men Can Take It*, a social and
sartorial manifesto that was published in 1939. Men, she suggested,
should stop looking at clothes as signifiers of gender and class and
just enjoy them. The reviews, from mostly male writers, were dispar-
aging. *Newsweek*'s review referred to her "Anschluss," a reference to
Germany's annexation of Austria the previous year. Another wrote
that Hawes needed to be stopped "before she goes completely hay-
wire . . . if she had her way males walking down Fifth Avenue would
look like a Mardi Gras parade."[60]

Although Hawes took fashion seriously, she liked to joke about
it, too, giving all her designs clever names that offered subtle social commentary. Her Lydia Pinkham negligee, for example, was
named after a tonic for "feminine complaints" whose high alcohol
content had given it a sales bump during Prohibition, while her

multihued Alimony evening dress suggested that the wearer might be having a good time on someone else's bill, especially when paired with the Misadventure cape. She could be staggeringly subversive. She accessorized the Alimony dress, for example, with a wood-and-suede handbag in the shape of a stylized penis and testicles.[61] Another evening gown, Pandora, was named after the Greek myth. Some scholars have interpreted Pandora's box as a symbol of the uterus, an analysis Hawes alluded to with a small, scarlet, pentagon-shaped insert on the bodice, placed between the breasts, the only splash of color on an otherwise cream silk gown.[62] The matching coat, also in cream silk, has vertical scarlet inserts that suggest the labia. In 1931, this was strong stuff.

Hawes took Lydia Pinkham and Pandora with her when, ignoring all precedent, she decided to stage a fashion show in Paris on the Fourth of July 1931, the first non-Paris-based American designer to bring her clothes to the mother ship. Her motive, she maintained, was not to undermine the French, whose country and food and clothes she loved. Rather, she wanted to let them know that "clothes are designed in America. All beautiful clothes are not designed in France. All women do not want French clothes."[63] She intended to show the French that their legend was nonsense.

She arrived in mid-June, and soon ran into her first problem: The American-owned, English-language *Paris Herald Tribune* would publish a story about the upcoming show—nothing that would offend the couturiers, they stressed—only if she took out an ad. Hawes needed the publicity, so she gritted her teeth, paid for the ad, and wrote the story herself, about why she was bringing the collection to Paris.[64] Then she moved on to her next challenge: The manager at Les Ambassadeurs, the restaurant where she had planned to stage her show, was out of town, and his underling professed to know nothing about any promises made to an American dress designer. She was eventually able to convince him to let her proceed, but he refused to allow any rehearsal time or allocate a dressing room for the models.[65] Undeterred, Hawes assembled her guest list, had the invitations printed, and sent them out. All but one of the couturiers she invited, her old boss, Nicole Groult, sent their regrets. She alleviated her stress by buying three expensive hats.[66]

Finally, the day arrived. The restaurant was packed. The models, American girls whom she had found via her ad in the *Tribune*, ended up having to change in the wings while fending off the waiters. Noble Sissle and his band played during the twenty-minute presentation, keeping tempo with the girls' slow, unrehearsed pace. There were a few boos and hisses, but by the time Hawes took her bow she was greeted with applause.

The next day, she eagerly scanned the French papers. She found only one mention of her show, and it did not identify her by name, although the writer did note that the clothes had "a distinct personality." [67] The rest of the papers ignored her completely. Given her self-described mission, it shouldn't have come as a shock. Still, it stung. "If I'd been French and come to America to undermine the [*sic*] U.S. Steel, I couldn't have had a colder reception," she said. Given the importance of fashion to the French economy, this was nearer to the truth than she might have realized.[68] In the United States, however, the Paris show put Hawes on the map. The photo taken of her on board the ship that brought her back to New York, wearing a polka-dot dress, her arms uplifted in triumph, was printed in newspapers across the country, with captions that ranged from *The New York Times*'s brisk "Shows U.S. Gowns in Paris" [69] to the Hearst Corporation's hyperbolic "She's Barred From France" (she wasn't).[70] Though Hawes might have been ignored in France, she had proven that Americans could compete at the very highest levels in fashion. To the *Times*, she spun a story of haughty couturiers threatened by a naïve young American. "I had no intention of trying to sell anything in Paris, nor any idea of opening a shop. Word somehow got circulated that I intended to do both, and the couturières [*sic*] were watching me closely."[71]

This quote—plucky, determined, faintly bemused by the fuddy-duddiness of the Paris fashion establishment—set the tone for Hawes's public persona. One profile, in *Redbook*, announced, "She's that daring American woman who sold the United States the idea of New York's fashion supremacy over Paris."[72] In the decade following her Paris show, she became the first American designer to be treated like a celebrity. She endorsed products as diverse as brandy,[73] soap flakes,[74] and cigarettes.[75] Hollywood starlet Joan Bennett wore one of her dresses in an ad for Doublemint Gum in which Hawes was described as "one of the greatest designers in the world."[76] *Vogue* and *Harper's Bazaar* featured her clothes, as did *The New Yorker, Ladies' Home Journal*, and *Good Housekeeping*. When *WWD* profiled her in 1935, the opening line of the article announced that Hawes "needed no introduction."[77] She made great copy, and she knew it. Instead of doing the conventional fashion-designer things, like going to Paris and the Riviera to keep abreast of trends, she might hop a freighter to South America, or wander around the markets in Haiti. Along with a pet skunk, she kept a pair of Afghan hounds that she brought to cocktail parties.[78] She was friends with the sculptor Alexander Calder, who made her a wire chastity belt as a joke. She wore shorts to work in the summer heat when fashion decreed that they only appear at the seaside or on a hike.[79] When their son, Gavrik, was born, Hawes's husband became his main caregiver.[80] Although in keeping with the couple's socialist beliefs in the fair distribution of labor, it was an extremely unusual arrangement for the era.

But it was her deliberately provocative first book, published in 1938 and followed by seven more, that made Hawes a star. Called *Fashion Is Spinach*, it offered an extensive critique of the fashion industry, including details about her escapades in France and a thorough exposé of the French Legend. In her contrarian way, Hawes dedicated the book to both Madeleine Vionnet and "the future designers of mass-produced clothes the world over."[81] The title was borrowed from a well-known *New Yorker* cartoon of the time that depicted a mother encouraging her child to eat her broccoli. "I say it's spinach," the tyke replies, "and I say the hell with it."[82] Fashion, Hawes informed her readers, was "that horrid little man with the evil eye" who nixes perfectly good clothes because they weren't "in" at the moment.[83] *Fashion Is Spinach* became a bestseller, and it earned Hawes a reputation as a troublemaker. In its review, *WWD* wrote, rather threateningly, "Fashion may be spinach and Miss Hawes may be in the business 'for her health,' but there are those who like spinach. There are those, too, who will consider it unfortunate that so clever a dressmaker should choose to be so destructive in her attitude."[84] Lois Long of *The New Yorker*, for whom Hawes had written her Parisite columns, and whose view of the fashion industry was less rosy, was supportive. "Memorandum to all those friends who ask me why *I* didn't have sense enough to write 'Fashion Is Spinach' before Hawes got around to it," she wrote in one of her widely read columns. "I don't write that good, even if I knew that much."[85]

Fashion Is Spinach was such a hit that there was talk of turning it into a film.[86] But as readers of her book could sense, Hawes was souring on fashion. While she still loved to design clothes that suited the precise needs of her made-to-order clients, she knew that the future was in ready-to-wear. She'd made several forays into this side of the industry, none of them satisfactory. When she'd had to outsource the manufacture of a leather jacket in 1931, the manufacturers went behind her back and sold it to Best & Co.; the department store retailed it for less than Hawes did and advertised it as a Schiaparelli. Hawes was livid and sued. She won the case, but a remark made by Mary Lewis, a vice president at Best & Co., stuck with her: "Ford makes all his money on Fords, not Lincolns," she told Hawes. In other words, mass production was a better business model than couture.[87]

A couple of years later, in 1933, Hawes designed a ready-to-wear collection that further deteriorated her regard for Seventh Avenue. She'd taken on the challenge in part to finance her made-to-order business, but she also felt strongly that all women, not just those who could pay several hundred dollars for a dress, should have access to fashion they felt good wearing. But when the clothes were delivered from the factory, her designs had been compromised, the colors were wrong, the sizing was off, and the fabrics were shoddy. Worst of all, only Hawes seemed to care. When she complained to the manufacturer that the clothes were hideous, he told her to relax.[88] To Hawes's intense frustration, no one seemed perturbed that women might buy clothes that were badly designed, garishly dyed, didn't fit properly, or would fall apart when they were cleaned. Of these disasters, she wrote, "My soul curdles. My stomach turns over eight times per second. My spine tingles and I vomit mentally."[89] Often, that was all women could afford, she knew. But she objected to such monstrosities being promoted, which suggested they were praiseworthy, especially when her name was attached to them.

One of her pet peeves was artificial silk, or rayon, which had a tendency to shrink in the wash. When she tried to get the manufacturer to upgrade from artificial to real silk, he refused to pay the extra fifteen cents a yard because only five hundred of the twenty-five thousand artificial silk dresses he'd sold the year before had been returned.[90] The stores had been recompensed for the returns, so they didn't have any reason to complain. And the women who were stuck with the ruined dresses would be enticed to buy new ones to replace them. Ready-to-wear, she was realizing, was all a matter of figuring out what the market would bear.

For Hawes, that wasn't acceptable. Just as she'd sworn in France in 1928, women deserved better. But as the 1930s wound down, she recognized that the time-consuming, expensive process of making clothes to order was dying out. As more women entered the workforce and navigated lives that were too busy for the leisurely process of attending multiple fittings or sewing their own clothes at home, they needed good design that could be mass-produced—they needed Fords. What needed to change was the quality of ready-to-wear clothes. The Fords needed to look and feel like Lincolns. When she'd been featured in the first batch of American designers to be promoted by Lord & Taylor in 1932, Hawes had been ambivalent. The attention was nice, but she was doubtful of the results. And although she liked the idea of promoting American designers, she didn't think they were ready to compete with the French.

By the end of the decade, she'd changed her mind. A generation of American designers had come to maturity since she'd returned to New York in 1928. They'd been well trained, and many were resentful of the French Legend. With her insider's perspective, Hawes knew their names, even if the public was not yet aware of them. She considered designing for wholesale again, even announcing as much in *WWD* in 1937.[91] Another idea was to have Hawes Inc. act as a lab for new designs that could be adapted by mass-market manufacturers. But in the end, she did neither. She knew she would chafe at making dresses for rich women while the world was in turmoil. And she understood that a small luxury business would struggle with the wartime rationing that was sure to come. In January 1940, she announced that she was closing Hawes Inc., although existing customers could continue to order from Hawes's Customers Inc., a cooperative enterprise run by the Hawes staff and overseen by Hawes's friend Narcissa Vanderlip. The future, she knew, was in ready-to-wear. And ready-to-wear meant American.

Hawes had been thinking about this long before the fall of Paris. In late 1938, just weeks after British prime minister Neville Chamberlain returned from Munich proclaiming "peace for our time," she placed an ad in *WWD* promoting her January 1939 resort collection. Resort collections consisted, as they still do, of clothes that the moneyed could wear while evading the chill of winter in locales like Palm Beach and the south of France. Hawes wrote her own advertising copy, and she was as fond of employing puns as she was of giving her designs winking names. Titled "It Cannes Happen Here!"—a play on the name of the French Riviera town now known chiefly for its annual film festival—the ad depicts a fashionably dressed couple who have just alighted from a touring car. Palm trees are visible, as is a sailboat. The only discordant note is the gas masks that obscure their faces. The copy explains that while Europe was "just ducky," it was rapidly sliding toward catastrophe. In which case, she suggested, "It begins to look as if America may have to look to itself for fashion inspiration. That really isn't too tragic."[92]

4

The Dress That Revolutionized the Industry

Claire McCardell

I belong to a mass-production country where any of us, all of us, deserve the right to good Fashion and where Fashion must be available to us all.

—CLAIRE MCCARDELL[1]

Claire McCardell was in a hurry. The walk from her Murray Hill apartment to the Townley Frocks showroom in Manhattan's Garment District didn't take long, but she was running late that morning. It was August 1938, the last day of work before her vacation began, and just weeks before the fall clothes she had designed would arrive in stores across the country. As Elizabeth Hawes was busy plotting the ad copy for her January 1939 resort collection, McCardell was dodging men pushing racks of dresses and garment workers rushing from the subway to the clothing factories that filled the loft buildings on either side of Seventh Avenue. Pausing only to get coffee, she dashed through Townley's door—and straight into a buyer from Best & Co. who was on his way out. The buyer had just wrapped up an early-morning appointment to look at the line, but he hadn't ordered much. Now, he turned and eyed the dress McCardell was wearing appraisingly. "Wait a minute," he said to the Townley sales rep who was walking him out. "You didn't show me that one."[2]

McCardell was taken aback. The dress was not one she'd designed for Townley, a wholesale manufacturer that specialized in sportswear. It was from her own wardrobe, and she'd sewn it herself, from nubby red wool cut on the bias so that it fell in graceful folds around the body, a design signature of McCardell's idol, Vionnet. It hung loose from the shoulders, shaped only by the wide belt she wore around her waist. The latter was a favorite trick of McCardell's, and one she had often tried to sell Townley's owner, Henry Geiss, on its merits. But Geiss just wanted his wayward designer to copy Paris styles and stop pushing original ideas that would never sell. McCardell had based the dress on a traditional Algerian caftan. She'd chosen it that morning because she was in a rush, and it was easy to throw on—she'd just dropped it over her head and buckled a black leather belt around her midsection. Still, it wasn't at all the sort of thing that department store buyers normally gravitated toward. The bias cut only came alive on the body, which meant it had none of the hanger appeal necessary to attract customers, and without the belt it looked like a limp tent. Clinching the dress's unusualness was its lack of a sewn-in waistline, a construction detail that was almost compulsory at the time.

But the buyer insisted, so McCardell changed out of her dress and handed it over to the patternmakers. Best ordered three dozen in rayon crepe in red, purple, spruce green, and black and priced them at just under $30, or about $630 today. For a dress that wasn't copied from a Paris design, it was expensive. Best placed it in the store's

Fifth Avenue display window, and took out an ad in *The New York Times* on Sunday, September 25, touting the "Nada dress in the new 'monastic silhouette.'"[3]

The dress had the Best & Co. label sewn into its neckline and, per convention, no mention was made of McCardell's name—to customers, it would have seemed that Best & Co. had come up with the design all by itself. By Monday afternoon, the buyer called Townley to place another order, twice as large as the first, which had already sold out. This, too, flew out the door, prompting a third order, this time for both the original street-length and a long evening version. Again, customers cleared the racks. Best & Co. could not keep the dress in stock. The store began preselling it on deposit, an extraordinary move for a thirty-dollar dress from a Seventh Avenue firm—previously, only expensive copies of haute couture designs had been sold this way.[4]

The Nada dress, better known today as the monastic dress, was one of the sleeper hits of the late 1930s. Within days of its appearance at Best & Co., it was being was copied for as little as $9 and for as much as $125.[5] Women loved it because it flattered every figure. Its streamlined design was so unusual that one manufacturer, on hearing of its fantastic success, was reputed to have told his staff, "Drop everything! There's a girl up the street making a dress with no back, no front, no waistline, and my god, no bust darts!"[6] To manufacturers accustomed to adapting intricate Paris designs, it was as though Best & Co. had persuaded women to garb themselves in thirty-dollar flour sacks.

By December 1938, when *Vogue* ran a feature on the monastic dress's astounding instantaneous popularity, it seemed as though every other woman in America was wearing some version of it, and every designer in the country was riffing on it—even Elizabeth Hawes.[7] *Vogue* counted negligees, evening gowns, exercise dresses, and coats inspired by McCardell's original. But once again, she received no credit. "Nobody knows exactly when or where it was born," the magazine declared airily, noting that two Paris couturiers, Alix and Madame Bruyère, were "surely . . . its godmothers."[8] And when a Best & Co. executive told the press, "It takes a genius to foist a uniform on the public," he neglected to mention the genius's name.[9]

Despite the blithe disregard for its designer, the monastic dress changed American fashion forever. It demonstrated that Paris, as Hawes had detailed in *Fashion Is Spinach* earlier that year, did not have a stranglehold on fashion. It proved that American women were happy to spend a considerable sum on mass-produced American design. Perhaps most significantly, it tackled head-on one of the major stumbling blocks faced by ready-to-wear manufacturers: fit. Copying Paris designs, the industry's standard practice, not only held American designers back, but also, as Hawes experienced in her forays into ready-to-wear, saddled American women with inconsistently fitting clothes.

The problem was that French and American fashion were focused on two different outcomes. Paris couturiers dressed one woman at a time, which gave them ample opportunities to make minute adjustments in fit. Convoluted cuts and finicky embellishments were not an issue for them. Nor were they for made-to-order American houses like Hattie Carnegie; in fact, the fitters who worked in these establishments were considered the best in the business, a result of their years of experience in adapting Paris designs. But every dress that an American ready-to-wear designer created had to fit hundreds or even thousands of different women, none of whom came in for fittings. And because standardized sizing was still a few years in the future, one manufacturer's idea of a size 12—today's equivalent of a 6—would not necessarily line up with a competitor's interpretation. This could work out just fine. But as Hawes described, a corner-cutting manufacturer could easily derail the integrity of a design. McCardell experienced this frustration, too. When she complained that a Townley design "didn't really fit the body," she was told to put a bow on the offending garment and move on.[10] By devising a dress that was expressly intended for the ready-to-wear customer, with an uncomplicated yet attractive fit that could be personalized with the tightening of a belt, she exposed a glaring inconsistency in the French Legend. Within the industry, the monastic dress made McCardell a star.

Emboldened by her success, McCardell asked Geiss if he would put her name on the Townley label, a courtesy that no American ready-to-wear designer had ever received. He refused. For Geiss, the monastic dress was the start of a living nightmare. Its extreme simplicity came with one major pitfall: Knocking it off was a snap. Wholesalers were churning it out faster than Townley could get its originals out the door. Although he'd been a devoted counterfeiter in the past—viz., the pleas for copies of Paris designs—Geiss launched one lawsuit after another against those who were replicating Townley's design. Before long, he hated the sight of the monastic dress. Meanwhile, McCardell was confident that she could steer it to even greater success, and proposed including it in the spring 1939 collection. But Geiss balked. Between his veto of McCardell's request for recognition and his rejection of her plea to design more monastics, a relationship that had always been strained deteriorated even further. Nor was this the end of Geiss's troubles—his mounting legal debts and the stress of the nonstop litigation were impacting his health. In late 1938, only three months after the monastic dress debuted, and on the verge of nervous collapse, he gave up. Townley Frocks went out of business, and America's first ready-to-wear rebel was out of a job.[11]

But ready-to-wear itself had already established its popularity. If we could peer into the closets of women from California to Connecticut in 1938, we'd find them filled with one of the unsung achievements of early twentieth-century American industry: reasonably priced, well-made clothes that didn't require multiple fittings or alterations. These clothes were the stars of *Vogue*'s first Americana issue, published in February 1938. But despite the issue's rah-rah, we-can-do-it theme, editors were torn between pride at the quality of American ready-to-wear and their first love: haute couture from Paris.

American women, *Vogue* reported, were widely considered to be the best dressed in the world. This was possible because of a robust ready-to-wear industry, which *Vogue* described as a "public benefactor" and lauded for its ability to "turn out masses of clothes to fit any figure or purse."[12] But in the next breath, the magazine qualified its statement: "A handful of top-flight Frenchwomen" were, *naturellement*, the *very* best dressed. It was the sheer numbers of well-turned-out Americans that tipped the scales in the country's favor.[13]

The New York–based ready-to-wear industry was a marvel of what Lois Long called "the American genius for mass production."[14] From its beginnings in the nineteenth century, when small firms turned out shirtwaists, coats, and tailored suits, ready-to-wear fashion had ballooned into a $12 billion-a-year industry.[15] Within a few square blocks on the West Side of Manhattan, about five thousand firms produced about 80 percent of the nation's clothes (the remaining 20 percent originated in regional hubs in New England, the South, Los Angeles, and the Midwest).[16] *Vogue* calculated that American women bought 170 million dresses a year, 97 percent of which sold for less than twenty dollars and 56 percent of which sold for less than six dollars. They acquired, on average, four pairs of shoes a year, leaving British women (two pairs), Frenchwomen (one and a half pairs), and German women (one and one-tenth pairs) in the dust as far as footwear went.[17] And they had a penchant for silk stockings that amazed European visitors. In the years before nylon, silk was the premier material for hosiery. But silk stockings were expensive, fragile, and, because of their lack of stretch, had to be put on with painstaking care. Yet American women wore them nonchalantly, choosing silk even for casual occasions when their Europeans sisters would have confined themselves to serviceable cotton lisle—a phenomenon McCardell had encountered in Paris, where sometimes even the models wore cotton lisle with the couture gowns they were showing.[18] As *Vogue* put it, "From cooks to college deans, and from movie stars to Girl Scout leaders we all wear silk stockings."[19] It's a sentence that sums up the democratic nature of American fashion: Everyone deserves to have nice things.

But although the American industry clothed millions of American women, for the most part it did so with clothes that were adapted from Paris designs. Despite Elizabeth Hawes's experience, inferior quality was not the norm, especially in the higher price points. But in adhering to a creative process that compelled them to adapt an haute couture garment to the demands of ready-to-wear, American designers were doomed to turn out good but not great work. This, along with the anonymity forced on them by their employers, made them seem like hacks rather than original talents. The French Legend had put them in a box that they struggled to break out of.

But McCardell refused to be boxed in. Although she had been obliged to copy Paris when she first started at Townley, as she grew in confidence, she didn't sit at her drawing table trying to answer the question "How can I make this French idea work for mass production?" Instead, she asked herself: "What do I want?" It was this curiosity that prompted Stanley Marcus, the president of Neiman Marcus, to later say of her, "Claire McCardell is one the few truly creative designers this country has ever produced, borrowing nothing from other designers."[20]

She believed that "clothes ought to be useful and comfortable," adding, "I've never understood why women's clothes had to be delicate—why couldn't they be practical and sturdy as well as feminine?"[21] Her logic-driven designs provided the answer. She designed what she—and, by extrapolation, other American women—needed, often because she encountered a problem that required a solution, like how to dress for an evening of dancing without freezing. McCardell's innovative cuts, many of which allowed the wearer to customize the fit of a garment, were as thoughtful as anything found in a Paris collection. Her fabric choices were often outside the accepted realm of high fashion—she liked sturdy, wash-and-wear weaves like denim, butcher's linen, men's cotton shirting, and cotton calico, and she used them for both casual clothes and formal ones, reasoning that if they worked in one category, they'd do just fine in another. And long before Lycra and neoprene were invented, she gravitated toward high-tech performance textiles like elasticized stretch cottons, which she fashioned into the wide belts that she used to give shape to everything from dresses to bathing suits.

McCardell was not the only designer pursuing this line of thinking, nor the only woman. In the 1930s, just as in Paris, American fashion design was dominated by women. McCardell's ready-to-wear peers included her friends Joset Walker and Mildred Orrick, as well as Clare Potter, Tina Leser, Vera Maxwell, and Bonnie Cashin, all of whom designed what was known at the time as sportswear—i.e., easygoing, comfortable, more or less informal clothes that could be worn for a variety of functions, including leisure pursuits like sports. Sportswear's antithesis was the sort of formal, citified, decorative clothing for which the French were worshipped—in fact, McCardell's preferred definition of sportswear was "clothes uninfluenced by Paris."[22] Although individual sportswear garments didn't necessarily originate in the United States, sportswear as a way of life came to be recognized as a uniquely American contribution to fashion. At its heart was the mythical all-American girl, described by *Life* magazine in 1946 as "the long-legged, tennis-playing swimming" type.[23]

McCardell was part of an illustrious cohort, all of whom worked in an American lexicon that set them apart from the French. But McCardell was singular in her ability to marry the rigor of Paris design with the relaxed spirit of sportswear. Her technical knowledge was second to none, and she had the perseverance and quiet confidence to demand recognition—she was the first of this group of talented women to join couturiers like Chanel, Vionnet, and Madame Grès in getting her name on the label of the clothes she conceived of and designed, a huge step forward for American designers. She also had the incredible good luck to eventually land at a firm that didn't dictate what her designs should look like. And in an industry that puts an enormous amount of stock in optics, the blond, five-foot-seven McCardell looked like a sportswear advertisement herself. Even when McCardell was approaching middle age, she was described as looking "exactly like . . . The Typical American Girl. Just as real as real, only prettier. She's glowing with health . . . Her figure is long and lithe . . . and she's young, fresh . . . full of slang and laughs."[24]

But all this was still in the future. First, McCardell had to pack up her office at Townley Frocks and start looking for another job. Although she was disappointed, she wasn't fazed. She'd been planning to find another position, and experience had taught her that when things didn't work out, it was best to cut your losses and move on. McCardell had always had an independent streak: Though her father wanted her to stay close to home after she'd graduated from high school in her hometown of Frederick, Maryland, she persuaded him to let her pursue fashion design at Parsons School of Design, then called the New York School of Fine and Applied Arts. Her goal, she wrote to a friend, was to "save the world from ugliness and dreary clothes."[25]

Her interest in clothing dated to her childhood. She was born in 1905, the eldest child and only girl in a family of four children. Her father was a bank manager, and her mother was a fashion-conscious Southern belle. By the time McCardell was five years old, she had accumulated a three-foot-high stack of her mother's old fashion magazines, from which she would cut out paper dolls. These rarely emerged from the pages of *Vogue* and *Harper's Bazaar* as they were drawn. Instead, McCardell confidently "improved" them, scissoring off sleeves or pairing the bodice of one dress with the skirt of another, a process that she later described as the point at which "my eyes began their training."[26] Equally important was the education in garment construction that she received from her family's dressmaker, who would first make a sketch, then drape fabric on a mannequin before drafting a pattern, cutting out the cloth, and stitching each piece together. This early grounding ensured that McCardell developed into a master of technique, always cognizant of the form that each garment would take and how to best translate her vision from sketch to finished product.[27]

She was also a natural athlete, which taught her from an early age that clothes should look pretty without "getting in the way"— they needed to allow the body freedom to move.[28] Having three brothers was useful, too. Whether they were climbing trees or playing baseball, she saw firsthand that their clothes were often more practical than her own. By the time she was a teenager, she was pilfering their shirts and jackets and refashioning them for herself, making them better, just as she had once done with the paper dolls cut from her mother's fashion magazines.[29]

McCardell arrived at Parsons in 1925, when the school was still located on the Upper West Side, on Broadway at West 80th Street. Like other girls from out of town, she roomed at the Three Arts Club on 85th Street, which provided housing for students pursuing careers in the arts and hosted cultural events and amateur theatricals. McCardell's roommates were Mildred Boykin, later Orrick, and Joset Legouy, later Walker.[30] The three became lifelong friends. For McCardell, one of the major perks of the Three Arts Club was that the society women who supported it would donate their old dresses to be used in the club's theater productions or to be sold to students for as little as five dollars apiece. Many were barely worn couture pieces from Paris, Chanels and Patous that had originally sold for hundreds of dollars. McCardell bought as many as she could. Their illustrious provenance didn't stop her from treating them as she had her brothers' shirts: She unpicked their seams and then reassembled them, learning something from each dress she dissected.

In the fall of 1926, McCardell and her two roommates arrived in Paris to begin their second year of study at Parsons's Place des Vosges campus. They were electrified by the city's creative energy, going dancing as often as they could, everywhere from street dances to public balls at the Opéra. In the spring of 1927, McCardell wrote up one of her adventures for her hometown newspaper, recounting how she and Orrick were at Le Dôme Café when a friend from the *Paris Herald Tribune* bundled them into a taxi and carried them off to Le Bourget airfield, where Charles Lindbergh was about to land after flying the Atlantic solo. They were swept up in the "wild screaming tornado" of joy that greeted the pilot, managing to touch his plane—"It escapes me why it was so important for us to touch the plane but we did," Orrick said—before losing, between them, the heel of a shoe and a hat. In the delirium of celebrating Lindbergh's achievement, they also lost their journalist friend, leaving the two girls to walk back to Paris. They hadn't gotten far when they ran into Harry MacElhone of Harry's New York Bar, the watering hole best known as the place where George Gershwin composed *An American in Paris*. MacElhone, who recognized the pair as regular customers, gave them a lift home.[31] For small-town girls, the Paris of the 1920s was heady beyond anything they could have imagined back home.

McCardell was less enthralled with the Paris fashion world. In her letters to her family, she described the same scene that Hawes was observing: "The person who can remember the models and sketch them for wholesale houses in the United States can make a fortune," she reported. Furthermore, American buyers "tried to get as many sketches as possible" without paying the couturiers the fee for copying their designs.[32] McCardell was impressed with what she saw in Paris, and eagerly made use of one of the chief advantages of being a Parsons student there, which was the opportunity to buy couture samples at the end of the season for as little as ten dollars. But when, three decades later, she reflected on the sense of freedom that had infused fashion during the years she spent in Paris, she didn't mention any of the couturiers. Instead, she zeroed in on the influence of sportswear: "The big change came in the twenties. Novelists of the time talked about it. Ernest Hemingway describes Lady Brett in *The Sun Also Rises*. 'She wore a slip-over jersey sweater and a tweed skirt, and her hair was brushed back like a boy's. She started all that.'"[33]

As McCardell knew, the most telling detail in Hemingway's

1926 passage about Lady Brett's choice of clothing is *where* she wore her sweater and skirt: not on a golf course or in the country, where it would have been perfectly acceptable, but at a bar in Paris, where every other woman would have worn something dressier, like a silk blouse and suit. Furthermore, McCardell continued, "Brett didn't wear a jersey because she was out of silk blouses. She wore it for amusement, because she liked it and felt comfortable in it."[34] McCardell could have been referring to herself. Throughout her career, comfort was the guiding principle of her designs.

One couturier whose work did resonate deeply with McCardell was Madeleine Vionnet, perhaps the most significant couturier of the twentieth century. Vionnet pioneered the use of the bias cut—that is, cutting her clothes crosswise rather than following the grain of the fabric, so that they clung to the body with an unparalleled, sinuous elegance. It was the same technique McCardell would use for her monastic dress, and one she would return to frequently in her career. In the couture sample sales, McCardell amassed as many Vionnets as she could and, to the horror of her friends, calmly took each apart so she could decipher the intricacies of the designer's innovative construction. Although Vionnet worked in the painstaking tradition of the haute couture and McCardell, who has been described as America's most American designer, made her career on Seventh Avenue, their perspectives were not dissimilar. Both disliked anything that contorted the body, and both had a knack for exploiting the qualities of the fabric they worked with. Both were individualists: Vionnet maintained that she never tried to make "fashion," just clothes she believed in, while McCardell once said, "Don't try to live up to Fashion . . . stay firmly you."[35] And as with Vionnet, McCardell's designs often looked simpler than they were. As the fashion historian Valerie Steele observed, her clothes were easy to wear and easy to make, but they weren't necessarily easy to design.[36]

McCardell returned to New York for her third and final year at Parsons and graduated in the spring of 1928. She moved in with Orrick, who easily found work. But McCardell struggled, going through a series of dead-end jobs, including as a lampshade painter, a pattern cutter for one disastrous day, a fit model at B. Altman, and as a sketcher for a designer who told her she'd never understand design.[37]

Finally, in 1929, McCardell was hired by a young designer named Robert Turk to be his assistant. One year later, Turk sold his business to Townley Frocks and became its designer. Turk had one condition for accepting the job: that he be allowed to bring McCardell along. This proviso was to prove instrumental in determining McCardell's future. A little over a year after joining Townley, over Memorial Day weekend of 1932, Turk drowned in a boating accident, leaving the fall collection half done. Like the tap-dancing understudy in a 1930s musical, McCardell stepped in and finished the job. Although she had ideas about what fashion should look like, she had yet to develop her signature aesthetic. Instead, as she later remembered, "I did what everybody else did in those days—copied Paris. The collection wasn't great, but it sold."[38]

It was enough of a success for Henry Geiss to promote McCardell to full designer, at a salary of $150 a week. The job came with one compelling perk: leisurely, semiannual trips to Europe to buy samples from the haute couture collections and sketch "good numbers" to adapt for American tastes. McCardell never denied how much she learned from the French, but after doing the obligatory rounds, she snuck away from Paris as often as she could, fitting in excursions to the south of France, or going farther afield, to

London, Venice, or Salzburg. Her companion on these European jaunts was often Joset Walker, her onetime Parsons roommate, who was designing for another Seventh Avenue firm. McCardell treated each destination as a design laboratory. In Austria, she became enamored of the dirndl, a full, gathered skirt that is part of Tyrolean folk costume. Comfortable and easygoing, it was perfect raw material for her. She put citified versions into a collection, but sales were initially slow. Much to Geiss's exasperation, two years later dirndls were, as he put it, "all over the place."[39] On an excursion to Budapest in 1939, McCardell was so enchanted with a trove of glass and crystal beads she uncovered at a flea market that she bought two brimming shoeboxfuls. Back in New York, she had them strung in triple strands of single-color beads and wrapped them around her models' waists.[40] She loved creating these kinds of accessories, or "props," as she referred to them.[41] Wide leather belts and cuffs, miles-long sashes, jersey head coverings—all were part of the total McCardell look.

As she traveled, McCardell assessed the faults in her own wardrobe, and turned her solutions into design ideas—what she called "problem solving." When a pretty but flimsy silk evening wrap proved insufficient on a chilly moonlight cruise, she designed a hooded one in wool tweed. To protect her ears from frostbite on ski trips, she devised a sleek hood in wool jersey. This grew into a favorite design detail, even appearing on a wedding gown. Tired of lugging a steamer trunk and several suitcases around Europe—in the days of ocean liners, people did not travel light—McCardell designed a system of mix-and-match separates in black wool jersey that could be easily packed in a small bag and emerge unwrinkled. Consisting of a low-necked halter top, a covered-up top, long and short skirts, and culottes, the pieces were simply cut and designed to adapt to every situation. The short skirt and covered-up top could be worn to work; the covered-up top and culottes could be used for bicycling or other sporty pursuits; the halter neck and the long skirt could go to a nightclub. With a change of accessories, they constituted what we would now call a capsule wardrobe. This day-to-night concept was far ahead of its time—so far that it confounded department store buyers. Although most stores were selling separates like wool sweaters and tweed jackets and skirts in the sportswear department, they didn't know where to put McCardell's category-defying proposal. In the 1930s, clothes were typically sold as ensembles: Either you bought a one-piece dress, or you bought all the components that made up a look. Faced with Claire's DIY concept, buyers were flummoxed. Would customers understand what they were being shown, they wondered? How were they supposed to merchandize clothes that sagged lifelessly from their hangers? And what if they were left with tops in one size and skirts in another? "Interesting, sure. Practical? Forget it" was the response. It would be two decades before the concept of separates gained traction with buyers. As late as 1985, when Donna Karan introduced her Seven Easy Pieces, a capsule wardrobe intended to meet every possible contingency, she was hailed as a visionary—fifty years after McCardell suggested that women might be interested in such a thing.

Even while she was having to shelve her most innovative ideas to placate shortsighted buyers and risk-averse executives, McCardell was being recognized for her imaginative personal style. She had a nonchalant, high-low flair that was both unique and influential. She liked menswear-style tweed, preferred flats to heels, and didn't usually bother with makeup, although she liked a dusting of silver eye shadow. She often styled her hair in braids, which she sometimes wound around her head. Or she might pull her hair up in a chignon and tie a piece of fabric that matched her dress around it.[42] When she wore an ankle-length, hooded French peasant's cloak on a skiing weekend in New Hampshire in February 1937, *WWD* wrote admiringly that McCardell "leaps a year ahead of the design trend and never hesitates to wear the most extreme costumes she has turned out."[43] Later that year, when she returned from Paris on the *Normandie* wearing a reindeer-fur coat, the first ever seen in North America, the paper again devoted a blurb to the news.[44] A striped taffeta gown with a full cut, contrary to the current vogue for slender lines, rated yet another mention.[45]

Although she was still subject to the Paris-knows-best rule that governed Seventh Avenue, by the second half of the '30s, McCardell was working out the axioms that would ground her mature style: comfort, practicality, an element of the unexpected. She eschewed extraneous details—if she put a button on a dress, it buttoned. Also jettisoned were complicated tailoring, boning, and padding. She had an aversion to closures that the wearer needed help to fasten, namely back zippers, which she couched in terms of independence. "A woman may live alone and like it," she noted, "but you may soon come to regret it if you wrench your arm trying to zip a back zipper into place."[46] McCardell herself didn't get married until 1943, when she was thirty-six. Her husband, Irving Drought Harris, an architect whom she met on a transatlantic voyage, had been married previously, and she became stepmother to his two children. Although she acquiesced to many of his preferences, including the heavy, English gentlemen's club–style decor of their apartment and a social life stacked with charity galas and theater openings, there was one area in which McCardell would not budge. Harris would have preferred that she stop working, but she refused. Her brother Bob later told a reporter that McCardell "was intent on having her career. It was her first love."[47]

Her emerging aesthetic was one that stood in complete opposition to Parisian chic—nature versus artifice. She made clothes that emphasized individual fits, especially wrap-and-tie styles; utilitarian details; practical fabrics; pockets in everything, then an anomaly in women's clothes; and, quite often, a healthy display of skin. To McCardell, being comfortable in both your body and your clothing was part of the sportswear attitude, and she taught her showroom models to personify it, an exercise that began from the skin out. A bra and girdle were standard accoutrements for even the slimmest woman in the 1930s, but McCardell didn't like anything that distorted the figure—her view was that "the girdle that ruins your muscular balance will also destroy the grace of the dress." [48] Her longtime showroom model Connie Polan remembered that the first thing McCardell had her do when she started working with her was discard these undergarments. That done, McCardell had Polan pull her hair back in a knot and cut short bangs and a few wispy tendrils to frame her face, a style similar to the designer's own. McCardell then demonstrated her dropped-shoulder, pelvis-forward gait and had Polan practice it. Today, this is the standard runway walk. In the 1930s, when models minced and pirouetted, it was considered inappropriately casual, a quality McCardell accentuated by having Polan stroll into the showroom barefoot, her hands tucked nonchalantly into her pockets. [49]

Despite the occasional raised eyebrows of buyers and the elevated blood pressure of Henry Geiss, McCardell's collections sold. Then came the monastic dress, and McCardell once again found herself out of a job. But while the general public still had no idea who she was, McCardell had made a name for herself on Seventh Avenue with her innovative designs. She was considered a maverick, however, and management viewed her warily. But the woman who offered her a job was savvier than the average Seventh Avenue garmento: Hattie Carnegie, the founder and owner of the most exclusive fashion house in New York.

As a young immigrant—born Henrietta Kanengeiser in Vienna in 1886—Carnegie had prophetically renamed herself for the richest man in America. She had started her career as a messenger at Macy's, then worked as a milliner before ascending to the summit of the American fashion industry. To keep abreast of trends, Carnegie visited Paris as often as seven times a year, a ritual that nothing, not even marriage, interfered with—hours after she said "I do" to husband number two, she set sail, by herself, to view the collections. In Paris, she was considered a bellwether, able to spot a hit dress at fifty paces.[50]

Small and brisk, Carnegie was known for her "little suits" and tasteful renditions of current trends, with anything outré carefully smoothed out so as not unsettle her well-heeled clients. The woman who shopped at Hattie Carnegie was never outré. She led a life that involved multiple residences, private club memberships, and indefatigable servants. If she could afford it, she had a dummy made to her exact measurements that was kept in the Carnegie workrooms above the salon on East 49th Street. This saved her the trouble of coming in for fittings. Ordering such a dummy signaled a significant commitment to Hattie Carnegie Inc.—one contemporary considered it the financial equivalent of owning a racehorse.[51] In return, the woman who was dressed by Hattie Carnegie was secure in the knowledge that she was always correctly turned out for every event in her appointment diary, from lunch at the Colony Club to winter in Palm Beach. The models at Hattie Carnegie did not saunter into the showroom barefoot.

Although Carnegie was not a designer herself—she was more akin to an editor in chief, skilled at separating the wheat from the chaff and then instructing her staff to make it so—she was a shrewd spotter of design talent. McCardell's Seventh Avenue background was unusual, but Carnegie recognized that her new find had both originality and skill. She moved swiftly, offering McCardell a position before she had a chance to look for something else, and let her bring most of the Townley workroom with her. What Carnegie proposed was that McCardell both design for private clients and create a line of casual but reassuringly expensive clothes known as Workshop Originals. As she had at Townley, McCardell would journey regularly to Paris to get inspired. Both she and Carnegie made the January 1940 voyage on the *Washington*, among the last fashion professionals to cross the Atlantic before German U-boats made that impossible. For McCardell, it was to be her final trip to see the haute couture collections. Even after the end of the war, she preferred to keep some intellectual space between herself and Paris.

Carnegie's arrangement with McCardell sounded good on paper, but the house's conservative clientele, who were accustomed to easily recognizable signifiers of wealth like sequins, were underwhelmed. "They thought Claire's things 'too plain for the money,'" remembered Polan, who followed McCardell to her new job across town.[52] Two exceptions were the richest woman in the world, Woolworth heiress Barbara Hutton, who was otherwise dressed by the haute-est of haute couturiers, and Diana Vreeland, who was then the fashion editor of *Harper's Bazaar*. Vreeland brought some French jersey to Carnegie and asked for "a little two-piece Chanel kind of uniform."[53] What she got instead was a McCardell, which so impressed her that she asked to meet the designer. She became one of McCardell's staunchest and most important supporters.

Although she was responsible for designing the Workshop Originals line, McCardell was still getting no credit for her work.[54] After almost two years of pleas for recognition and the inescapable reality that her aesthetic did not jibe with the firm's clientele, she and Carnegie parted ways. In the summer of 1940, McCardell returned to her mass-production roots, designing for a manufacturer of low-priced dresses with the dubious name of Win-Sum, located in the same Seventh Avenue building that had once housed Townley Frocks. McCardell was working for Win-Sum that fall when she stepped into one of the building's elevators and found herself face-to-face with her former boss Henry Geiss, his production manager, and a salesman she had never met, Adolph Klein.

During the short ride, McCardell learned that Geiss and Klein were restarting Townley Frocks in its old space. She congratulated them, gave Geiss a quick hug to show that she had no hard feelings, and prepared to go on with her life. But before she could step off the elevator, Klein, a sharp-witted young Brooklynite who was bored with selling Paris knockoffs, offered McCardell her old job back. She was astounded. Geiss was alarmed. But Klein, who was well aware of the infamous monastic dress—in his estimation, it "revolutionized the industry"—was determined. "In this business, you have to be exciting or basic," he said. "I figured we were too small to be basic, so we had to be exciting."[55]

Geiss insisted on a recent reference before he would commit to hiring McCardell. The first, from her boss at Win-Sum, did not mince words: "Better to throw your money out the window."[56] Geiss blanched and asked for a second reference—a good one, this time. It was no better. "If I were you, I'd go shoot craps with the money. It's not as much of a gamble as Claire McCardell" was the opinion of a Boston retailer Geiss contacted.[57] But Klein, impatient to get the first collection designed, had already hired McCardell by the time the retailer's letter reached New York—or so he told Geiss. In fact, it had arrived in plenty of time, but Klein thought it best to conceal its less-than-sterling endorsement until McCardell's hire was confirmed. At that point, even Klein wasn't certain she'd succeed—he gave her twenty-to-one odds—but it was a gamble he was willing to take.[58]

To the general astonishment of Seventh Avenue, Claire McCardell, who had once bankrupted the firm, was back at Townley Frocks. This time, however, she laid down some ground rules. Number one, management was not allowed in the design studio. Number two, clothes would be produced the way she designed them, with no unauthorized changes allowed—anything that needed to be adjusted could be done only with her knowledge. If a buyer didn't like her clothes, McCardell declared, they could buy something else.[59] While she was at it, she requested a redesign of the Townley space, which was outfitted to her specifications, with walls painted crisp shades of black, navy, beige, and bright white, and the floor covered with glossy black linoleum. It was a clean, modern look that complemented McCardell's clothes while providing a pointed contrast to the pastel-tinted, ersatz French château look that characterized other Garment District offices. Here, the design said, we don't copy.

Most important, McCardell finally got her name on the label. Both she and Klein thought "frocks" sounded old-fashioned, and after some persuasion, Geiss agreed. The new labels read "CLAIRE MCCARDELL CLOTHES by Townley." Just like Vionnet and Madame Grès, McCardell was finally getting the acknowledgment she deserved. Geiss had feared that if he gave in to McCardell's demands for recognition, she would become a diva, impossible to control. But Klein understood his new designer. He intuited that what she really craved was the freedom to create clothes the way she envisioned them. By steering clear of the design studio and demonstrating the company's good faith with the addition of her name to the label, he was confident McCardell would produce her best work.[60] He was eventually proved right, but initially almost everyone questioned his judgment, if not his sanity. "They said I was crazy," he later remembered. "But I figured why not have my own *couturière* right here instead of going to Paris every year? I almost kissed my money good-bye though. Nobody ever saw anything like the things Claire dreamed up." [61]

The kind of autonomy McCardell negotiated for herself was unprecedented in American fashion. Her old friend Joset Walker was openly, if good-naturedly, jealous of the arrangement McCardell had struck with Klein. "I can't tell you how I envied Claire," she said. "The day after my first showing [my boss] would whisk all the most exciting things off the racks and hide them in his office closet. The only fun I had was when Diana Vreeland would sweep past all the button-up-the-front dresses in the showroom, go right to the office, and say, 'Where are the lemons?'" [62] As Walker, McCardell, and every other designer on Seventh Avenue knew all too well, most manufacturers lived in terror of rocking the boat. In Klein, McCardell had found her champion. His trust in her freed McCardell to do her greatest work and ensured that even her more advanced designs—the ones Geiss termed "outlandish"—made it to stores. It was exactly the right moment for her to shine: With Paris out of the running, buyers were looking for American talent. Buoyed by the support of retailers and the press, the 1940s were McCardell's most creative period.

Her best-known design from the era is the Pop-over, which she created in 1942 at the request of Snow and Vreeland. They asked McCardell to come up with a dress for women who, due to wartime labor shortages, were now doing their own housework. McCardell, a strong believer in the modernist credo of form and function, devised a wrap-front denim coverall-cum-dress that came with its own attached pot holder. Klein ordered ten thousand yards of denim and, because he was able to have the dress classified as a "utility garment," priced it at $6.95. But the Lord & Taylor buyers sensed a hit, and suggested that he increase his denim order to a whopping seventy-five thousand yards. Klein begged McCardell to think up some other designs that they could use it for in case the Pop-over flopped; then, after a sleepless night, he took a deep breath and bought the extra yardage.

He needn't have worried. *Bazaar* photographed the Pop-over on the wife of a polo champion, suggesting even the well-to-do could benefit from it, and described the dress as ideal for "cooking, dusting, scrubbing, painting, pottering, or any odd job around the house," with a roomy pocket big enough for "matches, cigarettes, the morning mail, and the duster." [63] Within a year, Townley had sold seventy-five thousand of them and had scissored and stitched its way through 250,000 yards of denim. [64] The Pop-over was such a monumental success that it joined the monastic dress in becoming a permanent part of Claire's collections, tweaked and adjusted each season and worn far beyond the houses and gardens it was originally intended for. The two "just in case" denim looks McCardell had sketched for Klein, a suit and coat, also took off. Thanks to McCardell's ingenuity, denim, once relegated to men and children, was elevated to women's wardrobes.

As part of her unusual arrangement with Klein, McCardell was able to conceive of entire collections, from bathing suits to wedding dresses, rather than one category of garment—an approach that presaged the multipronged brands of today. This gave her imagination plenty of room to roam. Most of what she dreamed up were winners, like the winter "play clothes" that she decided women needed. We live in the modern equivalent of play clothes now, but in the mid-twentieth century, when everyday wear was much more formal and prescribed, play clothes were what women wore on vacations at the beach or other non-city locales and to participate in sports. A tennis dress qualified as play clothes, as did a skirt you could golf in or a swimsuit cover-up, and these were often featured in the spring and summer issues of fashion magazines. But McCardell reasoned that even when the weather cooled, women still wanted to remain active by going bicycling or bowling or walking in the country. She designed clothes for all these activities and more: for fall bicycling, striped knickers worn with a top whose hood could be pulled over the head or scrunched down around the neck or a cheery tartan jacket with matching long shorts; for winter walks, a fleece jumpsuit with a detachable hood and a bright, contrasting belt. She loved shorts and knee socks, capes, and hoods of any kind. Many of her cold-weather play clothes were layerable, to adjust for changes in temperature, and some had matching flat-soled booties. The effect, to eyes unaccustomed to today's leisurewear fashion-scape, was medieval page meets superhero, and buyers were at first skeptical, but these clothes were among McCardell's bestsellers. "No matter how far out, even outrageous, some of Claire's styles might seem to us at first, they almost always filled some need and ultimately became classics," said Mel Dawley, the CEO of Lord & Taylor.[65]

There were some ideas that were just too radical for their time, however. In 1943, shortly after the Pop-over triumph, McCardell designed leotards inspired by dancers' rehearsal clothes—essentially, she created embryonic athleisure clothing, the yoga pants and sports bras of her day. They were initially sketched for *Harper's Bazaar* by Mildred Orrick, but it was McCardell who followed through on the idea. Made of wool jersey in stripes or solids, the leotards came in two parts—basically, a bodysuit and leggings—and were worn under wool jersey sweaters and skirts or wraparound tweed jumpers. They were promoted as ideal for college girls living in underheated wartime dormitories, but because of their specialized manufacturing requirements were quite expensive. And to most people, they just looked odd. *Bazaar* was enthusiastic, but *The New Yorker* poked fun, and *Life* was outright bemused, putting them on the cover and captioning one image "Strange Looking Garments for Winter Wardrobes."[66] But in 1950, when *Vogue* wanted to define the look of the 1940s, the magazine had Irving Penn photograph two models in McCardell's leotards. Every detail, from the snood worn by women too busy to get their hair done to the McCardell slouch, was reproduced. The photo is a testament to McCardell's ability to craft an image for women.

More successful were McCardell's frankly sexy bathing suits. In the 1940s, before the invention of Lycra in 1958, women's swimwear had robust underpinnings that were reminiscent of nineteenth-century corsetry, and suits were often skirted and ruffled. McCardell's view of these suits was uncharacteristically tart: "I am afraid that little girl dresses worn as bathing suits suggests retrogression."[67] Her swimwear was fashioned from either woven cottons or lightweight wool jersey—if McCardell had been restricted to using only one fabric in her work, it would undoubtedly have been wool jersey, which she prized for its comfort, natural stretch, and temperature-regulating qualities. A McCardell bathing suit was neither boned nor padded, and could be revealing, especially when wet, qualities that earned her a reputation as a designer for the young and brave.[68] But in neutral shades of gray, beige, and black, they were never vulgar. A model wearing one on a beach in Cape Cod was once approached by choreographer and New York City Ballet co-founder George Balanchine, who introduced himself and told her she looked like a dancer—the epitome of beauty and grace.[69]

McCardell's suits still look dazzlingly contemporary, with cuts that range from a halter neck that crosses high on the chest, exposing most of the midriff and all of the back, to a short-sleeved style that fastens up the front with brass hooks. But McCardell's most famous swimwear design was her diaper bathing suit, which she first showed in 1942. In its simplest form it was made from a length of fabric that hung from the neck, passed between the legs, and then wrapped around the waist—elementary but daring. Polly Allen, who worked under Diana Vreeland at *Harper's Bazaar*, recalled McCardell whipping off her dress on the beach at Fishers Island to show off her new concept: "She was in a diaper—a diaper! Shocking, but she didn't care!"[70]

McCardell's evening dresses had that same aura of guileless sexiness. Some were inspired by early nineteenth-century little girls' dresses, with high drawstring waists and tiny puff sleeves. Others were mass-market riffs on the draped, bias-cut Grecian styles of Vionnet and Madame Grès. McCardell executed her gowns in silk jersey, a brilliant time-, labor-, and money-saving technique that looked as elegant as its haute couture inspirations. But the most forward-looking of her evening ideas was a silk gown she designed in 1945 and modeled herself in *Vogue*, which described it as a "future dress" made from "two triangles."[71] In fact, it's made of four squares that were rotated forty-five degrees to form diamonds, the lower points cut off to even out the hemline of the skirt and the upper points forming a halter that fastens around the neck at the front and back; a belt shapes the waist.[72] Cut from rust-colored silk, with double rows of contrast topstitching that take the formality down a notch, the dress is an exercise in geometry that could only have been executed by a master.

Other McCardell innovations were less about technical wizardry and more about her problem-solving approach to design.

In 1942, the War Production Board introduced Regulation L-85, which restricted the amount and types of fabrics designers could use. One of these fabrics was leather, which was required to make boots for the military. Keeping the services shod was, pun intended, no small feat. Foot soldiers in World War II went through boots almost as quickly as they went through C rations, which left very little leather for the civilian population—in fact, shoes were the only item of clothing that was rationed in the United States. McCardell, for whom L-85 was a challenge rather than a constriction, discovered that ballet slippers were exempt. In what we would now call a collaboration, a word that had a very different meaning in the World War II era, she partnered with Capezio, then a maker of pointe shoes and ballet slippers. Weeks later, the ballet flat, now considered a classic shoe design, was launched when models wore it to show McCardell's collection.

Threaded through these collections were design details known as "McCardellisms"—idiosyncratic motifs that she returned to again and again. Denim-style topstitching, which she adapted from men's workwear, was one. She loved hardware, especially brass hooks and eyes, and used them to fasten bathing suits and evening gowns alike. One editor described a row of them on a snug bodice as unexpectedly provocative, "as if inviting a man to unhook them," the sexiness all the more subversive because of their utilitarian appearance.[73]

But perhaps her favorite McCardellism were the long, skinny bias-cut ties that were nicknamed "spaghetti" by one of the women in her workroom and beloved by the designer for their ability so shape clothes while still allowing them to move. The latter was an obsession with McCardell—her statement "I like clothes to look alive" could be considered another McCardellism.[74] She often tacked spaghetti ties just under the arms of a dress in the hopes that the wearer would adopt her favorite Empire waistline, or even cross them in front, Grecian style. In effect, McCardell was letting her customers know that she wasn't telling them how to wear her clothes; instead, she saw design as a conversation. Her dresses were made by the hundreds, but each could be personalized by its wearer. The many separates she designed reinforce this idea—she fully expected that women would put them together in ways that she had not anticipated. McCardell was a partner, not an autocrat.

She summed up her fashion philosophy when she said, "Clothes are for real, live women, not for pedestals. They are made to be worn, to be lived in."[75] It's a view that was mirrored in an anecdote that appeared in a story that Betty Friedan, who would later go on to fame as the author of *The Feminine Mystique*, recounted in a 1955 profile she wrote about the designer. By that point, McCardell was famous. Earlier that year she'd appeared on the cover of *Time* magazine, one of the very few fashion designers ever accorded that honor. Friedan asked McCardell if, after more than twenty years on Seventh Avenue, she still found clothes exciting. McCardell, who was in a denim suit of her own design that Friedan noted she'd seen her wear eight times already that month, responded by pulling out a thank-you note she had received from a customer, a trapeze artist who wrote to tell her that she'd worn the designer's purple cotton dress

> as a dressing gown, housedress, beach robe and maternity dress, travelling with the circus across two Americas; given birth to her third child in it in a primitive hospital in Peru; gone down on her knees in it to wash diapers on a filthy Amazon River steamer; had it smeared with crayon, coffee, eggs and baby-wet on the plane back to New York; and proceeded to wear it two years as a party dress.[76]

She wanted to thank McCardell for "this good, useful dress."

Most of the women who bought McCardell's clothes didn't subject them to such rigors. But they treasured what they bought from her. McCardell made her customers feel beautiful. She never tried to persuade them to wear a skirt that shortened their stride or a jacket that rode up when they raised their arms. She didn't load them down with useless garnishes, and she understood that a dress had to meet the wearer, not the other way around. She knew that they needed to stay warm in the winter and cool in the summer. She gave them solutions and she gave them confidence. In the absence of Paris, American women might have thought they'd have to settle for good-enough clothes. McCardell gave them extraordinary ones.

But she couldn't have accomplished any of this without the retailer that recognized her genius. Enter: Lord & Taylor.

5

The Most Exciting Store in the Country

Marjorie Griswold and Dorothy Shaver

If I think something is right, I know it's right and nobody
can budge me . . . A bell rings inside me. Call it instinct.
Then I see to it that other people know it's right.

—MARJORIE GRISWOLD[1]

I believe that the American Look is and will continue to be
the most important style trend in the world today.

—DOROTHY SHAVER[2]

In 1940, department stores were where the majority of American
women shopped for clothes. Even small cities supported several,
and whether they catered to the budget-conscious or the affluent,
women's ready-to-wear was integral to their identities. This was
rooted in their origin story: Department stores evolved from the
old dry goods stores—like the one at which Charles Frederick
Worth had gotten his start—where women had shopped for fab-

rics, trims, shawls, and the like. The transition to the larger, more diverse department stores began in the mid-nineteenth century, a result of rapid urbanization, better and faster transport links, a growing middle class, and the revolutionary new concept of leisure time.

As their name suggests, department stores had a management structure that differed significantly from the independent traders they put out of business. Goods were classified and organized by category, or department. Buyers were responsible for choosing and acquiring goods for individual departments, as though they were running a small boutique within the larger structure of the store. Profits and losses were tallied up by each department, while management provided services such as window and departmental displays, advertising, and promotions.

One quality that department stores retained, however, was their predominantly feminine customer base. This was due in part to the importance of women's fashion to their businesses. But perhaps more critically, department stores provided a place where women could respectably socialize in public at a time when such venues were scarce. Although this was no longer the case by the mid-twentieth century, the radical idea that department stores had disseminated—that shopping was not a task but a social pastime— had become an indelible part of consumer culture.

Department store managers were ingenious at promoting this perception. Unlike the cramped, old-fashioned shops they replaced, department stores were often the largest and most impressive buildings in town, with soaring ceilings and opulent decor. Their design made use of new technologies like escalators, elevators, steel-frame construction, and electric light; later, department stores were among the first public buildings to have air-conditioning. They had lounges where customers could rest between bouts of shopping, and generally had at least one restaurant, café, or tearoom; some had all three. Larger stores even boasted amenities like skating rinks, art galleries, and supervised children's play areas. You could spend an entire day in a department store, having morning coffee, planning a holiday at the travel bureau, eating lunch, getting a treatment at the beauty salon, taking a dancing lesson, and, by the mid-1930s, unwinding with a cocktail.

Commerce, the main purpose of the department store, was also designed to be exciting. The dry goods stores had kept merchandise behind the counter, out of reach and under the control of supercilious clerks. Department stores did away with that barrier by piling merchandise on tables for customers to touch and feel before they handed over their money, a munificent tactic that gave the customer a feeling of control. Management ramped up the emotions with a continual influx of new items, seasonal sales, surprise discounts, and liberal return policies, strategies that drew huge crowds and encouraged frequent visits. As detailed in Émile Zola's great department store novel of 1883, *The Ladies' Paradise*, about a fictionalized version of Paris's Le Bon Marché, these practices were fatal for the old dry goods merchants, who could not afford such largesse. Zola vividly evokes the seductive qualities of the gargantuan new stores, and how their dizzying array of goods could cause a shopper to lose all self-restraint. The eroticism of his language leaves no doubt as to the potent attraction of these retail palaces. He describes Octave Mouret, the owner of the Ladies' Paradise, as obsessed with "the conquest of Woman . . . His tactics were to intoxicate her with amorous attentions, to trade on her desires, and to exploit her excitement." Unsurprisingly, Zola's novel also includes a storyline about the new phenomenon of the shoplifter.[3]

In the United States, the ready-to-wear industry and the department store developed in tandem. At first, accessories and trims made up the better part of department store's fashion offerings. But beginning in the 1890s, with the advent of the mass-produced skirt and the shirtwaist (or blouse)—garments that, unlike dresses, did not need to be painstakingly fitted—ready-to-wear departments began to claim more floor space. By the 1920s, fashion had simplified enough to make women's ready-to-wear garments of all types, from the tubular "flapper" dress to the bandeau bras that replaced corsets, easy and inexpensive to manufacture. Many women switched from sewing their own clothes to buying them ready-made. Guiding them through this process were the department stores, which interpreted fashion—which, bien sûr, came from Paris—for the overwhelming majority of women who would never order an haute couture garment. The French Legend, which had once spread its gospel individually, via dressmakers and home sewers, thus breached the closet of the ready-made customer.

From the beginning, the relationship between the haute couture and American department stores was mutually beneficial. To borrow the Fred Astaire–Ginger Rogers analogy—he gave her class, she gave him sex appeal—Paris gave department stores authority, department stores gave Paris the masses. It was a connection retailers leaned on unashamedly. As Elizabeth Hawes found when she was hired to report on Paris trends for a Wilkes-Barre department store in 1925, references to "our Paris bureau" were a familiar refrain in the advertising of the time, even if that bureau was a lone girl writing up bulletins in her rented room and the garment being advertised a cheap cotton housedress.[4]

More sophisticated stores stressed their relationship to high style via elaborate promotions and tie-ins, like the Surrealist window displays designed by Salvador Dalí for Bonwit Teller in December 1936. Surrealism, born in Paris and beloved by the fashion set, was at that moment getting its first big outing in the United

States via exhibitions at the Museum of Modern Art and the avant-garde Julien Levy Gallery.[5] These inspired the Bonwit window, which featured disembodied arms protruding from the walls, a teaspoon-strewn floor, and mannequins whose heads were obscured by a profusion of paper roses. In lieu of telephone receivers, the mannequins grasped lobsters, an allusion to Dalí's *Lobster Telephone*, a Surrealist object he created that same year.[6] Much to Dalí's disgust, Bonwit Teller tried to persuade him to make do with papier-mâché ones; he insisted on the shells of real boiled lobsters and fitted them into the mannequins' wax hands himself.[7]

Despite the expense of (presumably) acquiring fresh seafood every day, the windows were a huge hit, and sparked a spate of Surrealist displays by other retailers. Eager to repeat the success, Bonwit invited Dalí back again in 1939, but this time the results were not so happy. The theme of the second window was his interpretation of narcissism: A mannequin wrapped in a coq-feather cape stepping into a fur bathtub, surrounded by quilted satin walls mounted with hand mirrors. Unbeknownst to Dalí, the store had made last-minute alterations to his design. When the window was unveiled, he became enraged. As the stunned crowd assembled on the sidewalk watched, he picked up the bathtub, which was made of aluminum covered with Persian lamb, and hurled it through Bonwit's plateglass window onto Fifth Avenue.[8]

Although the Bonwit-Dalí collaboration was an extreme example, it was by no means unusual for department stores to host art and design exhibitions, lectures, and other educational events, all intended to whip up interest in new merchandise. As Andy Warhol would later observe, department stores are like museums. Today, when they're irrelevant to most people's shopping experiences, his comparison is not obvious. But in their heyday, department stores were institutions in which one could discover the material goods that defined a prosperous and cultivated life. They were "lands of desire" that made real the "dream life of capitalism."[9] The difference, of course, was that in department stores, unlike in museums, the objects on display could be purchased. Department stores didn't sell necessities—few stocked basic food items, for example— but rather products that symbolized the buyer's taste and aspirations and conveyed, in physical form, abstract concepts like success, femininity, discernment, and patriotism. And because they bought large quantities of goods, department stores were able to lower prices on items that were once reserved for the wealthy, like stylish clothes and furniture, and bring them to a wider audience. As the consumer historian Jan Whitaker noted, in the middle years of the twentieth century, when discretionary income and consumer spending soared, department stores "exercised an almost moral authority to define in material terms what it was to live as a middle-class American."[10]

New York, as the center of the American fashion industry, boasted dozens of department stores in 1940, each with its own personality. At the highest end were the specialty retailers. Saks Fifth Avenue was snooty and hushed, the purlieu of wealthy matrons and their debutante daughters; here, all was *luxe, calme et volupté*. Best & Co. was sedate and dignified, a purveyor of correct tweed skirts and sweaters, as well as refined layettes for the most privileged infants in the tristate area. Far more New Yorkers patronized R. H. Macy & Co., whose busiest department was sewing notions. There, where home seamstresses shopped for small items like buttons and thread, the average sale rang up at fifty-three cents, and the turnover was $1 million a year.[11] In Brooklyn, Abraham & Strauss, which was as central to the borough's identity as the Dodgers, catered to an immigrant clientele, with interpreters available for speakers of twenty different languages.[12]

But for those who worked in fashion, the department store against which all others were measured was Lord & Taylor. Perched on Fifth Avenue at 39th Street, it was, *Life* fashion editor Sally Kirkland said, "the most exciting store in the country."[13] Its buyers were brave and its promotions and advertising executives bold, a combination that exposed the store's clientele to a continual influx of stimulating ideas. This clientele was the envy of every other retailer in the United States—neither extravagantly wealthy nor striving, but solidly upper-middle class, interested in good rather than high style, predominantly but not exclusively urban, it was a demographic dubbed "mass-class" by *Vogue*.[14]

Although it was the oldest American department store, founded in 1826 in Lower Manhattan, everything about Lord & Taylor suggested a forward-looking attitude, from its dramatic full-page ads to its attention to niceties like its practice of providing coffee, served in china cups, to shoppers who arrived before the store opened for the day. Its American Beauty rose emblem, which the store formally adopted in 1946, stood for everything that Lord & Taylor represented: quiet tastefulness and an unwavering belief in the rightness of the American way of life, just as its distinctive handwritten logo promised individuality and finesse. Even the demanding Lois Long loved it. "Every time I go there," she wrote, "I realize anew that this shop is second to none in the matter of good taste, chic, and an avoidance of obvious tricks in detail that are easily cheapened."[15] Year after year, it was the store that every other specialty department store attempted to imitate. "They did things with such heart and passion," Diana Vreeland recalled. "I used to call Marjorie five times a week."[16]

"Marjorie" was Marjorie Griswold, and in September 1940, she had just begun working at Lord & Taylor as the new sportswear buyer. Griswold was a department store veteran. She'd started out in Macy's executive training program, which she'd joined in 1928, after earning her degree in Romance languages from Stanford University. The store was then in the process of turning itself from a no-frills purveyor of homely bargains like seventy spools of thread for one penny to a stylish retailer whose buyers were welcome in the most elegant salons in Paris. But Macy's never abandoned its commitment to bargains. Instead, it convinced the public that bargains were modish—as the store's famous slogan advised, "It's smart to be thrifty." This bait and switch was accomplished by expanding the store's buying policy to include the most refined luxury items alongside more prosaic items like cast-iron skillets while raising the tone of its advertising. From fine Danish silver to the latest millinery from the avenue Montaigne, you could get it at Macy's, alongside those seventy spools of thread.[17] That the store stocked one luxury item—say, for example, a duck press like the one used at the Tour d'Argent restaurant in Paris—for every thousand cast-iron skillets sold was beside the point; the duck press was advertised just as rigorously as the skillet. Those who had a use for the duck press felt sure it was a bargain because it was sold alongside the skillets, while those who came in for a skillet felt they were getting it from a high-class establishment. Bernice Fitz-Gibbon, the legendary copywriter who coined Macy's slogan in 1928, said this strategic use of reverse psychology turned the retailer into "the General Motors of all department stores."[18]

For Marjorie Griswold, it was also a valuable lesson in the power of perception. Her rise through the ranks at Macy's was swift. By 1938, she'd been appointed the store's merchandise manager for all fashion accessories. Her brilliance was evident to all—one editor thought that given another year, Griswold would be running the entire store.[19] Instead, she quit.[20] Bored with bargains and tired of Macy's unrelenting pace, she retreated to suburban

Westchester with her chemist husband and young son, to lead a life of domestic concerns punctuated by the occasional game of tennis. This self-imposed exile lasted all of eighteen months. Unadulterated domesticity, Griswold discovered, was not for her. "After having worked," she said, "I was wretchedly dissatisfied as a housewife."[21] When she was offered the buyer job at Lord & Taylor, which came with the promise of more creative merchandising, the freedom to buy what she believed in, and the opportunity to work with Dorothy Shaver—the store's progressive vice president, who was already making the kind of innovative changes that Griswold longed to enact—she leapt at the chance.

In choosing to work in fashion, specifically in fashion retail, Griswold was not alone. From salesclerks to executives, department stores were staffed by women, who found in the fashion industry one of the best places they could build careers: By 1940, 84 percent of American women who held executive positions worked in fashion.[22] Of the job titles available to them, one of the most glamorous was that of buyer. To become a buyer at Lord & Taylor, the most well-respected specialty retailer in fashion, was a coup.

Although most buyers worked for small department stores outside of major cities, the media invariably portrayed them as worldly tastemakers with enviable wardrobes and lively social lives, like the Chicago-based Carson Pirie Scott buyer who was the subject of a photo essay in *Good Housekeeping* in 1941. She was depicted, among other things, journeying to New York—on an *airplane*, the magazine emphasized. There, readers were told, she would frequently buy a thousand dresses in one fell swoop. To make darting back and forth between the two cities less stressful, she kept a trunk full of clothes at the Algonquin Hotel, her residence of choice in New York City. She frequented the Pump Room in Chicago, "one of the smartest night clubs in America"; bought a new hat—a major

investment in those millinery-mad days—for every meeting of the
Fashion Group, which had by then established branches in cities
around North America; and directed photo shoots with starlets
like Gloria Stuart (known to audiences today as the aged Rose
DeWitt Bukater in *Titanic*).[23] Compared with clerical work or
domestic duties, being a buyer was like stepping into a Technicolor
daydream.

By becoming a buyer at the country's most exciting store just
as the first collections with zero input from Paris were launching,
Griswold was in a unique position to shape the look of American
fashion. Sportswear, the department that she ran, was already recognized as one in which Americans excelled, and there was every
indication that it would continue to improve.

Griswold was still settling into her new office when she got a
call from Adolph Klein, who announced that he had something
"new and exciting" to show her. It would be well worth her while,
he continued, for her to stroll over to the Townley showroom,
which was just a few blocks from Lord & Taylor. Although Klein
had been willing to take a chance on Claire McCardell, he wasn't
such a gambler that he trusted the market to clasp her to its bosom
unprompted. To bring McCardell to the masses, Klein knew, he
had to persuade a major department store, one known for its fashion leadership, to get behind her.

Griswold groaned inwardly—every manufacturer in town
promised something "new and exciting." But she agreed to stop by
to have a look. "I came to be nice," she said. As she sat waiting for
the presentation to begin, Griswold didn't have high expectations.
She was being polite, she reminded herself, and would not commit
to buying anything. Then the first model stepped out and Griswold
snapped to attention. "I saw this simple collarless dress stitched in
white like blue jeans," she remembered. "I stopped being a good

Samaritan. This was original."[24] The dress had neither a sewn-in waistline or darts to give it shape, but it nevertheless looked coolly, self-assuredly expensive. So did the ones that followed. Griswold sensed revolution. She placed her first order even before she left the showroom.

As it happened, Griswold was exactly who McCardell envisioned wearing her clothes—a busy woman who enjoyed working, spending time with her family, athletic pursuits, and an active social life. Although McCardell was a skier rather than a tennis player, she and Griswold were leading essentially similar lives, as were millions of other American women. Gilbert Adrian, the Hollywood costume designer and couturier who was famous enough to go by the single name of Adrian, summed up their attitude to fashion when he said, "The American wants to look attractive, but she wants to arrive there by a short cut . . . she likes to be able to jump into a little dress and look charming."[25] From the moment she saw McCardell's first collection—modeled by fresh-faced models who strolled, hands in pockets, through Townley's snazzily painted showroom—Griswold knew that she was looking at the future of American fashion.

Placing an order was the second hurdle in getting McCardell's clothes to the public. Next, Griswold had to persuade her customers that these radical new garments were the answer to their needs. She had ideas about how to merchandise them, but she needed the help of her boss, Dorothy Shaver, to put those ideas into action.

In 1940, Shaver was Lord & Taylor's first vice president of advertising, display, and publicity, and already the most important woman in American retailing.[26] She'd been at Lord & Taylor since the mid-1920s and had made her first big splash in 1928, when she persuaded the store's then president, Samuel Reyburn, to spend $125,000 to import and exhibit the finest modern French furniture and homeware. Shaver spent six months in France personally hunting down pieces that she felt would resonate with the American public, and secured an impressive array of advisers, collaborators, and patrons, including Norman Bel Geddes, Otto Kahn, Condé Nast, Eleanor Roosevelt, and Lucien Vogel, the fashion editor of Paris *Vogue* and *Gazette du Bon Ton*. The final exhibition, which took up Lord & Taylor's entire seventh floor, featured model rooms by Émile-Jacques Ruhlmann, Jean Dunand, Vera Choukhaeff, Louis Süe and André Mare, Pierre Chareau, Francis Jourdain, René Joubert, and Philippe Petit, as well as some of the first paintings by Picasso, Braque, and Utrillo ever seen in the United States.[27]

Style moderne, or Art Deco, a term derived from the hugely influential Paris World's Fair of 1925, the Exposition Internationale des Arts Décoratifs et Industriels Modernes, had been a dominant theme in France for more than a decade. But the American government turned down the invitation to participate in the fair, and the style was slower to catch on in the United States. Shaver's exhibition was described in the press as a sort of experiment, to gauge whether the American public would warm to this streamlined new aesthetic.[28] The opening night was orchestrated like a theatrical premiere, with banks of red roses massed around the store, floodlights, and New York's social elite in evening clothes sipping champagne. The guest of honor was the French ambassador, Paul Claudel, who traveled from Washington for the event. Presiding over it all was Shaver, resplendent in a white evening gown. Over the thirty-two days that the exhibition was open, an astonishing three hundred thousand people, perhaps half the number of visitors that a major museum might attract in a year, trooped through the large gallery hung with paintings and the nine model rooms Shaver had furnished.[29] It was, *Vogue* reported, "a tremendous impetus to the acceptance of modern design," as well as "the night Lord & Taylor

arrived as part of New York's social life, a mover in the arts, and a
battler for the improvement of taste."[30]

Years later, when Shaver was reflecting on her career, she described the Lord & Taylor she first joined as an excellent store that
"had no more showmanship than a high school play; it was busy
selling clothes and furniture but not fashions and living and ideas."[31]
The Exposition of Modern French Decorative Art changed all of
that, and established Shaver's reputation as a cultural avatar and visionary retailer. From then on, Lord & Taylor operated in the Shaver
mode of dramatic flair buttressed by high culture and class.

Despite her support for new art forms and design movements,
nothing in Shaver's appearance or demeanor suggested the avant-
garde. She dressed quietly, in black or navy blue suits accessorized
with gold earrings that set off her deep brown eyes. In an era when
fashion editors wore hats even at their desks, she almost always
went bareheaded. She never visited a beauty salon, preferring to
arrange her brown hair in its habitual updo herself each morning.
She shared a penthouse apartment with her younger sister, Elsie—
neither ever married—in Manhattan's East 50s.[32] The apartment's
decor reflected their mingled tastes: walls painted with daisies and
forget-me-nots by Elsie, an artist, and important pieces of furniture
chosen by Dorothy, like the $3,500 andirons for their fireplace that
she bought with one night's winnings in Monte Carlo.[33]

Her coiffure in order, Shaver stepped into a limousine for the
twenty-block ride downtown. She alighted at the 39th Street entrance and was then whisked up to the ninth floor by one of the
store's elevator operators. Her large office, located just off the lamp
department, was decorated to look like the library in a wealthy
home, down to the pale pine paneling that had originally lined an
eighteenth-century English gentleman's study, ancestral portraits
(in this case Lord & Taylor founder Samuel Lord and Mrs. Lord),

and an antique Chippendale desk, the latter of which was set to one side rather than placed in the center of the room, to encourage informal discussion. Buyers, display designers, and copywriters were in and out constantly and knew to be prepared to answer any question Shaver might lob at them. When she was very pleased, she'd pronounce an idea "tops, tops, tops." Proposals that met with her displeasure were dismissed with a curt "That's 1929 modern."[34]

Shaver, who was born in Arkansas in 1893, had a manner that combined the ladylike helplessness of her Victorian youth with the shrewdness of a natural business leader. Thunderstorms made her apprehensive, and despite living almost her entire adult life in New York City, she found crossing streets a source of anxiety. She carried a linen handkerchief in her sleeve and thought open-toed shoes "monstrous" (a view shared by her friend Edna Woolman Chase, who pontificated against this vulgar new fad in the pages of *Vogue*).[35] Shaver was also the first woman in the United States to run a retailer the size of Lord & Taylor, which turned over $32 million in the mid-1940s, and the first to earn a six-figure salary, making $110,000 a year when she was named president of the store in 1945, a sum that was in keeping with what the retailer paid its male executives.[36] When another woman asked her how she got along with the men she worked with, Shaver replied in her soft voice, "The best answer to that is that I have survived three changes of management and got a promotion each time."[37]

The Shaver sisters arrived in New York, after first trying and rejecting Chicago, in 1920. They were pondering their next steps when Elsie began crafting a series of whimsical dolls. Christened Princess Olie-ge-wob, Ketsey Piper, Patsy Doola, Baby Olie-ge-wob, and Thomas Squeelix, names originally given to the sisters' childhood dolls by their grandfather, they had cotton bodies, silk-floss hair, painted features, and amusing backstories that Elsie invented.[38]

Dorothy approached Lord & Taylor's Samuel Reyburn—variously described as a distant Shaver cousin and a family friend—and, using her uncanny powers of persuasion, convinced him to sell the dolls in his department store. The Little Shavers, as they became known, were an instant hit, and the sisters soon set up their own little shop. "Friends came by at night and showed me how to keep books," remembered Shaver. "I found out I had a sense of organization. We made a fortune."[39] But after four years, Elsie tired of the whole venture and returned to her first love, painting (she specialized in gauzily rendered, huge-eyed children). The sisters closed their shop, and Shaver went to work for Lord & Taylor.

Her first assignment was being a comparison shopper at other department stores. After a few months of this, she suggested that it would be more expedient to simply concentrate on improving Lord & Taylor's products, an observation that led to her appointment, in 1924, to the head of the comparison bureau. A year later, she became director of fashions and interior decorations. In short order, she joined the board of directors and became one of the store's vice presidents. She was promoted to first vice president in sole charge of all advertising, display, and publicity in 1936, a position she held until she reached the very top of the corporate hierarchy in 1945.[40] She was not the only woman, or the first, to be named the president of a department store—Hortense Odlum had been the president of Bonwit Teller from 1934 to 1940, and Beatrice Fox Auerbach was president of G. Fox & Co. in Hartford, Connecticut, but both came to their jobs via marriage. Although "she knew the boss," as her employees acknowledged, Shaver had worked her way up. Her success was a source of fascination to the nation's journalists, who profiled her, frequently quoted her, and generally regarded her as a go-to interviewee for anything to do with fashion. In 1947, *Life* deemed her the "No. 1 American career woman."[41]

Although Shaver enjoyed a varied social life and was a member of the boards of several museums, Lord & Taylor, or "the store," as she always called it, was the center of her life, and there were few areas of it that weren't subject to her penetrating gaze. Her innovations contrived to make each customer feel special, as though shopping at Lord & Taylor was like visiting a friend rather than parting with money. Every bride who bought her trousseau at Lord & Taylor was given a seed pearl heart charm, and every baby whose layette was ordered there received a rattle. The glove counter, then a busy area in any department store, was outfitted with elbow rests of red felt to make trying on gloves more comfortable. In the tenth-floor men's department, Scotch broth and deep-dish apple cobbler with rum sauce were dispensed by a wise-cracking counterman in an oversized chef's toque.[42] On the fifth floor, in the Bird Cage tearoom, individual diners could sit in armchairs equipped with trays; in a nod to the then almost universal habit of smoking, they were given a complimentary cigarette at the end of their meal. Shaver created the store's distinctive, handwritten logo, and it was at her behest that Lord & Taylor's awnings were swapped out seasonally, with green ones in the spring, rose-patterned ones in the summer, and russet in the autumn. New Yorkers, it was said, could tell the time of year by looking at Lord & Taylor. The first petites department was launched at Lord & Taylor, as was the first maternity department and the first teenagers' department. But its most famed department was its College Shop, which was strategically located across from the Bird Cage and staffed by recent college graduates who were hired to advise prospective coeds on campus essentials like polo coats and saddle shoes.[43] In reality, women of all ages shopped there, because the casual clothes fit the increasingly informal style of dress that Americans preferred. In some ways, the College Shop was the most fashion-forward department in the entire store—*Vogue* was known to poach staff from its ranks. The concept was copied by retailers all over the country, further disseminating the appeal of sportswear.

Generally, Shaver preferred to under- rather than oversell. In 1943, she stripped Lord & Taylor's already spare ads even further, limiting each to a single illustration and eliminating the copy that gave information about prices, sizes, colors, and location of the item within the store. In effect, she made them more like magazine editorials than hard-charging sales tools. "The strategy is not to sell a specific item," she explained. "It is to plant the idea that we know fashion." [44]

Conversely, she could be brash when she judged it warranted. In November 1938, when unseasonably warm autumn weather was depressing winter coat sales, she used Epsom salts, chemically bleached cornflakes, powerful fans, and a record player that broadcast the sound of howling winds to simulate a blizzard in Lord & Taylor's Fifth Avenue windows. [45] Coat sales shot up 50 percent over the previous year, and New Yorkers stood with their children three deep to witness the spectacle. Those who couldn't make it to the store straightaway jammed its telephone exchange—Wisconsin 7-3300—with calls to inquire how long the storm would be raging. [46] But the raucous display violated the rules of the Fifth Avenue Association, which strove to maintain a high tone on Manhattan's most refined thoroughfare. Moving objects and sound effects were verboten, an infraction that store executives appealed by arguing that no merchandise was displayed. [47]

Shifting from the absurd to the sublime, Shaver continued her fall 1938 roll by keeping the windows empty of merchandise during the busy holiday shopping season. Through the end of December of that year, the only items in Lord & Taylor's windows were large, gently tolling golden Christmas bells. [48] Like the best of Shaver's display windows, it was created for the amusement of the public rather than the ensnaring of the buyer. Less agile merchants watched in fascinated despair.

But it was her conviction that American designers deserved the same attention enjoyed by their Paris peers that has made Shaver a retail legend. After the success of her French furniture exhibition, she considered mounting a similar show to highlight American art and design. But on reflection, she decided it made more sense to focus on American fashion. "It occurred to me that it was about time we recognized what a tremendously capable job this country was doing in turning out 'ready-to-wear,'" she told a reporter. "Every little side street shop had chic wearable models. Every small town in the country had crisp, fresh, smart looking clothes that have somehow been translated into the American vernacular." Ignoring this wellspring of talent, she added, was holding back American fashion. "No human being can do his best work without encouragement. Anonymity makes for unimaginative, mediocre, slipshod work. We all need the stimulation of praise, or recognition to develop our full capacities."[49]

In 1932, after a two-year search, Shaver launched a coordinated promotional campaign that, over the course of its eight-year run, brought the names of more than seventy-five American designers to the attention of the public. In window displays, in-store promotions, and newspaper advertising, Shaver took pains to present each designer as a relatable fellow citizen rather than a Parisian-style demigod. Window displays, for example, included large photos of the designers, and customers were able to meet and interact with them on designated days.[50]

Shaver requested that each designer provide a small collection of designs for three different Lord & Taylor departments: the Young New Yorkers Shop, the moderately priced dress department, and the higher-end salon. By offering American design at prices that ranged from $10.75 to $125, she was able to reach a wide swath of women, and prove that stylish, well-made clothes did not have to be expensive.

Although Shaver was a staunch believer in American design, supporting it had an underlying economic motive. The idea came to her, she said, when she was "wrestling with the problem of what to do to stimulate business" during the Depression.[51] The Wall Street crash of 1929 and the subsequent higher import taxes had made Paris fashion far more expensive than it had been just a few years earlier, and women who had once thought nothing of spending several hundred dollars on a dress with a French label were no longer so free with their money. (This was dire for the French couturiers, who reported a drop of 40 percent in exports between 1926 and 1930.)[52] Stocking American designers was patriotic—Shaver even co-opted Edward Bok's slogan, "American Fashions for American Women"—but it was also practical and timely. Bok's crusade had been premature, Shaver told the press. The combination of the more mature domestic fashion industry and the higher prices being charged for French imports meant that American designers were now ready to be given their due.[53] And whereas Bok and his followers had not been able to pinpoint how American fashion was different from Paris fashion, Shaver had an answer: sportswear, which she considered native to the United States. American women, she insisted, were unique in their athleticism and active lifestyles, and so "we must have sports clothes that fit in with our needs."[54]

In the press, the American Fashions campaign was hailed in patriotic terms, with Shaver described as the "general" leading the revolt against Paris.[55] But *Vogue*, the publication that then held the final word on fashion, was less impressed, describing nationalism as the "fetish of the day," a reference that contemporary readers would have recognized as an allusion to the rise of fascism in Europe. It was commendable of Shaver to promote American designers, its editors acknowledged, but "let us admit that Paris sets the mode and the majority of American designers interpret it."[56]

Shaver, however, was not to be dissuaded. During the course of her American Fashion campaign, she brought to light—or, as *Vogue* less flatteringly put it, "ferreted out"—dozens of American designers, including future sportswear stars Clare Potter, Vera Maxwell, Tina Leser, and Bonnie Cashin. In 1933, she expanded the campaign to encompass industrial designers, tapping, among others, Donald Deskey, who was responsible for the Art Deco interiors of Radio City Music Hall, to create exclusive textiles for Lord & Taylor. Five years later, she scaled her pet project up again, by inaugurating the Lord & Taylor American Design Awards. That first year, they were presented to two fashion designers, Clare Potter and Nettie Rosenstein, and two textile designers, Dorothy Liebes and Stanislav V'Soske. Each dropped by the store individually to collect their $1,000 prize. That was a little too subdued for Shaver's liking. She used to tell her staff, "Don't give me dits and dats"— Shaver-speak for anything picayune. "Give me four big public relations ideas a year and you can relax the rest of the time."[57] By 1945, 1,800 guests attended the awards ceremony at the Waldorf Astoria hotel, where each place setting was adorned with Lord & Taylor's signature American Beauty rose. The under secretary of the navy spoke, and a prize of $25,000 was given to members of the National Academy of Sciences for their work developing, among other discoveries, penicillin, DDT, and, months before the public knew of its existence, the atomic bomb. No one could accuse Shaver of thinking small. As one guest commented, "[Shaver] will hitch Mars onto Lord & Taylor."[58]

While it sounds odd for a department store to give awards to scientists, for Shaver it made perfect sense. She viewed Lord & Taylor as upholding the tradition of the Medicis and other great merchants of the Italian Renaissance, rendering service to the community by uniting commerce, art, and science.[59] To her, Lord & Taylor was nothing less than an engine of American greatness. When she was asked to join the advisory board of the resources division of the Office of the Quartermaster General, which oversaw the designing and standardization of all the items used in the clothing and feeding of the army, in May 1942, Shaver didn't hesitate. But neither did she give up her job at Lord & Taylor. Instead, she commuted weekly between Washington, DC, and New York.[60]

It was this deep-rooted patriotism that underlay Shaver's support of American fashion. She had no issues with the French, but she thought them unsuited to the business of clothing Americans. "We believe," she said, "there must be clothes which are intrinsically American and that only the American designer can create them."[61] The majority of her peers, however, had to be forcibly disconnected from the French Legend. At the July 11, 1940, meeting of the Fashion Group, Mary Lewis, a former Best & Co. executive turned designer and boutique owner, acknowledged as much. Speaking one month after the fall of Paris, she told her fellow attendees, "I for one have always felt that never would we know our own strength, so to speak, until we were physically cut off from Paris. The present unfortunate events in the world spell adversity for our fashion trades—but they also spell opportunity."[62] Demanding, "Are we mice or designers?" Lewis called for individual designers to be identified by name.

Shaver, meanwhile, was looking ahead. She knew that American designers needed more than recognition—they needed guidance. In a lengthy response to "the question so much discussed since the German invasion of Paris—the question as to where the fashion trades in this country will find style guidance formerly supplied by France," Shaver told *WWD* that the solution was to "design the American way . . . Paris has built up a splendid fashion structure suited to the character and traditions of her people, and appropriate to her workers. It would be nonsense for us to impose the same setup on our country and it would not succeed." Instead, she continued, the United States needed to play to its strengths, i.e., its world-leading mass-production capabilities and a population primed for fashion consumption by retailers and the press—two qualities that the French, who concentrated on selling labor-intensive designs to a select group of women, couldn't claim. "The French," Shaver acknowledged, "had a precious possession in their Haute Couture. And I hope and believe they will regain their property." But Americans, she continued, needed to "develop a property of our own, which will complement and not imitate [the French]." [63]

Then Shaver made her pitch: Those best qualified to "evolve" American fashion were American retailers. It was they who presented women with a hat-to-slingbacks picture of fashion, she explained, which made it easier to introduce new ideas. Stores were in a unique position to promote the fashions they believed in and, in doing so, to impart authority to designers. Because they were in constant contact with both designers and customers, retailers were ideally placed to let one know what the other was thinking—when a trend was winding down, or whether a new color might prove successful. These customers, she pointed out, were a diverse lot. Nowhere else, Shaver said, did "women of wealth and social position frequently buy ready-made clothes in the same store in which the young stenographer does her shopping. And often pay as much as they would buying a French model in Paris." Moreover, American retailers were recognized for their inventive merchandising and promotions—even the French borrowed ideas from them.[64] Finally, Shaver delivered the coup de grâce: It was American retailers who had given the French the wide distribution that they had come to count on. Who better to give the same status and prestige to the designers of the United States?[65]

She put these ideals into action just after Labor Day 1940, when Lord & Taylor's Designers' Shop opened. Located on the third floor, it showcased dresses by ten American ready-to-wear designers, all of whom had been working anonymously for Seventh Avenue manufacturers. In a strikingly illustrated two-page ad that appeared in *Vogue* that month, the ten designers were counted off the fingers of two manicured and bejeweled hands. The copy describes them as "the most successful designers in the American fashion field who will create exclusive dresses for Lord & Taylor" and whose labels "you can wear with pride." The fall 1940 collection, readers were told, "centers around THE BOUND HIPLINE and THE ELONGATED SILHOUETTE, which we predict will be the outstanding silhouettes of autumn, and which each of our ten designers has interpreted with his or her own special flair." The illustrated hands could just as well have been counting off the points in Shaver's pitch to *WWD*: support, promotion, trend direction, and education. The tone was friendly but authoritative and its intent was clear: Lord & Taylor was giving American designers the red-carpet treatment because they deserved it.

One of the designers who would benefit from the full weight of Lord & Taylor's support was Claire McCardell. But it would take a while for Griswold to convince customers that they wanted what McCardell was offering. The problem, she recognized, was one of perception. Jo Copeland, one of McCardell's fellow New York designers, once commented that the trouble with French clothes was that they were so perfect in and of themselves that they were "complete without the woman." Yet when Copeland imagined her clothes, it was always in the context of how they would be worn, even if "they looked like nothing in the hand." [66] Although Copeland was referencing her own designs, her observation was very much true of McCardell's, whose clothes drooped without a body to give them life—or to "perform," as she might have said.

This was a distinct disadvantage on the sales floor, where McCardell's penchant for soft, unconstructed cuts and wrap-and-tie fastenings meant her dresses and tops often slipped off their hangers and puddled on the floor. That first year, the dresses and play suits that had made Griswold sit up in her chair in the Townley showroom were often relegated to the markdown rack. To combat this, Griswold decided on a strategy that combined aggressive promotion with a laissez-faire take on presentation. If the dresses slid to the floor, she instructed sales staff, let them be. Sooner or later, a curious customer would pick one up and try it on, especially if they recognized the name on the label as one that Lord & Taylor believed in. It was at that point, she was confident, that a sale would be made.

Griswold's merchandising instincts proved correct. Sally Kirkland, the *Life* fashion editor who wore the designer's clothes in her personal life, recounted that "women took up limp-looking bargain-priced McCardells home in a what-have-we-got-to-lose spirit, discovered they could wear and enjoy them, and returned with their friends to buy more at full price." [67] Clothes that had once seemed radical or puzzling were, on the body, revealed to be easy, modern, and sophisticated.

Griswold loved how McCardell played with contradiction to make clothes that were both modest and sensual, a quality that was underscored in her favorite McCardell window display. It starred a series of halters and crop tops McCardell had made from floral voile, a fabric Griswold associated with "little old ladies rocking on their porches all day long." The store's display department slyly alluded to this by putting these pieces on mannequins sitting in a row of rocking chairs—the sexiest grannies on Fifth Avenue.[68]

Although getting McCardell into the nation's closets took time, Griswold didn't let her customer's initial wariness influence her buying. For years, McCardell had been trying to get buyers interested in her six-piece capsule wardrobe of hand-washable, packable separates. And for years, she had been told that women wouldn't understand the concept. Griswold thought that was nonsense—in her view it was the buyers, not women, who were confused. She bought McCardell's capsule wardrobes and put them on the sales floor. Finally, in September 1944, ten years after McCardell first designed it, her capsule wardrobe was featured in *Harper's Bazaar*. The story, titled "Be Nifty—Be New—Be Interchangeable," demystified the concept by telling readers that the idea "was your own—mixing up your skirts and shirts and jackets until a small wardrobe looked like 'the works.' Fashion has caught up with you. Now clothes are *designed* to be switched. They're all in parts, and the parts are interchangeable."[69] Underlying this explanation was the idea that American fashion was a conversation between the designer and the customer. A ready-to-wear designer, unlike a couturier, didn't lecture their customer—they collaborated with her. The customer was an equal rather than a follower.

The writer then outlined several scenarios, each illustrated, in which the six pieces could be worn. On the opposite page is a capsule wardrobe by McCardell's onetime employer, Hattie Carnegie, styled with the ballet flats McCardell had made popular. Carnegie, with her impeccable sense of timing, had judged the moment right to convince her customers of the merits of separates. Despite *Bazaar*'s assertion, Carnegie's decision to add a capsule wardrobe to her collection suggests that fashion had finally caught up to McCardell.

But her fame really began in 1945, when Shaver launched the campaign with which McCardell would become synonymous. It was the most successful advertising campaign in Lord & Taylor's history, and it dubbed McCardell and her fellow sportswear designers the exponents of "the American Look."

Unlike Shaver's promotion of American designers in the 1930s, this new effort focused not on individual creators and their specific aesthetic, but on the broader concept of American fashion and its interpretation by American women. The ads spotlighted various types, like "America's own product—the successful businesswoman" and "the girl striding across a thousand campuses," all of whom embodied the qualities of the American Look, which were, according to Shaver, "a natural manner, freshness and enthusiasm, a friendly smile, an easy confident stride with head held high, an unaffected elegance in make-up and dress."[70]

She announced the new campaign's launch in *WWD* on January 12, 1945—almost five years to the day after McCardell, Carnegie, and others in the American fashion contingent had set sail for their last trip to see the Paris collections before the Nazi invasion. During that time, Shaver said, American designers had come of age. Now they were the ones in a position to launch the trends—and stave off what would certainly be a determined comeback effort by the couturiers of Paris. *WWD* quoted her at length, including this majestic ode to the power of American fashion: "Just as our way of living is influencing the entire world, the way the American woman looks is as significant a tendency as any artistic movement or development."[71]

After four years of war—years that required major adjustments on the part of designers and manufacturers—the American Look had come into focus. Shaver was confident that it would have a "strong, virile influence and will continue to grow, even when the European markets are at our disposal," which was code for "even when we can copy Paris again if we want to."[72] Clearly, Shaver did not think that was the way to proceed. With her "American Fashions for American Women" campaign of the previous decade, she had sought to educate an American audience. But now, her postwar vision was bigger. The American Look, Shaver predicted, would have a global impact. She told *The New York Times*, "The American Look will be copied widely . . . just as our movies and jeeps are distinct contributions, our casual pretty clothes will exert international influence." Soon, she added, women all over the world would take it as a compliment to be told, "My dear, you look so American."[73]

Again, Shaver borrowed the name of her campaign, this time from Mary Lewis, who had used the term "the American Look" in the late 1920s, when she was the advertising director at Best & Co. Like Bok, Lewis had misjudged her timing. Shaver was able to capitalize not only on the patriotic fervor of the war years and the stellar work that now-confident American designers were producing, but also on the sum total of her efforts to position Lord & Taylor as a trendsetting market leader.

The American Look campaign was multifaceted, with store window displays, and ads in *Vogue*, *Harper's Bazaar*, and the Sunday editions of newspapers all over the country. The campaign was also covered in the national press, with the biggest story, a multipage photo essay, appearing in *Life* on May 21, 1945. Titled "What Is the American Look?" it's really an extended press release for Shaver, who provides the answers to the question—good grooming, a ready smile, youthfulness, confidence, etc.—which are then illustrated with a series of photo vignettes, including one of Shaver and her staff selecting American Look models. Like earlier celebrations of American fashion, it has a nationalistic slant, with the writer praising everything from the country's mass-production capabilities and dime stores stocked with cosmetics to the widespread availability of orange juice, fresh vegetables, and bathtubs, all of which were judged to play a part in the healthy, scrubbed-clean charm of the American Look.[74] But the overall message was one that McCardell herself might have written: The American Look was an expression of the modernistic principle that form should follow function, and it was deeply rooted in the democratic tradition. But only five years out from obeisance to Paris, and with that city's couturiers once again producing collections and claiming the attention of the press, there was still a need to define the American Look in terms of what it was not. Four months later, *Life* ran a similar story on "the French Look," concluding that it was "sexier and less natural than the American Look . . . the result of effort and ingenuity."[75]

Although McCardell was not the only designer whose career was buoyed by the American Look campaign, the sure-handedness with which she established its tenets made her its biggest star. She was the designer whose view of what fashion could be meshed most readily with that of Griswold and Shaver, who moved her from the sportswear department to the main designer department, where her bathing-suit-to-evening-gown approach to fashion made more sense. All three understood that women's lives were changing, and they needed clothes that could keep up with them. The American Look campaign was the start of McCardell's transition to nationwide recognition—a woman might walk into Lord & Taylor and ask to see "the Claire McCardells" as she had once asked to see the Chanels. By the late 1940s, Townley was Lord & Taylor's biggest domestic account, McCardell was a household name, and the humble pieces on which her career was founded, sportswear and interchangeable separates, had become the backbone of American women's wardrobes.

Lord & Taylor, meanwhile, didn't forget its position as the retailer that had done the most, for the longest, to convince Americans of the ability of their designers. When *Life* published a story in the spring of 1944 on what its editors considered the ten leading American designers, the store responded with a humorous ad chiding the magazine for underestimating the breadth of the country's talent while stressing the democratic reach of the American Look. "Tsk, tsk, *Life* Magazine," the ad ran. "We think you're pretty good, but—take another look around and learn something about the fashion business!"

> We'd say it should be MANY TIMES that number. We know, because we were the first store in America to publicize and promote American designers . . . It's like that old business of the "ten best dressed women." You'd think, from the sound of it, there were only ten women in the country who knew how to dress. Ten? There are hundreds of thousands![76]

By the time this ad ran, the press had been writing almost exclusively about American fashion for almost four years—an idea that would have been unimaginable in the early days of 1940, when Paris was still synonymous with style leadership. For most journalists, covering American fashion came with a steep learning curve. Two exceptions were Lois Long and Virginia Pope, the fashion editors of, respectively, *The New Yorker* and *The New*

York Times, both of whom had been attuned to the possibility of American ready-to-wear for years. When the fall of Paris put the city's couturiers *hors de combat*, they recognized the importance of the moment: It was time to convince consumers of the greatness of American design.

6

A Good Designer Need Not Breathe the Air of Paris

Lois Long and Virginia Pope

It has been easy and tempting for us to lean on Paris and to get into the lazy habit of adapting instead of creating . . . now that this prop has been removed, we shall develop numbers of great designers of our own.

—LOIS LONG[1]

New York was definitely established as the fashion center of the Western Hemisphere, as one magnificent costume after another swept in review before the gasping crowd of onlookers.

—VIRGINIA POPE[2]

On Thursday, September 5, 1940, three days after Labor Day marked the unofficial end of the most stressful summer the American fashion industry had ever experienced, *Vogue* took out a large ad in *The New York Times*. Its purpose was ostensibly to promote the magazine's two September issues, the first ever to contain only American fashions. But what it was really doing was assuring women that this was nothing to worry about.

Newspapers across the country might be demanding, "Can America Design?" and Edna Woolman Chase and her editors not only had the answer ("*Vogue* says, YES!"), but they also were reporting on the all-American fall collections with "the same critical judgment, the same brilliant picturing" that had characterized the coverage of the Paris collections for the past fifty years. In "these confusing times," to whom would the country look for fashion guidance? "To VOGUE . . . *as always!*" The cheery, patriotic tone was reinforced by a photo of two models in tailored woolens posed in front of the sculpture of a bald eagle, wings spread and beak raised triumphantly to the sky.[3] Although Chase, a devout Republican, might not have sanctioned the analogy, the ad was her magazine's version of one of FDR's fireside chats, a soothing assurance that the authorities—she and her staff—knew what they were doing.[4]

Had Lois Long, *The New Yorker*'s fashion critic and a former *Vogue* staffer, read the *Times* that day, she would have rolled her eyes. Long filed her first column of the new season, dated September 7, from California. All summer long, she wrote, New York fashion journalists had poured "out of every airplane and streamliner from the East." They'd made the journey to beg Hollywood designers like Howard Greer, Adrian, and Travis Banton to take the place of the absent couturiers by creating clothes for Seventh Avenue to copy.[5]

Long, who did some writing for Paramount in the '30s and would visit the studios of the Hollywood designers when she was in town, was the rare New York fashion editor who was not sniffy about the work of the film industry's costume designers.[6] We love the costumes of Hollywood's Golden Age today, but to the fashion elite of the era, they were vulgar and showy, the opposite of refined Parisian good taste. Yet these same critics had so little faith in the ready-to-wear designers of New York that they'd turned to the closest thing Americans had to fashion royalty. The creators of the gowns worn by screen goddesses like Marlene Dietrich and Joan Crawford were now sought after to replace the temporarily missing French masters, "without a word of apology for the snubs of the past."[7] It was an ill-conceived plan, but also a backhanded compliment. Unlike the country's fashion designers, Hollywood costume designers had never had the luxury of using Paris as their template. Production schedules meant that sketches were finalized months before a film was released. If Adrian had to design the costumes for a contemporary picture in December, he couldn't wait around for February to see what Schiaparelli was thinking—he had to push ahead on his own. The Californians advised their New York friends to do what they did: look to other sources—get costume books, they suggested—knuckle down, and get to work.

Long was less sanguine, or perhaps more realistic. Designers, she said, were in a state of stark terror. And as for the journalists, they were bewildered. "While experts in other fields have been continually geared to record a state of uncertainty in a moment of crisis, fashion writers in the past have had only to think up synonyms for words like 'elegant' and 'suave,'" she wryly observed. "Thus, the present situation catches them woefully unprepared."[8] She wasn't kidding. Many American fashion journalists, including those who worked for Chase, had not attended a single American opening before—this was virgin territory for them. So much for *Vogue*'s confident assurances that all was well.

The 1930s were a critical period in the development of American fashion. Primed by Elizabeth Hawes's insistence that the French Legend was a folderol and Dorothy Shaver's vigorous promotion of homegrown talent at Lord & Taylor, American designers had gained, albeit slowly, in confidence and prestige. But they had yet to win the respect, or in some cases the attention, of the press. Those who worked at the couture end of the spectrum, like Hawes, could count on some coverage, although not on the scale of a headlining Paris name like Vionnet or Schiaparelli. Those who were employed by the made-to-order departments of big retailers like Bergdorf Goodman or Seventh Avenue ready-to-wear firms might see their designs in print, but their individual identities were obscured by those of their employers. It was, as one journalist recalled decades later, "Just Paris, Paris, Paris . . . It made it hard for American design."[9]

From the press's point of view, covering New York designers was a headache. There was no organized show schedule—the fall of 1940, when a group of Fifth Avenue retailers banded together to stage coordinated fashion shows, marked the first tentative steps toward a system of any sort—and many manufacturers showed their collections only to buyers. When they deigned to invite journalists, it was with the proviso that nothing about the collection be published until it arrived in stores, a delay of at least a month. This was because manufacturers were paranoid about being knocked off (they were right to feel that way—American designers still don't own the intellectual property rights to their designs, meaning anyone can copy anything). But the result was that their fashions seemed like old news, especially in comparison to the French, who showed well ahead of editorial deadlines—and always invited the press.[10] Nor were New York fashion shows the elaborate, colorful affairs that Parisian ones were. They took place in grimy buildings on the West Side of Manhattan, not *hô-tels particuliers* near the Seine. No one would mistake them for a cocktail party—they were no-frills, businesslike gatherings, and the models, who announced both the number of the ensemble they were wearing and its price, were trained to get buyers to place orders.[11]

In Paris, the Chambre Syndicale de la Couture Parisienne not only organized fashion shows into a manageable timetable, allowing journalists to visit all the major houses in a ten-day visit, it also provided press releases that could be converted into ready-made stories (smaller newspapers that lacked their own fashion reporters sometimes reprinted these verbatim).[12] Engraved invitations were issued, chilled champagne was served, and for nighttime shows, guests wore evening dress.[13] And then there were the many enjoyable little flourishes that the couturiers exercised in their wooing of the press—the flowers, the dinners, the generous discounts on clothing orders. Most important, Paris fashion retained the aura of exclusivity that it had enjoyed since the days of Louis XIV, a quality that is to fashion what gasoline is to the internal combustion engine. The press went to Paris to hunt for new ideas, which they turned into magazine pages and column inches. Manufacturers and retailers went to look for new ideas, too, but with the added burden of having to translate those ideas into actual clothing, a fairly daunting caveat that most journalists never really grasped the intricacies of.

The Paris designs that were selected by buyers to be copied or adapted for the American market came complete with a toile, or pattern; a set of construction details; and a list of suppliers for materials. For high-end retailers who made exact replicas of haute couture designs, the process was fairly straightforward. Using the instructions and suppliers provided, the design was copied, line for line, for each customer who ordered it. For mass-market manufacturers, the receipt of the garment, the toile, the construction details, and the list of suppliers was just the start of the technically challenging process of turning an haute couture design into one that could be cut out and stitched by the hundreds or thousands. The patterns needed to be drastically simplified, and then graded for each size that the garment would be sold in, a painstaking process that required dozens of precise measurements. On top of that, less expensive materials needed to be sourced. The whole operation took time, which the press, in its hurry to publish the big news of the season from Paris, didn't take into consideration. This meant that manufacturers rushed to get "Paris" designs on the sales floor to coincide with their appearance in the fashion glossies. These sped-up adaptations often ended up being marked down because all the hiccups of fit hadn't been ironed out.

This financial drain wasn't limited to the ready-to-wear side of the industry—the haute couture salons of exclusive department stores also suffered losses. Andrew Goodman, the owner of Bergdorf Goodman, once complained, "I wouldn't mind charging so much in custom if only we could show a little profit. And I wouldn't mind losing so much if we were selling our merchandise and services at a low price. But to charge so much and still lose, I find that downright embarrassing."[14]

The durable charm of Paris had kept the system going, but it led to bad feeling all around, especially between the press and manufacturers. Manufacturers resented the high-handedness of the press, and the press were contemptuous of manufacturers, whom they regarded as unimaginative and drearily obsessed with the bottom line. For many American fashion editors and writers, homegrown ready-to-wear was a fine concept, but it was the French Legend that kept them enthralled.

Long, who wrote about Paris clothes but didn't travel to Paris for the collections, might have found that this made it easier to write about what she really believed. And because she worked at *The New Yorker*, she wasn't beholden to the whims of fashion advertisers. Her colleague Virginia Pope, of *The New York Times*, was in a similarly advantageous position. Both had considerable respect for the traditions and output of the haute couture, while consistently giving space to American designers. When it came time to review the collections of the fall of 1940, they were ready. They'd been assessing American design for years, and they were familiar with its strengths and weaknesses.

The similarities, however, ended there. Long, whom one colleague described as so thoroughly embodying the rollicking spirit of the 1920s that "she could have posed for Miss Jazz Age," was a minister's daughter turned Manhattan sophisticate, and one of the few women to gain entry to *The New Yorker*'s inner circle.[15] Pope, who was sixteen years older and known for her charm and old-fashioned manners, always wore pristine white gloves, the right one removed so she could take notes. Everyone who met her described her as "a lady," and the sign on her seat at fashion shows read "The Dean of American Fashion Editors."[16]

But these differences were of style, not substance. Each woman was a staunch supporter of American fashion, albeit in her own way. Long, who was one of the ablest writers ever to make fashion her subject, was credited by her longtime editor, William Shawn, with inventing fashion criticism. She was, he said, "the first American fashion critic to approach fashion as an art and to criticize women's clothes with independence, humor, and literary style."[17] Long's belief in American fashion wasn't inspired by patriotism or disregard for the French, but by the simple conviction that it was good. She interpreted her role as a critic to mean that she should encourage when praise was warranted, and when it was not, explain why. Throughout her career, she paid American designers the respectful compliment of being as stringent with them as she was with the French.

Pope, too, wrote perceptively about American fashion throughout the '30s. But it was her genius at harnessing the power of *The New York Times* to promote American designers and the clothes they created that is her most enduring legacy. She had a flair for showmanship that her refined appearance belied, and when she dug in her heels, she usually prevailed. Long and Pope's combined efforts were crucial in establishing the legitimacy of American design.

Lois Bancroft Long was born in 1901 in Stamford, Connecticut. Although she was younger than Pope, she was the first to begin reporting on fashion. She joined *The New Yorker* in May 1925, landing there via Vassar (where she earned a bachelor's degree in English literature in 1922) followed by stints at *Vogue* and *Vanity Fair*. She was working as the latter's theater critic when Harold Ross, who had recently launched *The New Yorker* with his wife, Jane Grant, hired her to write his new magazine's nightlife column, "Tables for Two." To her colleague Brendan Gill, Long's appeal was obvious: "Ross never doubted that the ideal *New Yorker* writer, to say nothing of the ideal *New Yorker* reader, would be someone as like Lois Long as possible."[18] Ross offered her a salary of fifty dollars a week, fifteen more than she was making at *Vanity Fair*, and set her loose.[19]

Prior to the 1920s, it was possible, certainly in large cities like New York, for men to go out for an evening of food or drink or entertainment. But nightlife as we now think of it, with buzzy

restaurants and themed clubs, was a product of the Jazz Age, as
was the revolutionary idea that women could participate. Instead of
killing this fledgling industry, Prohibition, which came into effect
on January 17, 1920, simply pushed it to the margins. Speakeasies
sprang up to meet the demand for after-dark carousing, and within
a few years New York City was roaring like never before, fueled by
rivers of illegal booze.

Long and her roommate, the actress Kay Francis, who would
go on to be known as the best-dressed woman in 1930s Hollywood,
were habitués of all the best nightspots in town, from the 300 Club
on West 54th Street, where the hostess was the brassy Texas Gui-
nan, to Chumley's in Greenwich Village, where the literati drank.
They had their own bootlegger, a man named Frankie Costello,
who sold them gin for twelve dollars a case. Francis liked to down
a tumbler for breakfast.[20] Long was no slouch as an imbiber, either:
Her renown among Manhattan's bartenders was such that a cocktail was named in her honor. Not her *real* name, but the sobriquet
under which she wrote "Tables for Two"—Lipstick, a feminine re-
tort to her predecessor, who'd written as Top Hat. The Lipstick,
Long explained, was so called because "it tastes sweet and innocuous and has an awful wallop."[21]

The two women shared a minuscule apartment on East 39th
Street that had no kitchen and a single bedroom so small that it was
impossible to get to the bed by the window without climbing over
the one by the door. They did, however, have three phones, which
rang constantly, mostly with men calling up to make plans for the
evening. These plans could sometimes go quite dangerously awry.
The pair were at the Owl Club on West 45th Street with their dates
one night when it was held up—Prohibition had caused organized
crime to surge—and had to dive for cover behind an overturned

table as the bullets flew.[22] If incidents like this shook them up, they hid it behind a scrim of bravado. It was, Long later recalled, a reckless era. "You were thought to be good at holding your liquor in those days if you could make it to the ladies' room before throwing up," she said. "It was customary to give two dollars to the cabdriver if you threw up in his cab."[23] The birth control available wasn't always reliable, so Long's crowd relied on a woman doctor they knew when they needed an abortion. She would take a vacation over Christmas to rest up for the inevitable post–New Year's rush.[24] "We women had been emancipated and weren't sure what we were supposed to do with all the freedom and equal rights, so we were going to hell laughing and singing," Long remembered.[25] Attempting suicide, she added, "was almost a fad."[26]

For her new gig, Long visited four or five nightclubs, cabarets, and restaurants a night. "We'd start at '21' and go on to Tony's after '21' closed. Drinks were a dollar twenty-five. We thought brandy was the only safe thing to drink, because, we were told, a bootlegger couldn't fake the smell and taste of cognac."[27] If she couldn't make it to all the clubs on her roster, she'd outsource a few to Francis and ask her to take notes.[28]

To preserve her anonymity, the lanky, dark-haired Long variously described herself as "a short, squat maiden of forty who wears steel-rimmed spectacles" or "the kindly, bearded old gentleman who signs himself—LIPSTICK."[29] Her nocturnal escapades she rendered as a series of screwball comedy scenes. During a raid on one establishment, "one of those movie affairs, where burly cops kick down the doors . . . and waiters shriek and start throwing bottles out of windows," she recounted being rescued by an Irish cop who looked at her, said, "Kid, you're too good for this dump," and helped her evade arrest by directing her out a window to a fire escape.[30]

Long managed to keep her identity a secret until her marriage to Peter Arno, *The New Yorker*'s star cartoonist, was announced in August 1927. Like Long, Arno was a good-looking, elegantly dressed hell-raiser. To match her Seven Sisters–minister's daughter pedigree, he was the Yale-educated son of a judge. Together, they were the magazine's version of Zelda and Scott Fitzgerald— glamorous and lawless. One morning, after a long night of drinking, they were discovered passed out naked on a sofa at the basement club Ross maintained for *New Yorker* employees. Long thought that perhaps they'd forgotten they were married and had an apartment to go to. Ross, however, wasn't amused and shut the place down permanently.[31] In the end, like the Cole Porter lyric, the Long-Arno romance was too hot not to cool down; they divorced in 1931, after four years of marriage and the birth of one child, a daughter.

But Long got into plenty of mischief on her own. Her antics in the early years of *The New Yorker* read like they were lifted from a Preston Sturges script. Because writing "Tables for Two" required her to go out almost every evening, she would often write her column in the small hours of the morning. If she had forgotten the key to her office, she would kick off her shoes and clamber over the transom; in hot weather, she was known to strip down to her slip to type her column. When she and her assistant were assigned desks at opposite ends of the floor, they took to roller-skating back and forth.[32]

As entertaining as Long's after-dark dispatches were, it was her fashion reportage that made her name. She began writing "Feminine Fashions," one of a series of shopping columns that appeared under the umbrella title "On and Off the Avenue," soon after she joined

The New Yorker. Unlike her titillating nightlife adventures, this new column was conceived of as practical and service-oriented: "smart copy about smart clothes contrived to lure readers and advertisers alike."[33] "Smart" in 1920s jargon meant made-to-order, and most of the fashion Long covered was from this higher end of the market. But she admired better-quality ready-to-wear, especially sportswear, and that, too, found its way into her column. In 1927, "Tables for Two" was retired (it was revived in the late 1990s as the magazine's restaurant review column), and Long began covering fashion full time.

One of the more unusual qualities of "Feminine Fashions" was that it included neither illustrations nor photographs. In fact, during Long's entire tenure there, *The New Yorker* did not publish a single photograph (and would not do so until Tina Brown became editor in chief in 1992, sixty-seven years after the magazine's founding). The only way Long could make her readers "see" an item of clothing was with accurate and concise description, a challenge at which she excelled.

Apart from this constriction, she enjoyed an exceptional amount of freedom. Because *The New Yorker* was not dependent on fashion advertising, she could be far more honest than her peers at publications like *Vogue* and *Harper's Bazaar*. And because her editor, Ross, was not a professional cheerleader for the industry, she was not obliged to engage in what a colleague called "the sedulous puffing of certain favored shops and designers."[34] If Long didn't like something, she said so. She established this editorial independence early on when she asked Ross how she should describe some jewelry she thought was terrible. Having worked at *Vogue*, she knew that honesty was not always appreciated or even expected in fashion writing. But Ross replied, simply, "Say it's terrible."[35] It was advice that helped to shape the integrity and humor of her column.

Long saw her mission as twofold: She educated her readers and she entertained them, and she did both in a spirit of camaraderie. She was well aware that many fashion writers "sat in their offices and told their awestruck public that Vionnet was Vionnet and that any model she turned out, no matter what it did to your charm, was automatically veddy smawt," and the knowledge clearly irritated her (one of the more appealing qualities of Long's writing was that she wasn't afraid to show her emotion, and not infrequently referred to how elated or exasperated fashion made her, sometimes in the same column). As far as she was concerned, it was nonsense to pretend that Vionnet was infallible. And while Grecian drapery was all well and good, the ancient Greeks hadn't worn girdles. And they definitely hadn't smothered themselves in pleated chiffon, a Vionnet weakness that she found grating.[36]

That Long was willing to badmouth Madeleine Vionnet, who, along with Chanel and Schiaparelli, was among the most celebrated Paris couturiers in the years before World War II, was a sign of her moxie. In American fashion magazines, praise for them was just shy of gushing. Long, however, had no patience with the French Legend. In a column published on January 1, 1927, she levelheadedly assessed the quality of the House of Chanel, the most successful *maison de couture* of the decade: "Go ahead and buy an original little Chanel around here if you want to. And watch it fall to pieces on your back [on] the second wearing . . . reproductions may not give you the same feeling as a celebrated label, but they do stay together longer." American women, Long added, should smarten up about French clothes.[37]

Long had high expectations of Coco Chanel, as she did for every designer she admired. She delighted in Chanel's sleek modernity, wore her clothes, and continued to refer in print to the purity of her designs into the 1960s. But for Long, every designer was only as good as their last dress. When she wrote of Chanel a few years later, "Her good things are so simple (except in detail), so wearable, and so young that they defy description; her bad things would make a Hollywood star feel too dressed-up," both her irritation and her disappointment are evident.[38]

When a designer who was capable of excellence created what Long considered an epic failure, she could be apoplectic. Of Vionnet, who revolutionized fashion with her bias cuts and was revered by both Elizabeth Hawes and Claire McCardell, not to mention countless fashion lovers then and since, she once fumed:

> I am still enraged by a chiffon evening thing at Saks Fifth Avenue which, so far, stands unchallenged as the horror of the season: huge harem trousers, very full front and back so that you can't avoid looking dumpy, and those unspeakable full Vionnet folds, crossing high at the front and back to wrap around the neck. I could howl.[39]

Long wasn't being spiteful—in this same column she praised two other Vionnet dresses, calling one "divine" and the other "a honey." But the horror she could not unsee. Meanwhile, Long's beef with Schiaparelli was rooted in what she interpreted as the latter's tendency to expose her clients to ridicule:

> She enjoys . . . putting colored net gloves and cellophane parachutes and butterflies on horse-faced women. The trouble is, once we take one of these whims seriously, she doesn't respect us anymore. She's forever suggesting we drape hyacinths around ourselves at 7,000 francs a throw, and then refusing to speak to us socially if we have them on.[40]

It was this skill at parsing fashion, all the while slinging zingers, that made Long so well respected. Fashion writers of the era who wrote for newspapers followed the ups and downs of hemlines and the permutations of silhouettes with dogged intensity, but for the most part without any deeper scrutiny, with Pope as the notable exception. Those who worked for fashion magazines, mindful that the subjects of their photo shoots and commentary were also their main advertisers, didn't find fault, or at least not publicly. They interpreted fashion, issuing instructions couched in the imperative (thus revealing the fashion editor's true identity; she is a bully), like this order from *Vogue*'s September 1, 1939, issue: "Wear one colour—the new taupe—from head to foot. Taupe hat, taupe suit, taupe fur, taupe gloves, shoes." [41] Long took a different tack. She *analyzed* fashion.

In her view, it was not enough for a dress to be "veddy smawt." For a garment to succeed, it also had to fit well, flatter the wearer, and be both comfortable and practical—whether it was an evening dress or a winter coat, it had to make sense in the life of the woman who wore it. A French-designed dress or coat could do all of this; as Long once confessed, "Despite my irreverent jeers, I look to Paris for a great deal." [42] But the customer who mistook a Paris label for a guarantee of chic, she warned, was a chump: "Possibly you don't realize how few clothes made in France keep a Parisian tone after being transplanted." [43]

In spelling out a fact that was usually ignored—that French designers could fail—Long was implicitly acknowledging the corollary: that American designers could succeed. She was not, however, ceding an inch of critical ground. In the first half of the '30s, she considered very few of them good enough to rate a mention in her column. (One who made the grade was Hawes, who was both a friend and Long's former Paris correspondent. Long once affectionately described her as "the incorrigible brat of American design.")[44]

But rather than ignoring American designers, Long used her column as a forum for encouragement and guidance, doling out witty lessons in how to compete with the French. Know what you do well, she counseled. "Where the beach is concerned, California and Seventh Avenue rule the world. No couturier can touch our ingenious manufacturers when it comes to clothes that are utterly in rapport with the lolling life."[45] However tempting it might be, do not indulge in "defiant eccentricity" or endeavor to out-French the French with tortured elegance, two pitfalls that Long thought American designers were prone to. Playing to their strengths was fine, but Seventh Avenue's designers needed to push themselves: "Turning out clothes that are wearable and becoming is part of the American genius for mass production, but it is not enough—there has to be a point of view, adroitly expressed, to put fashion designers up among the other artists."[46]

When it came to originality, for most of the 1930s Long believed that Paris maintained an edge on New York. Although by no means an unquestioning supporter of the French Legend, she felt it was important for American designers to remember that they faced stiff competition if they wished to succeed at the highest level, explaining, "I am sentimental about the surly spirit of the French. They should continue to ritz [sic] us by giving us their best."[47] But despite what the magazines and the couturiers might say, she reminded her readers, it was not Paris that set the styles or New York, or even Hollywood, "but the people who wear them . . . These are the judges, and they appear all over the map." Nor were those who created fashions confined to one location: "A good designer is a person who senses the direction in which fashions inevitably move and need not breathe the air of Paris for inspiration."[48]

Long wrote those words in 1936. Two years later, in February 1938, she reported that she was no longer the only one who felt so inclined: "Of late a rapidly increasing group of people have agreed that a good designer in Des Moines is a good designer just the same and worthy of having a footpath beaten to his doors, but the influence of this group is slight as yet."[49] The following month, she noted that these designers were making their presence felt, observing that the "deathly, five-in-the-morning hush which used to hold the fashion girls rigid as they awaited the arrival of the French clothes is barely noticeable this season." Instead, they were impressed by the New York collections, which were "as nonchalant as they are independent."[50]

These "fashion girls"—the editors and buyers who shaped each season's fashion message for public consumption—were a persistent source of frustration for Long, who saw them as "destroying the independence of American women" by enthusiastically backing every Paris fad, no matter how ridiculous it looked in the cold light of day. One that particularly galled her was the much-ballyhooed return of the corset in the fall of 1939. Corsets were uncomfortable, Long pointed out, and the timing of their revival was lousy; women who hadn't been able to draw a deep breath since war broke out on the first of September didn't want to be laced into a state of even greater stress. But most pertinent was her observation that the corset fad was not only stupid but pointless. The silhouette of the new season was not that different from that of the previous one, for which no corsetry had been required—it was only being pushed because fashion writers and retailers needed something to promote.[51] The French Legend was adept at meeting the endless need for hyperbole, throwing out just enough newness to get the typewriters going but not enough to scare retail executives. This was something else American designers, who specialized in wearable clothes, would have to contend with if they wanted to compete in what Long called the Big League.

But by September 1940, American designers had been thrown headlong into the Big League, like it or not, and the eyes of every fashion girl, department store president, manufacturer, and advertising executive were trained on them. Despite her self-proclaimed wariness, Long found herself pleasantly surprised by what she saw during that first season of Paris-less design. Fittingly, it was the ready-to-wear collections that she found most pleasing:

> Though disturbances are rocking the civilized world, the Average Woman may rest assured that right at this moment, at the drop of a moderate sum, she can step into clothes which are smart, practical, and attractive, and be ready to face whatever comes.[52]

Long's words were a paean to what truly made American fashion unique: the general availability of good, affordable clothing. When she exhorted American designers to trust their instincts and lean into their strengths, to forget about French standards of chic and concentrate on developing their own ideas of elegance, it was this type of clothing that Long was referring to. She knew that those who could afford to have their wardrobes made to order would always have recourse to top-notch design, no matter where they lived. But it was the homegrown "genius for mass production" that kept most women clothed.

The qualities of New York ready-to-wear versus those of Paris haute couture was the topic of a long article Pope published on August 18, just a few weeks before the debut of the fall 1940 collections. She characterized New York as democratic and Paris as aristocratic; in the former, "thought is devoted to dressing the multitude"; in the latter, "the consideration was for the individual." Although working without the guidance of Paris was a new challenge for New York designers, they were ready for it: "For a quarter of a century [New York] has been training for such an opportunity." And in the years when Paris was supreme, she said, the French learned just as much from their American visitors as the visitors learned from their hosts.[53]

This was essentially a summary of Pope's views on fashion, restating and condensing the ideas she had been exploring since she became the *Times* fashion editor seven years earlier. In fashion designing for America, she told Vassar students in 1937, "Paris is like the brain while New York represents the hand. Without the hand the brain would be unable to work."[54] This was a version of the line that every fashion authority used to describe the relationship that existed between the two cities, but Pope's interpretation, that it was the hand that facilitated the brain, was definitely not the orthodox view.

A diminutive woman with a ramrod posture and an extensive hat collection, Virginia Pope was born in Chicago in 1885. When she was five, her father died, and she and her mother and siblings left the United States to live in Europe, like a family in a Henry James novel. They remained for the next fifteen years, during which young Virginia became fluent in French, German, and Italian. Back in the US, she tried several careers before she settled on journalism, including a brief stint as a dancer on Broadway. But it was the language skills she acquired during her peripatetic childhood that got her in the door at the *Times*: Her first articles, which appeared in 1923, were an interview with German Passion play performers and a report on Christmas in Little Italy. She joined the paper's Sunday staff two years later.[55]

Although Pope didn't wield the semantic flourishes or engage in the wordplay that make reading Long a delight, she was a sure and knowledgeable writer who treated fashion as a topic as worthy of serious attention as architecture or economics. Her tone was smart and practical, and she related fashion to wider artistic and cultural ideas. She might compare a gown to a Sargent portrait or trace a trend for Indian-style draperies to the appearance of an Indian princess in a sari at the Paris opera or link the popularity of Tyrolean-style hats to the newly fashionable sport of skiing.[56] The *Times*'s fashion pages included illustrations and later photographs, so Pope had visual aids in depicting the fashion she covered. But like Long, she also had a major restriction to contend with: the *Times*'s draconian fashion-credit policy.

Its origins extended back many years, to when a department store had inadvertently been left out of a story on Fifth Avenue fashion merchants and had pulled thousands of dollars' worth of advertising in retaliation. Smarting from the loss of revenue, the *Times* management vowed to never again expose the paper to such a financial hit. The solution was a blanket ban on all fashion credits except for French ones.[57] When Pope became the *Times* fashion editor in 1933, she could credit French designers, but not the American retailers who sold them. Nor could she credit American couturiers, ready-to-wear firms, or the made-to-order departments of department stores. What she could do was drop clues about designers' identities. On November 5, 1935, for example, Pope referred to a designer "with an especially fine sense of materials" who "is able to merge the picturesque and the sophisticated." The visitor to her salon would find "no model parade . . . instead she presents a series of sketches, made by herself, which portray her silhouettes and fabric treatments."[58] The exceptionally well-informed reader might have discerned that Pope was referring to Muriel King, an illustrator turned designer who was a favorite of fashion insiders and known for her detailed sketches and elegant referencing of period details (Long was a fan as well as a customer—she called King "a top flight designer").[59] But the average reader of the *Times* would likely come away from passages like this, which seemed as though they were redacted by a censor, utterly mystified.

Pope was eventually able to convince her employers to add a query box to the fashion pages, which directed readers who wished to obtain more information about the clothing depicted to write or call the fashion desk. But it wasn't until September 1940 that the *Times*, bowing to pressure to support American design, gave in and updated its editorial policy: All designers and retailers could now be credited. Pope clearly savored the moment. She published sixteen stories that month about the New York collections—among her favorites were the ten ready-to-wear designers Lord & Taylor was promoting that season, whom she thought "demonstrated effectively what the American designer can do when he has a chance"—and each one had full credits.[60]

Almost as soon as the new policy went into effect, the *Times* began getting letters from retailers and manufacturers insisting that it must be Pope, not one of her staff, who covered their shows.[61] It was a demand that reflected Pope's stature, as well as her sympathy for American design, which had been evident from the beginning of her tenure as the *Times* fashion editor. In her articles, Pope would acknowledge the influence of Paris, but with the caveat that American designers did things their way.[62] She described their clothes and quoted them—albeit anonymously—in ways that made their authority clear. "One or two of the manufacturers saw what

I was trying to do," Pope later said. "I was trying to promote the American designer." [63]

Although Pope spoke of it as promotion, what she really did was report. This was in keeping with the way the *Times* viewed fashion. In a memo to *Times* publisher Arthur Hays Sulzberger, Lester Markel, the Sunday editor, explained: "We publish fashions because they are news, and not because they are 'publicity' . . . We feel that, as a newspaper, we must print the news, and that, without question, fashion is part of the news—and an important part." [64] Because of the *Times*'s status as a paper of record, its decision to treat fashion as weighty and topical impacted newsrooms around the country. Tobé Coller Davis, who published a widely read weekly trend-forecasting newsletter for retailers called the *Tobe Report* (it still exists today, albeit in digital form), summed up the effect of the *Times*'s authority in October 1940: "All the other papers no doubt said, well, if the *Times* puts the O.K. on fashion, and since there's lots of controversy about it this year, let's shoot the works." The result, the *Report* continued, was that newspapers began to print "reams and reams of fashion news." [65]

Once paper was rationed for the war effort, however, newspapers were obliged to trim the number of pages they printed. In an effort to rein in the size of the paper, the *Times* abridged articles and turned away advertising. [66] But it didn't drop its fashion coverage. Instead, the regular Sunday fashion page was eliminated in September 1942, and replaced with Fashion Forecasts, a seasonal feature that mixed fashion shoots with reportage. It was, in essence, the *Times* version of a fashion magazine, edited by Pope and folded into *The New York Times Magazine*. The first issue, published on September 13, 1942, took up thirty-five of the magazine's sixty-four pages. [67] It featured interviews with ten designers, who were asked to predict how American fashion would develop, and articles on timely topics like fashion in Britain ("Fashion Survives the Blitz") and the rationing of materials such as metal, leather, and rubber ("Shall we have to go without girdles? Certainly not."). Fashion Forecasts was a hit with readers and advertisers alike, but Pope had even bigger plans.

Two days after Fashion Forecasts first appeared, the *Times* announced that it would host four public fashion shows to benefit the Army Emergency Relief fund at New York Times Hall on West 44th Street. *Fashions of the Times*, as the four-show package was christened, was Pope's brainchild. She decided on the theme—fashion in wartime—chose the fashions, wrote the script, directed the entire production, and personally delivered an invitation to Mayor Fiorello La Guardia in his office at city hall (La Guardia's response was an enthusiastic yes—he was, he said, in favor of anything that strengthened New York's fashion industry).[68] She also edited the Fashions of the Times section of the Sunday magazine, which appeared the week after the shows (this was expanded into a stand-alone supplement in 1946, and remained the name of the *Times* fashion supplement until the launch of its replacement, *T: The New York Times Style Magazine*, in 2004).[69]

The first iteration of *Fashions of the Times*, on October 6 and 7, 1942, with matinee and evening performances on each day—all of which sold out—was relatively modest. Models appeared in a series of vignettes that represented scenes from the lives of American women, from "the business girl at home and saving fuel oil," who was bundled up in wool jersey slacks and a hand-loomed fringed shawl, to a bride gowned for an informal wartime wedding in a white wool flannel knee-length dress with eyelet embroidery. And the "Fashions of the Future" segment featured fabrics that were not yet available to the public, like the red nylon fleece—nylon had tantalizingly debuted in the form of stockings in 1940, only to be yanked off the market two years later, when it was requisitioned for military use—that Claire McCardell used for a sporty coverall.[70]

But *Fashions of the Times* did more than raise money for a good cause; it also provided romance, a quality that was sorely lacking in New York's factory-dominated, business-oriented rag trade. Pope divined that New York required a bit of fantasy to engage the imaginations of tastemakers who were accustomed to the practiced delights of Paris. But rather than trying to compete directly, with hauteur and refinement, she used the very American idiom of the Broadway show to achieve her aim. And she opened it to the public, selling tickets to anyone who wanted them.

The industry responded eagerly to Pope's *Ziegfeld Follies*–meets–fashion shoot extravaganzas. Subsequent productions raised the glamour quotient and the production values—perhaps Pope drew on her brief stint as a Broadway hoofer for inspiration—with twelve to fourteen different tableaux on a three-tiered stage, a musical score, and professionally designed sets, lighting, and choreography.[71] By 1946, one model, playing "the American girl" in a scene entitled "Breakfast at Dawn," arrived at a penthouse-apartment set via helicopter.[72] But despite the abundance of vivacity and glamour, the fashion remained grounded in reality, chosen to suit a variety of lifestyles and incomes, a formula that led to rave reviews.[73]

Bill Cunningham, who would go on to fame as the *Times*'s street-style photographer, was then a young milliner. He remembered the thrill that swept through the audience when the curtain went up on *Fashions of the Times*, and the dazzling array of clothes that were shown, from bathing suits to ball gowns. In the nine years it lasted, the stage version of *Fashions of the Times* gave the verve of an opening night to American fashion (Hollywood designers, too, would eventually participate). For the final show, in

1951, the price of a ticket was $1.65. Unofficially, people paid $25 for what had become one of the most in-demand seats in town.[74] By then, the money raised was going to the Fashion Institute of Technology, which had been founded in 1944 and would become the linchpin of fashion education in the United States.[75]

On June 6, 1944, D-Day, 160,000 Allied troops crossed the English Channel and landed on the beaches of Normandy in northwestern France. The first French town to be liberated was Bayeux, followed by Cherbourg, Saint-Lô, and Caen. The battle for Paris began on August 19 and went on for six tense days. Finally, on August 24, just before midnight, the French 2nd Armored Division under General Jacques-Philippe Leclerc arrived at the Hôtel de Ville. The next day, German general Dietrich von Choltitz surrendered to the French. Unwilling or unable to be remembered as the man who had leveled the city at the heart of Western culture, he had disobeyed Hitler's order to destroy Paris's landmarks, blow up its bridges, and burn what remained to the ground.

Along with the front-page story of the French capital's liberation, the *Times* published a piece on the reaction of New York's fashion industry to the news, headlined "Clothing Designers Overjoyed at Liberation of Paris, Doubt City Will Dominate Fashion."[76] Among the designers quoted was Hattie Carnegie, who said, "I'll always go back—but I'll always work on my own."[77] Five days later, on August 29, the first report on Paris fashion, by Lee Carson of the International News Service, one of World War II's few women war correspondents, appeared. The women of Paris, Carson wrote, were wearing bright prints and platform shoes, and styled their hair in enormous pompadours. Despite all they had suffered, she judged them as chic as ever.[78] Although they were elated at the news that Paris was once again free, New York's fashion designers were wary of returning to the prewar status quo. Many had expressed a desire to retain their independence in a series of profiles of American designers the *Times* had run earlier that year. "We can never go back," Jo Copeland had said. "We have learned what it means to do our own initial research; we won't be satisfied with second-hand inspirations again."[79]

It was a legitimate concern. Long's first postliberation column, published in September 1944, was characteristically wry about the eagerness with which the country's fashion professionals were rushing to reembrace Paris. Long had heard rumors that copying would soon be back, "and I might as well say that I would hate that." American designers, she continued, "shouldn't be allowed to relax; that might encourage the Paris designers to be complacent and take things easy themselves."[80]

The following month, the *Times* published a story about the haute couture titled "French Ready to Export Gowns As Soon as They Get Transport."[81] Pope, meanwhile, redoubled her efforts to promote American designers, a tactic that prompted Eleanor Darnton, the women's editor of the *Times*, to complain of her colleague:

> She is so almost hysterically opposed to Paris at the moment that she can't see any story out there, whereas I think some of them have news, as well as fashion value. To counteract the Paris coverage, she tends to puff up local stories . . . today I have from her a Bergdorf Goodman piece that runs to 1300 words.[82]

Long, although she was of the opinion that Paris was too important for New York to call itself the center of the fashion world, was also irked by the presumption that the French would simply reclaim their best-in-class status as though they could step back in time four years.[83] She had mellowed during the war. Her preference

for trimness and sleek lines meant that the fashion produced under
the L-85 order, which trimmed excess yardage and unnecessary
flourishes from women's clothing, satisfied her.

But the following September, with the war over and Paris
firmly back in the game, Long's temper flared. The first target of
her ire was Lucien Lelong, the president of the Chambre Syndicale
de la Couture Parisienne, who had "generously" told the press that
there was "a place" for Americans in fashion. Lelong's lukewarm
words, she argued, were haughty and insulting, "Because the boys
and girls in this country did just swell. People who had never liked
being just copyists or adapters were at last allowed to think up designs on their own." These were the sorts of easygoing styles that
best suited the national temperament, she continued. So why, then,
were designers looking to the fashion that had been produced under the Nazi occupation for inspiration, turning out "clothes so utterly gauche and clumsy that you wonder if all hands have decided
to toss the whole business of designing back to Paris as a gift."[84]
The slow burn of her column ended with a warning: "We are being told to throw away that celebrated 'American look,' which is
streamlined and sleek and effortless, and become dumpy and fussy
in a hurry. Will anybody join me at the barricades?"[85]

Long was invoking the language of revolution, which, in a sense,
is what had just occurred. In four years, New York had mounted
the first ever credible rival to the haute couture and, in doing so, had
challenged a fashion system that had existed for decades. But with
the French—the erstwhile ruling class—now back in the game, the
upstarts from New York would have to work even harder to retain
the ground they had won.

Luckily, they had developed more than their design skills in
the years since the fall of Paris. Like the French of the sixteenth

century, they had finally come to understand the power of marketing. Leading the charge was Eleanor Lambert, the woman who invented the profession of fashion publicist. By the time Paris was back in play, Lambert had taught New York designers how to beat the French at their own game.

7

The Godmother of American Fashion

Eleanor Lambert

You must always be alert and see the things right in front of you that have not been done and should be done.

—ELEANOR LAMBERT[1]

In mid-December 1940, two and a half months after her headline-generating lecture at Lord & Taylor, in which she'd told the overflow crowd that New York could never rival Paris for fashion dominance, Elsa Schiaparelli was back in Manhattan. It was the last stop on what had been a rapid-fire, forty-city lecture tour, after which she would journey back to Paris. Since leaving New York in September, Schiaparelli had crisscrossed the continent by air and rail, venturing as far north as Montreal and as far south as Dallas. By the time she reached San Francisco, the seventeenth city on her itinerary, in late October, she was exhausted. She wearily told a journalist from the *San Francisco Examiner* that she didn't want to talk about American fashion; moreover, she had yet to receive any inspiration from her time in the United States. The only thing that perked Schiaparelli up, the reporter noted, were the letters she had received from Paris telling her that the couturiers had reopened their houses.[2]

Schiaparelli's final lecture, delivered on December 10 at Town Hall on West 43rd Street, unfolded along the same lines as her first New York appearance. American sportswear was fine, she told the crowd, but it wasn't going to supplant Paris couture. And American women, she insinuated, were unsuited to be fashion leaders because they didn't sufficiently appreciate quality.[3] For Julius Hochman, the vice president of the 240,000-member-strong International Ladies Garment Workers Union (ILGWU), described by one journalist as "one of the smartest and best-run unions in the country," this was the final straw.[4] The couturier's most recent disparagements, he told *WWD*, "insulted both our industry and the American woman." The need to respond to Schiaparelli forcefully, he continued, was one reason that he was advocating for the New York fashion industry to unite in a common promotional campaign.[5]

The couturier's dismissal of New York was a timely emotional hook, and Hochman was irritated by Schiaparelli's cavalier attitude. But what really concerned him was the growing strength of regional garment-production centers like Los Angeles and St. Louis, which posed a direct challenge to New York's long-established superiority. In Dallas, one department store had even had the temerity to bill itself as "America's Dress Center," a title everyone on Seventh Avenue considered rightly belonged to them. One observer said it was as though the city's fashion industry was slipping down around its own ankles like a stocking unmoored from a garter belt. Even Mayor Fiorello La Guardia expressed concern.[6]

This apprehension led Hochman to push for an unprecedented alliance between labor, management, La Guardia, and Governor

Herbert Lehman that culminated in the March 1941 announcement of the hastily founded New York Dress Institute (NYDI).[7] Funded by dues from the manufacturers, who pledged one-half of 1 percent of their profits, an amount they promised would amount to between $3 and $4 million over the next three years, the NYDI vowed to launch an ad campaign that would secure New York's status as the country's fashion capital by emphasizing the talent and creativity of its designers.[8] Every garment made by a participating firm, a number that amounted to 90 percent of the dresses made in the United States, would be finished with a label that read "New York Creation" and which certified that the garment was made by an ILGWU member.[9] The first of these labels were sewn in on Monday, July 7, 1941, under the supervision of the mayor. As First Lady Eleanor Roosevelt looked on, La Guardia shouted, "Ready . . . set . . . sew!" and twenty seamstresses wielding golden needles stitched them into dresses that were priced at just under $2 to almost $300, a range that reflected just how many women the city's garment industry catered to.[10]

To create the ad campaign for "That New York Look," the NYDI hired the J. Walter Thompson agency, the same firm that had capitalized on the previously obscure medical term "halitosis" to shame Americans into buying Listerine mouthwash. Its plan to promote the NYDI relied on similar tactics. The agency's maiden effort—print ads that debuted in several New York City newspapers in October 1941—were centered on a character called One-Dress Beulah, who always wore the same black dress. The first ad established the hectoring tone of the series, explaining that Beulah represented the 67 percent of women who thought one basic dress sufficed for every occasion, a selfish attitude that reduced profits for retailers all over America. The illustration depicted a crowd of

men and women—none of whom wore black—smirking and point-
ing at the hapless Beulah.[11]

If J. Walter Thompson's executives thought that scolding American women for liking black dresses and portraying them as shal-
low, competitive, and unpatriotic would earn it accolades, they
were wrong. Not only were black dresses the backbone of many
manufacturers and retailers' businesses, but the smug quality of the
ads was tone-deaf.[12] NYDI members protested, and a fresh series
of ads was commissioned from J. Walter Thompson. This second
campaign capitalized on the recent entry of the United States into
World War II. Its protagonist was a dressed-to-the-nines Martha
Washington, who inspired lovesick-looking soldiers of the Revolutionary War with her modishness ("At the very sight of her, fresh
and lovely in that desolate camp, new courage sprang up in the
hearts of George Washington and all around him").[13] These, too,
fell flat. NYDI members began to complain that they were paying
dues but not getting anything in return.[14]

Retailers like Dorothy Shaver had been watching J. Walter
Thompson's bright ideas with mounting horror. In early 1941, they
took action. Shaver—along with Henri Bendel, owner of the epon-
ymous department store; Andrew Goodman of Bergdorf Goodman; William M. Holmes of Bonwit Teller; and Adam Gimbel of
Saks Fifth Avenue—approached the NYDI leadership and told
them that the promotional campaign needed a complete overhaul.
There was only one woman for the job, and they demanded that the
NYDI hire her: Eleanor Lambert.[15]

It would be impossible to tell the story of American fashion
without Lambert. She's been described variously as its impresario,
its ringmaster, and its architect. But these analogies fail to fully
grasp the Herculean nature of the role she played in dragging it

onto the world stage. Lambert was not just the impresario, but also the director of the play, the stage manager, and the box office cashier. She was not just the architect, but also the construction worker, the real estate agent, and the decorator. Her efforts on the part of American fashion were, by any definition, indefatigable. Blond and slight in stature, Lambert exuded authority. She was, her son said, "determined to be the best at whatever she did, even if that meant she had to invent a new profession."[16] The profession she invented was that of fashion publicist.

Lambert was born in 1903 in Crawfordsville, Indiana, the youngest of her parents' five children by twelve years. Her father, a former journalist, had abandoned his family to become an advance man for Ringling Bros. long before Lambert was born; she was conceived on one of his rare visits home.[17] Although he was only a sporadic presence in her childhood, Lambert, always attuned to a good backstory, liked to say that she got her PR moxie from him. But while Clay Lambert had literally run away to join the circus, he had more traditional aspirations for his youngest child. When father and daughter were briefly reunited in New York City in the 1920s, he put her on a train back to Crawfordsville, which he considered a more suitable milieu for a well-brought-up young woman. Lambert nimbly exited the train on the other side and proceeded with her life.[18]

Her first ambition was to be a sculptor. To save money for art classes, she made packed lunches for students at a college in Crawfordsville. She left her hometown at eighteen for art school in Indianapolis, paying her way by writing a fashion column for two Indiana newspapers. She eventually enrolled at the Art Institute of Chicago, where she met her first husband, Willis Conner. The couple moved to New York in December 1925. By that point, Lambert had decided that she was a mediocre sculptor. New York, she felt, was the place to find something at which she could excel.

The couple rented an apartment in Queens, and Lambert found two part-time jobs, each of which paid her sixteen dollars a week. In the morning, she wrote for a fashion-trend report called *The Breath of the Avenue*. In the afternoon, she designed book jackets for a publicist named Franklin Spear.[19] Her life during this period spanned the thrifty to the fabulous. She ate at the Automat to save money, but spent her evenings at the Algonquin Hotel, then in its Round Table heyday, to see what the city's writers and artists were up to. That's where she met Dorothy Parker, who took her along on an expedition to a Bowery tattoo parlor one evening. Anxious to fit in, and not yet the assertive personality she would become, Lambert ended up with a small blue star inked on her right ankle— "the most discreet thing I could do in the most discreet place"—a permanent souvenir of a night out with one of the most celebrated wits of the twentieth century (Parker reportedly got an identical tattoo, albeit on the inside of her biceps).[20]

Lambert learned to write concise descriptions of clothes at *The Breath of the Avenue*, but it was her job with Spear that determined the course of her future. The office was small, with Spear and four employees all sitting in one room, so she couldn't help but over-hear his phone conversations. Many involved cajoling celebrities like Douglas Fairbanks and Mary Pickford, the reigning king and queen of Hollywood, into giving their thoughts on books, a public-ity strategy that now seems as quaint as the rotary telephone Spear used. Lambert, still a relatively new Midwestern transplant, was enchanted by this proximity to stardom.[21]

"I was such a celebrity hound that I would sit open mouthed," while Spear dialed and wheedled, she remembered. Finally, he looked across the room and suggested that Lambert try making the calls. She turned out to be a natural, as adept at schmoozing celebrities as Clara Bow was at oozing joie de vivre. Impressed by her zeal, Spear encouraged his protégée to start her own business. He offered her the use of a desk in his office if she paid for her own phone line and threw in a bonus piece of advice: Peddle what you know. What she knew, Lambert realized, was art. And so began her career as an art publicist.[22]

Her method for signing clients was simple: She went to 57th Street, then the main gallery district in New York, and pitched her services. "The first day I went up there, I got ten galleries in a row, from Park Avenue to Madison. That was at ten dollars a week," she later told an interviewer.[23] Although she didn't detail her technique, those who worked with, and especially for, Lambert remembered her as exacting, tough, incredibly persuasive, and sometimes downright scary. "Her clients were terrified of her," one colleague recalled.[24]

Within a few years, Lambert was representing some of the biggest names in American art, including Alexander Calder, Jackson Pollock, Walt Kuhn, George Bellows, Jacob Epstein, John Curry, and Isamu Noguchi, who gifted her a portrait bust when he couldn't afford to pay her.[25] She became an integral part of the nascent New York art scene, involved in the creation of the Art Dealers Association of America, the Parke-Bernet auction galleries (acquired by Sotheby's in 1964), the Museum of Modern Art, and the Whitney Museum of American Art, for which she served as press director.[26] In 1937, she helped Irene Lewinsohn, a wealthy heiress with a large collection of antique clothing and folk costumes, and Aline Bernstein, a costume designer, found the Museum of Costume Art.[27] One of its prize possessions, the Mainbocher wedding dress of the Duchess of Windsor, formerly Bessie Wallis Warfield of Baltimore, was acquired by Lambert personally, who dryly noted, "She realized it wasn't going to be in a British museum."[28] When the Museum of Costume Art moved to the Metropolitan Museum in 1946 and became the Costume Institute, it was Lambert who came up with the idea for funding it via what she called "the Party of the Year." This was the genesis of today's Met Gala, whose red carpet is fashion's equivalent of the Olympics crossed with the Academy Awards. Had her career gone no further, these alone would have been impressive credentials.

Lambert was working for the Whitney in 1934 when she was sent to the Venice Biennale. Her mission was to have a portrait of the actress Marion Davies removed from the Whitney-sponsored American pavilion, on the grounds that its Polish creator wasn't entitled to exhibit there. Davies was the mistress of William Randolph Hearst, who was intent on keeping the portrait on display. Hearst's emissary was Seymour Berkson, the general manager of his International News Service. Lambert and Berkson met for dinner, each prepared to argue their case. Instead, they fell in love. "I looked across the table and knew we belonged together," Lambert said.[29] As relationship origin stories go, theirs was pure 1930s Hollywood.

There were significant complications, however. Both were married, and Berkson's wife, the journalist Jane Eads, was pregnant. Lambert was separated from Conner, but she still supported him, even paying for him to study art in Paris. Conner used his wife's money to bankroll his relationship with a woman he met there, but his attempt to buy a yacht with funds drawn on Lambert's account was the final straw. The check bounced, and Lambert divorced him.[30] Berkson divorced his wife, too, and two years after they met, the couple wed, the bride in a dress made by Elizabeth Hawes.[31]

Their marriage lasted twenty-four years, until Berkson died of a heart attack in 1959, when he was only fifty-two. Lambert was devastated. For twenty years after her husband's death, she wrote him love letters, something the couple's only child, Bill Berkson, discovered after Lambert herself died.[32] His parents' marriage looked perfect to outsiders, but it wasn't easy being their son. In his memoir, Bill Berkson recounted meeting an acquaintance of theirs as a young adult. "My god, you're alive!" she cried. "I never thought there was room for anyone else in that house, what with their being so involved with each other and their work."[33]

Lambert's commitment to her work was total. "She was a tough boss," Bill Berkson said. "She would chew people out. But apparently no one ever stomped out of there. Her line was always 'I work as hard as anybody, and I expect people to work as hard as me.'" Until she retired at ninety-nine, Lambert tirelessly pitched stories on behalf of her clients. By that point she had long since shifted her focus to fashion, which she had first dipped a toe into as a founding, if not especially involved, member of the Fashion Group (she objected to its women-only policy).[34]

Her real entrée into fashion began, Lambert said, "completely by accident," thanks to a phone call she received in the summer of 1932.[35] The voice on the other end of the line belonged to the fashion designer Annette Simpson, who was featured in Dorothy Shaver's "American Fashions for American Women" campaign. Simpson had read a newspaper interview that Lambert snagged for one of her artist clients and wanted to know if she could get her the same sort of press coverage. Her competitive nature piqued, Lambert said yes and agreed to take Simpson on as a client. The relationship was short-lived and rocky: By December of that year, the two women had parted ways and Lambert had decided that her erstwhile client was "crazy."[36] Five years later, still owed more than $2,000, a considerable sum during the Depression, Lambert took Simpson to court for breach of contract.[37]

Lambert never got her money, but the experience proved invaluable. When she began working as an art publicist in the mid-1920s, it was the galleries that got attention, not artists. Lambert changed that. In the 1930s, the names of manufacturers and retailers were known, but the designers who created the clothes that made their businesses successful were anonymous. Having had a peek into the workings of the fashion industry, Lambert saw intriguing parallels. Why, she asked herself, couldn't she do the same thing for American designers that she had done for American artists? And why shouldn't American fashion enjoy the same recognition that American art did? Years earlier, a fortune teller in Chicago had told Lambert that she would never be an artist herself but would always work with them.[38] In her view, fashion designers were as much artists as the painters and sculptors she currently represented. This, she decided, was the path she was meant to take.

When she divulged her idea to her friend Diana Vreeland over lunch, she received a dubious stare in return. "Eleanor," Vreeland exclaimed, "you are such an amateur!"[39] To an insider, the idea that American fashion designers could stand shoulder to shoulder with the couturiers of Paris was plainly ridiculous. But Lambert was undeterred. Like Louis XIV three centuries earlier, she considered her country's fashion potential limitless. This wasn't the only quality Lambert shared with the Sun King: She had a penchant for red heels, which she had custom-made for the Hélène Arpels pumps she habitually wore (the same shade of leather was used to line the interior of the succession of black Buick convertibles she drove), and she could be peremptory with just about everyone.[40] Her assistant John Tiffany recalled that on his first day in Lambert's employ, the Queen Mother called the office. "Ms. Lambert was yelling at her, 'Why are you calling me during the day? Don't you have something to do? Now, what is it you want?' That's how she started her conversations with people." [41]

Lambert rejected the French model of promotion, in which couturiers were positioned as lofty beings who dictated from above, as antithetical to American sensibilities. Instead, drawing on her experience of packaging artists into what she called "personalities with well-rounded appearances," she portrayed fashion designers as creative individuals, with jobs, families, and hobbies—people not unlike the women who bought their clothes. [42]

The designer she had the most success with was Claire McCardell. True, McCardell was a paragon of a client. With her rangy good looks and warm smile, she was her own best model, while her friendly, down-to-earth manner made her someone a customer could imagine as a friend. But she was also a mid-market designer working on Seventh Avenue, which meant overcoming the prejudice of the made-to-order-fixated press. Undeterred, Lambert shrewdly positioned McCardell to maximize her appeal. In a 1941 press release, she described how McCardell knew from personal experience that "girls who are struggling for their place in the sun have good tastes to support with their two-figure bank balances," a phrase that summed up her appeal to the young. Lambert then pivoted, describing McCardell as a bold innovator who had created exercise clothes for the celebrated ballerina Vera Zorina, co-opted men's shirting for women's clothes, and set the fashion for tweed evening coats and wool jersey dinner suits, all points that argued the designer's case to a more sophisticated, moneyed customer. The press release concluded, "In fact, Claire McCardell, The Typical American Girl, has a taste and a designing talent so unusual, that it makes the word Typical turn to irony in the mouth." [43] Zing!

For McCardell, as she did for all her clients, Lambert spun a compelling narrative that invited journalists to pick up its threads and easily weave them into stories of their own. With Lambert guiding her public image, McCardell became a star. Her name was so widely recognized that she received lucrative endorsements from Chrysler and Chevrolet, as well as the country's best-selling hair dye, Miss Clairol (the ads McCardell appeared in trumpeted "made-to-order" hair color, an ironic association for a designer who'd made her name in ready-to-wear).[44]

Another early Lambert client was Valentina, who was *not* one for whom the relatable angle worked. Lambert's attempts to get biographical details from the mercurial designer were futile— Valentina spun one lie after another. Why write about Valentina? she asked Lambert. Let the public dream about her instead. Eventually, Lambert went on to represent every American designer of importance, including Hattie Carnegie, Lilly Daché, Norman Norell, Bonnie Cashin, Vera Maxwell, Pauline Trigère, Ralph Lauren, Oscar de la Renta, Halston, and more. Joe Eula, an illustrator who worked with Lambert in the late 1940s and '50s, said of her, "There wasn't a soul on Seventh Avenue who didn't have Eleanor behind her. If you couldn't afford her and you wanted her, she'd work for free."[45] She could presumably afford to: By the late 1940s, one journalist speculated that Lambert's yearly income was in the neighborhood of $50,000 a year.[46]

In 1940, however, all of this had yet to transpire. Although Lambert had accrued notable clients, including several major specialty department stores (hence the relationship with Shaver and other retailers), she was not yet the imposing figure she would become. She did, however, have one invaluable asset: a robust social network. Lambert and Berkson loved to entertain, first in their apartment on West 72nd Street, and then in the thirteen-room apartment on Fifth Avenue with two fireplaces, a suite of maids' rooms, and a view of the Central Park Reservoir that they moved into in 1942. Their guests were part of a high-powered crowd that drew on their intersecting professional worlds—fashion people, politicians, journalists, stars of the stage and screen, and what was then called café society, an assortment that made Lambert one of the best-connected people in New York City, with friends and clients who represented a Venn diagram of mid-twentieth-century celebrity. The Duke and Duchess of Windsor were frequent guests, as were Clare Boothe Luce, Judy Garland, and Cecil Beaton.

One client was Gayelord Hauser, an early celebrity health faddist—think a male, Germanic Gwyneth Paltrow—who rose to fame promoting the merits of his five "superfoods": blackstrap molasses, brewer's yeast, skimmed milk, wheat germ, and yogurt, any one of which qualified as exotic in the America of the day. Hauser's disciples included Greta Garbo, whom he introduced to Lambert at a dinner party she hosted just before the war. Another guest, who had very recently arrived from Berlin, enthused to Garbo that Hitler had been so impressed by her new film, *Ninotchka*, that he had watched it three times over the course of the previous weekend. To the astonishment of everyone present, Garbo replied, "I know. I could go to Germany. And I could see Hitler. And I could kill him." [47]

Lambert, who subsequently became quite close to Garbo, brought her to Valentina to upgrade her wardrobe (only on-screen was the reclusive star a fashion plate). She thus unwittingly set in motion a decades-long affair between Garbo and George Schlee, the designer's husband. With remarkable chutzpah, Schlee persuaded Garbo to move into the same apartment building he and Valentina lived in, at 450 East 52nd Street. [48] The two women, who physically closely resembled each other, were such bitter frenemies that the elevator operators knew not to stop at one's floor if the other was already aboard.

Another figure in the Lambert orbit was Louella Parsons, the all-seeing, vindictive Hollywood gossip columnist who had a lifetime contract with the Hearst Corporation, an arrangement that was rumored to result from some damaging information she had on the boss. As a child, Bill Berkson would answer the phone and hear what he described as Parsons's "alarming nasal," calling to give his father her latest scoop.[49] Parsons once reversed the flow of information by leaking a Lambert press release, a major faux pas she had to rectify with a groveling letter of apology.[50]

To socially prominent business leaders like Shaver, Lambert was not just a colleague but a friend, someone who moved in the same circles they did and understood their views. When they prevailed on the NYDI to hire her, it was with the certainty that she could deliver exactly what they wanted. As one NYDI employee said, "She had made all the right social connections—we wanted the society ladies to wear our clothes—and she was a snob: Her nose was way up in the air. But she was also very focused, extremely businesslike, completely dedicated. Our mission was to change the image of American fashion and we were very successful."[51]

Initially, Lambert wanted to replace Beulah and Martha Washington with ads that trumpeted individual designers by name. But the largest contributors to the NYDI fund were big firms like Julius "Jack" Davis's Jay Day Dress Co., which at its high point shipped two hundred thousand dresses a month to retailers around the country.[52] Davis and his colleagues didn't put labels in their garments because retailers insisted on sewing in their own, so they had nothing to gain from Lambert's proposal. Finally, she took a different tack. Let's promote a few of the most creative designers by name, to be chosen by you, she told the NYDI. This faction, which included Claire McCardell, Jo Copeland, Nettie Rosenstein, and Adele Simpson, would be known (loftily, if erroneously) as

the Couture Group. A second, more general campaign, emphasizing the greatness of all New York designers, would cover everyone
else.[53]

Although the ads in this second group mentioned no names,
they did convey that New York was as essential to fashion as flour
is to bread. One linked the city's arts scene to the creativity of its
designers: "The overtones of Manhattan's music, like a thousand
other of its fabulous sights and sounds, contribute to the incom-
parable fashions for which New York is famous."[54] Another, under the headline "Pattern for Leadership," referenced the "sensitive
touch" of New York's designers, which made it possible for them
to "divine the future, and confidently point the way to the fashions that have always made you the best dressed woman in the
world." The visuals combined dress pattern pieces with an image
of the city's skyline, suggesting that fashion was entwined with the
very structure of the city.[55]

Elevating the tone of the NYDI's advertising was the remit that
Lambert was tasked with. But what turned out to be of far greater
importance in raising the prestige of American designers was a trio
of innovations that she conceived of and implemented: the International Best-Dressed List, the Coty Awards, and National Press
Week. Beginning in 1924, the wire services had carried year-end
stories about the women who had been named to the "Paris Dressmakers' Best-Dressed Women Poll." Various couturiers weighed
in on the winners, although rumor had it that Chicago-born
Mainbocher was its mastermind. The final couturier-orchestrated
poll was released in early 1940, just a few months before Paris fell
to the Nazis. It was, as usual, heavy on titled names—*The New
York Times* covered it under the headline "British Duchesses Are
Best Dressed."[56] Lambert, who had been following the list on the
grounds that it was a historical artifact, guessed that the war would

put an end to it and, with tactical foresight, acquired it for the NYDI. She couched this maneuver as a form of aid for Paris, saying she would carry the torch until the city could pick it up again.[57] This, clearly, was nonsense. Once the keeping of the list, and the authority that conferred, moved to New York, there was no way Lambert would have relinquished control.

In the fall of 1940, she posted fifty mimeographed ballots to her chosen judges, mainly clients and others in the New York fashion world she thought had good taste, including the design staff at Bergdorf Goodman and the fashion editors of *Harper's Bazaar* and *Vogue*. Never a voter herself, she tabulated the results, fashioned them into a press release, and sent it out as a missive from the NYDI. The release included the unmistakable suggestion that New York, with its immense ready-to-wear capabilities, was the new fashion power: "America is a huge country full of well-dressed women," Lambert wrote. "The Paris designers spoke for Paris alone, while we must speak for the world."[58]

The New York Times published the all-American list on December 27, noting that it had been "taken over this Winter for the first time by the key designers, fashion authorities and members of the fashion press, as the world's new style center," a phrase that was lifted verbatim from Lambert's release.[59] Topping the list was one of its habitual denizens, Mrs. Harrison Williams, who started life as Mona Strader, the daughter of a Kentucky horse breeder, and ended it, via her penultimate marriage, as Countess von Bismarck. In a forty-year stretch from the 1920s through the 1960s, her name, whatever it was at the time, was a byword for refinement. Fashion editors gushed over everything from her lawn, "probably the greatest in Palm Beach,"[60] to her discernment in the clothes she chose: "She never orders the 'successes' in a collection, but instead, the costume which is noticeable only on a second glance."[61] When

Williams's preferred couturier, Balenciaga, from whom she ordered everything down to her gardening shorts, shuttered his couture house in 1968, Diana Vreeland, who was staying with her, reported that Williams retreated to the bedroom of her villa on Capri for three days to mourn.

Williams was hardly the only wealthy woman on the 1940 Best-Dressed List, but perhaps because it was released just weeks after the attack on Pearl Harbor and the United States' subsequent entry into the war, the net worth of its inductees was downplayed. Gone were the quotes about spending tens of thousands of dollars on clothes that had accompanied past iterations. Instead, the 1940 list tilted more humblebrag, with one nominee insisting she had bought only a couple of dresses in the past year.[62] The egalitarian note, genuine or not, indicated a shift in attitude. Throughout the war years, when American women could buy only domestically designed and made clothes, plus a few British exports, Lambert skillfully positioned the Best-Dressed List as a celebration of both American designers and the unfussy style of American women. She was so successful that even Eleanor Roosevelt, whose most ardent admirer would have to admit was no clotheshorse, clamored to be on the Best-Dressed List.[63]

When a newspaper editorial accused Lambert of elitism, challenging her to "name ten women who dress best on three or four $30 dresses," she noted privately that being named to the list was "as descriptive and worthy as the honor awarded annually to writers by the Pulitzer Prize committee, the Hollywood Academy, or any other body which tries to set recognizable standards and milestones of progress for an art or industry."[64] Fashion, Lambert believed, was art, and American fashion was in no way inferior to that of the French. "America has its fine painters, such as Benton, and France has Picasso," she told a journalist. "There is no reason why a Benton and a Picasso cannot hang in the same room. And certainly there is no reason why a gown by a French dressmaker and one by an American cannot hang in the same clothes closet!"[65]

Although some nominees affected indifference, being named to its rolls was a major coup, and resulted in a flurry of favorable press mentions. Designers, Lambert decided, needed the same validation—and attention. She approached Grover Whalen, the chairman of the board of Coty Inc., the cosmetics manufacturer, and pitched him the idea of sponsoring what she christened the American Fashion Critics' Award, to be given annually to an American designer for excellence. Whalen, a politician turned official greeter for New York City—he invented that NYC institution of the ticker-tape parade—readily agreed. In January 1942, the creation of what were soon being referred to as the Coty Awards was announced via an ad Lambert wrote for *WWD*. Coty, Lambert's copy stated, was "keenly aware of America's dominance as a world fashion center, and of the necessity of stimulating our great fashion industry during the war effort and afterwards." It went on to spell out how the new awards would work: Secret ballots would be sent to "the fashion editors of national magazines, newspaper syndicates and metropolitan newspapers" in December of that year. In January 1943, "and in each January thereafter," the awards would be announced and presented.[66]

On January 22, 1943, in a ceremony at the Metropolitan Museum of Art that was attended by Mayor Fiorello La Guardia, the inaugural Coty Awards were presented. Not even the war, La Guardia said in his remarks, would interrupt "creative art, whether it be a monument, a painting, or a beautiful dress."[67] First prize, for outstanding fashion design in 1942, went to Norman Norell, who worked for a high-end Seventh Avenue firm called Traina-Norell. Like McCardell, he was the rare designer with his name on the label; unlike McCardell, he had been obliged to accept a lower salary for the honor.[68] Norell was presented with $1,000 in war bonds and a gilt bronze trophy in the shape of a female nude lightly draped with fabric and nicknamed "Winnie." Second prize went to the milliner Lilly Daché, who received the trophy and $500 in war bonds. Among the honorable mentions was McCardell, who was singled out for her hugely successful Pop-over dress. In bestowing the award on Norell, a Hattie Carnegie–trained creator of elegant suits and glamorous evening gowns, the selection committee wanted to demonstrate that an American designer was capable of Paris-style work. But Norell later admitted that it was McCardell who should have been the first American designer to be given the top honor. "I worked in the couture tradition—expensive fabrics, hand stitching, exclusivity, all that," he said, "but Claire could take five dollars' worth of common cotton calico and turn out a dress a smart woman would wear anywhere."[69]

The following year, McCardell got her Coty Award. The chairman of the selection committee, Gertrude Bailey, the fashion editor of the *New York World-Telegram*, specified that it wanted to honor the designers who had shown the greatest ingenuity in the face of wartime difficulties.[70] McCardell, who embraced the challenge of the fabric restrictions posed by L-85, was the obvious choice.

For the next four decades, the Coty Awards celebrated the greatest names in American design, from Hattie Carnegie, Clare Potter, Pauline Trigère, Bonnie Cashin, and Charles James to Oscar de la Renta, Anne Klein, Stephen Burrows, Calvin Klein, Ralph Lauren, Donna Karan, and Willi Smith. Before the Coty Awards, said Trigère, who won her Winnie in 1949, "People were making clothes, but nobody was paying attention."[71] The awards ceremonies were glamorous black-tie affairs, part of Lambert's gambit to shift the perception of the industry from its rag-trade roots to one of cultural and creative significance. The next morning, Lambert would blanket the country's fashion editors and women's page writers with press releases, ensuring that the names of the winning designers were printed in newspapers from coast to coast.

Despite this outpouring of press attention, Seventh Avenue retained its old suspicion of journalists. The attitude of a manufacturer named Ben Reig was fairly typical. At a meeting of the Couture Group, Reig asked Lambert what to do about "those newspaper women from out-of-town horning in with the buyers" to view his designers' collections. Should he show them the door, he wondered, or let them in? Everyone in the room understood the subtext to Reig's question: Journalists were dangerous because they were possible design thieves. Lambert, however, didn't hesitate. "I think you should not only let them in but invite them!" she retorted.[72] From that exchange sprang Lambert's plan for National Press Week, which paid the expenses of journalists from around the United States to travel to New York to view the collections. Press Week evolved into New York Fashion Week, a biannual event that now adds close to $900 million to the city's coffers.[73] New York Fashion Week was so successful that Lambert was asked to recreate her formula for both Paris and Milan; today, this triumvirate makes up three-quarters of the Big Four fashion weeks.[74]

Prior to Lambert's organization of Press Week, New York's garment manufacturers couldn't even agree on a show schedule. "Eleanor Lambert was the first one—the only one—to organize Seventh Avenue. No one had ever done it before. No one had even *thought* of doing it," said one editor.[75] Working with NYDI director Adelia Bird Ellis, Lambert's office drew up a show schedule, contacted journalists (all, in this gender-siloed era, women), organized train tickets, booked hotel rooms, and arranged for guides to show the out-of-towners around the city.[76]

New York's maiden Press Week, which occurred in July 1943, attracted about thirty journalists; the follow-up, in January 1944, was attended by twice that number. "First there were eight reporters at a show," Trigère remembered, "then twelve, then one hundred and twenty-five."[77] Soon New York–based journalists, not wanting to miss out, began attending, too. Lambert, meanwhile, was being described as "a young woman publicist from whose mind ideas emerge with the ease and speed of pop-ups popping from children's books."[78]

Press Week, said Polly Allen, then a junior fashion editor at *Harper's Bazaar*, energized the American industry. "It was so exciting, I ran to work every day," she remembered. "It was a whole different way of dressing. Less fancy. Less uptight. Much more interesting to a young person. I think it started Europe looking at us, the American market."[79]

There were, inevitably, wrinkles to be smoothed. The first go-around, hostesses called the hotel rooms of visiting reporters—known as delegates, as though they were attending a political convention instead of looking at clothes—at nine A.M. every morning, chirruping, "I just want to make sure you are happy, my dear!" Even more irritating from the point of view of the out-of-town journalists, the NYDI gave their hotel details to anyone who asked for them, so they were barraged with fifteen or twenty phone calls and telegrams a day, asking them to breakfast, lunch at the Stork Club, or out for drinks. "It may sound like fun," complained one writer, "but the moment you opened the door of your hotel room, the phone began to jangle, and it kept up until you were nearly crazy." Meanwhile, the official daily program included several fashion shows, two or three cocktail parties, and excursions to restaurants and the theater in the evenings. Out of a sense of self-preservation, most of the invitees discarded the name badges they were given rather than leave themselves open to more invitations.[80]

The NYDI had neglected to set up a press room, a necessity for any journalist who had to file copy with an expectant editor back home and didn't own a portable typewriter. One cub reporter stayed up all night writing her story by hand. She printed, she explained to colleagues who inquired about her bandaged wrist the next morning, because she didn't think Western Union would accept a message written in cursive.[81]

Being journalists, the delegates had no trouble expressing their dissatisfaction with aspects of their Press Week experience. One embittered reporter wanted to know why the event's organizers kept talking about Paris and how New York stacked up against it. "Maybe Paris was once the capital of all the arts, the inspiration for every Seventh Avenue manufacturer to copy, but in the language of the girl in the street: SO WHAT?" she demanded to know. "Let's keep Paris buried. Paris should never have dressed America anyway."[82]

By the time the second Press Week rolled around, the NYDI had rectified some of its early missteps. A press room was set up, complete with sixteen typewriters for those on deadline, and accommodation details were kept private. Moreover, the January 1944 Press Week generated its first nationwide trend: milliner Lilly Daché's brightly colored hairnets fashioned from thick cotton cord. The French-born Daché had immigrated to the United States in 1924, when she was about sixteen. In short order, she got a job at a hat shop, took over the hat shop, and established herself as one of the country's most expensive milliners. By transforming the hairnet, a drab accessory associated with waitresses and cafeteria workers, into a fashionable snood rendered in meant-to-be-seen colors like bright red, geranium pink, and brilliant green, she made it possible to turn around what we would now call a bad hair day. In a seeding gambit that has become routine, journalists who attended the Press Week launch were each given six complimentary Daché hairnets. They wore their new accessories back in their hometowns and in due course thousands sold, many to women whose newly busy schedules of war work and domestic responsibilities left little time for the salon.[83]

Getting a free accessory and stepping into the role of trendsetter was fun, but many of the journalists who attended the Lilly Daché press conference understood little of what was happening. Ideally, Lambert would have invited fashion journalists to cover Press Week. But in 1943, there simply weren't enough of them. Most worked in New York already and had no use for Lambert's offer to cover travel expenses. Many of the reporters who attended Press Week in the early years had little or no experience writing about fashion. Some wrote for their publication's "women's page," covering topics like cooking and childcare. Others were general interest reporters. Many didn't even recognize the organizer of the junket they were on. One afternoon Lambert found herself on an elevator with a couple of oblivious delegates and overheard one ask the other if she was planning on attending a particular designer's presentation. No, she replied, "his clothes don't fit me." Lambert had to stop herself from telling the woman that being a fashion journalist is not the same as shopping for one's personal wardrobe.[84]

The effusiveness with which the president of the company that manufactured the hairnets spoke of Daché, and that with which she spoke of him, a standard fashion practice, puzzled delegates, as did the continual references to the "launch" of the hairnets. Now that everything from face creams to sneakers are launched, we take this usage in stride. But eighty years ago, most people asked to use the verb "launch" in a sentence would have paired it with "ship." Hence the cracks that a few of the more irreverent attendees made about having a bottle of champagne broken across their backsides.[85]

Even more confusing was the collection Norman Norell showed that season, which was inspired by his favorite fashion period, the 1920s. Today, it's commonly understood that fashion designers allude to past decades in their work. Norell was hardly the first to do so—designers in the 1930s, for example, were fixated on the 1890s. But most people in the 1940s would only have seen this sort of referencing after it had been interpreted by a fashion magazine or a department store stylist. Moreover, it takes an experienced fashion journalist to recognize how a collection will be rendered less extreme and therefore more commercially viable when it goes into production. Lacking this context, many reporters took Norell's collection at face value and left the show thinking he was trying to foist their mothers' dropped-waist shifts and cloche hats on them.[86] In fact, the Traina-Norell collection that arrived in stores a few months later had only the remotest '20s details: tunic-style tops that vaguely suggested a shift dress; hats with deep, cloche-style crowns; and shoes with a strap across the instep.[87]

Also mystifying to the newly formed American fashion press corps was the personal style of the fashion professionals they encountered in Manhattan. The popular conception of 1940s fashion follows the Betty Grable–Ginger Rogers paradigm: high pompadours, linebacker shoulder pads, and ankle-strap platform shoes worn with stockings no matter how high the mercury climbed. Makeup consisted of powder and lipstick. For many women of the era, this was indeed the ideal. But fashion people were a breed apart. Rosamond Bernier, a journalist who later became famous for the lectures she gave at the Metropolitan Museum of Art, described herself as "terrified" of the almost alien chic of her *Vogue*

colleagues when she arrived there just after World War II. Her
first morning in the office, the sight of editors sitting at their typewriters in veiled hats, with masses of rhinestones twined around
their necks and dangling from their earlobes, details that to civil-
ians denoted evening attire, unnerved her. "I looked with absolute
wonder!" she said. To fit in, she did what all the other *Vogue* girls
who wanted to keep their jobs did: She bought a hat from Tati-
ana Liberman, the milliner wife of the magazine's art director, that
cost a week's salary.[88] Another neophyte magazine editor, a recent
Mount Holyoke graduate who was "too inexperienced to compre-
hend these women who looked and smelled like five o'clock instead
of 9 A.M.," described the typical accessories of the fashion editor
of the day: "Arpège [perfume] by the quart and turquoise eyelids";
also "a cigarette holder worn out of the side of the mouth, the way
a flamenco dancer bites a rose."[89]

Even among this cohort there were standouts. Babs Willaumez,
a flamboyant fashion editor at *Vogue*, was known to flaunt her
midriff in the office at a time when this body part was seen only
at the beach or in daring evening clothes.[90] She grew her toenails
long and painted them white, a quirk of grooming she highlighted
by wearing sandals year-round, even in the depths of winter.[91] A
colleague who spotted Willaumez getting out of a cab on Seventh
Avenue one summer morning in 1940 with her assistant (later to
become Best-Dressed List habitué Babe Paley) remembered, "Both
had brilliant turbans twisted round their heads, bare legs, and open
toed sandals at a time when Edna Woolman Chase was crusading
against the open-toed shoe so violently that shoe manufacturers
were taking their advertising out of *Vogue*." Completing the look
were armloads of jangling bracelets and huge drawstring handbags
"that looked like feed sacks."[92] The latter were likely made by the
American brand Phelps, a favorite of wartime fashion editors and

the originator of the giant-bag trend (it took the general public a few more years to adopt this new style).[93]

Sally Kirkland, the *Vogue* editor who would go on to be the fashion editor of *Life*, was Willaumez's polar opposite, a pared-down McCardell devotee ("No figure ever looked more completely removed from Paris," said one of her office mates).[94] She eschewed the pompadour for a flat pageboy bob, and accessorized McCardell's narrow wool jersey sheaths with wide, silver-studded leather belts; giant shoulder bags from Phelps; and leopard-skin buskins, the mid-calf, open-toe, lace-up boots worn by Roman soldiers.[95]

But it was McCardell, whose sophisticated, idiosyncratic style was so admired by her peers, who was singled out for derision. Her nemesis was a delegate who hid behind the pen name Cornelia Stokes, purported fashion editor of the fictitious *Willow Prairie Bugle*. She cast her opinions in the form of a satirical letter to her grandmother, and submitted it to *WWD*, which published it soon after the first Press Week wrapped up. Stokes's complaints about her experience were lengthy and detailed, from the lack of ashtrays to the overly ambitious scheduling. Mayor La Guardia was condescending—all New Yorkers were, she grumbled—and the clothes were disappointing and overpriced. She compared Lambert's hat to a birthday party balloon, and skewered the mannerisms of a designer named Ruth Kass, "who speaks only what is known around here as 'Seventh avenue-ese.'" But what most galled her was the sight of "a thin, tired gal . . . in slightly worn red shoes." Everything the thin woman wore, from the blue mesh stockings on her skinny legs to her snood—still six months away from being popularized by Lilly Daché—Stokes decried as freakish. She felt sorry for this pathetic creature, she maintained, until she realized who she was. "After one look at Claire McCardell I figure I can get away with absolutely anything from now on," Stokes declared.[96]

As Marjorie Griswold of Lord & Taylor diplomatically phrased it, a certain cosmopolitan polish was required to appreciate McCardell, at least in the early days. Stokes apparently didn't have what it took.

A brisk response to Stokes's tirade arrived the following week, when Laura O. Miller—her real name—the fashion and beauty writer of the *Indianapolis News*, wrote a piece for *WWD* that made it clear that the former's hatchet piece was neither amusing nor clever. Miller suggested that journalists who wanted to speak their minds freely should pay their own way, as she had. And when they did criticize something, they should do so plainly instead of indulging in "some rather unfunny bile." Finally, before they sat down at their typewriters, they might want to educate themselves; a five-day visit to Seventh Avenue did not confer world-weary expertise. "What you saw in New York, while planning to stick your stiletto in the back of the NYDI," Miller wrote, "were the trendsetters, the cream of the crop."[97] The styles these designers created would be adapted by less expensive manufacturers, just as New York designers once adapted Paris models, she pointed out. And those adaptations would be sold all over the United States, including "Willow Prairie."

In creating Press Week, Lambert taught Seventh Avenue how to deal with the media. But just as importantly, she taught the press how to cover their new beat, and designers how to present and talk about their collections. She encouraged them to think big, and to innovate. As early as the mid-1940s, she hired Black models for Press Week fashion shows, a precedent that would not be matched for decades.[98]

"Eleanor's vision was always very much that fashion had a place in the world," said one fashion editor.[99] From her office at 598 Madison Avenue, Lambert and her staff constructed the image of American fashion, one phone call, designer bio, and press release—

printed on her firm's signature pink paper—at a time.[100] Every request for a photo or quote, no matter how small the publication in question, was filled. When journalists came to town, Lambert made sure they went to important exhibitions and shows, arranged for them to meet up-and-coming performers, and took them to lunch. She spoke of fashion as one of the arts and encouraged designers to consider themselves the equal not just of painters and sculptors, but of the French couturiers. "When Americans come to recognize design in dress, then we will have achieved what we have been fighting for in recent years—equal recognition—not supremacy!" she told a reporter in 1945.[101]

To the designer Oleg Cassini, what she did was simple: "It was as if she had opened a school to teach fashion to the rest of the country," he said.[102]

In 1947, four years after Press Week was launched, Alice Hughes, a charter member of the Fashion Group and the author of a widely syndicated column called "A Woman's New York," called Lambert the "No. 1 Fashion Instigator" of the United States. When the history of American fashion was written, she wrote, Lambert would have a prominent place in it because "she has made American styles and their designers' names known in all of America and abroad."[103]

Lambert had succeeded in making Americans pay attention to their fashion designers. But it would take two other women to teach them what their native style looked like. Over at *Harper's Bazaar*, Diana Vreeland and the photographer Louise Dahl-Wolfe used the war years to craft editorials that combined American locations with fresh-faced models wearing sportswear that announced its independence from Paris in every line. It would become known as the American Look.

8

The American Look

Diana Vreeland and Louise Dahl-Wolfe

I was always fascinated by the absurdities and the luxuries and the snobbism of the world that fashion magazines showed . . . I was always of that world, at least in my imagination.

—DIANA VREELAND[1]

I believe that the camera is a medium of light, that one actually paints with light.

—LOUISE DAHL-WOLFE[2]

The girl on the cover of the March 1943 issue of *Harper's Bazaar* had "a bit of the panther about her," thought Nancy "Slim" Hawks. Her gaze was direct, just this side of insolent, suggesting she would direct a saucy comment at you while you lit her cigarette or mixed her a drink. She was dressed in a tiny white skullcap-style hat, a white blouse, and a navy blue suit, the collar of which flared out behind her tawny blond head and called attention to her hooded eyes. Behind her was a windowed door lettered with the words "American Red Cross Blood Donor Service"; a woman in a nurse's uniform was visible through the glass. It was a nod to both the urgent need to stock blood banks and the new roles women had assumed since the United States had declared war on Japan and Germany. *Bazaar*'s art director, the legendary Alexey Brodovitch, had been unsure about this cover. The model, he thought, looked too "decadent" to be associated with the Red Cross.[3] But it's this loucheness, offset by the tailored clothes and patriotic theme, that produced the arresting image that caught Slim's attention.

The model, she said, "was certainly my taste in beauty. Scrubbed clean, healthy, shining, and golden."[4] She showed the magazine to her husband, the director Howard Hawks, and suggested that this was the leading lady he had been looking for. Hawks had the girl fly out to California and gave her a screen test. She made her film debut the following year, at nineteen, opposite the much older and more famous actor she would soon marry. By the time the film, *To Have and Have Not*, loosely based on the Hemingway novel of the same name, was released in October 1944, Betty Bacal, née Betty Joan Perske, had become Lauren Bacall.

In the film, Bacall's character is known as Slim. She wears clothes copied from Slim Hawks's wardrobe and speaks dialogue that she fed to her husband, including the memorable line "You know how to whistle, don't you? Just put your lips together and blow." Bacall's on-screen persona—smart, independent, quick with a comeback, and elegantly but never fussily dressed—was one that Slim Hawks had earlier perfected. Her archetypically American style, a mix of sophistication and freshness, had already caught the eye of the editors of *Harper's Bazaar*. Carmel Snow was so impressed with Slim, who is often called the first California Girl, that she offered her the job of West Coast editor. Slim turned it down when she discovered she was pregnant, so the magazine had to be content with photographing her instead.[5] She appeared in *Bazaar*'s pages in a mitered striped suit by Adrian; in a white halter top, cuddling her dog, Meatball; posed in a fringed buckskin jacket by the paddock where she kept her horse; in a ribbed wool sweater, her hair pulled back in her habitual ponytail.[6] In 1944, *Bazaar* even photographed Hawks and Bacall together for two separate issues, looking like sisters in evening clothes by Adrian in one and blue jeans and plaid shirts in another. Two years later, Slim Hawks topped the Best-Dressed List, an honor she professed had about as much meaning to her as if she had been named Wisconsin's Miss Butterfat Week.[7] Making a big to-do about clothes was antithetical to her style.

Slim Hawks and her on-screen alter ego personified the American Look just as it was becoming a catchphrase for American style. But it was the women behind the Bacall cover who defined and codified that style. Bacall owed her appearance there, and arguably her subsequent Hollywood career, to the greatest team of image makers in fashion history: fashion editor Diana Vreeland and photographer Louise Dahl-Wolfe.

Bacall had done a little modeling before she was introduced to Vreeland in 1942 but had never encountered anyone remotely like *Bazaar*'s fashion editor, that "extraordinary looking woman," as she later described her. Vreeland was very thin, Bacall remembered, and dressed all in black, with her boot-polish-black hair held in place with a net snood topped with a flat bow. She took Bacall's chin in her red-nailed hands and turned it to the right and left as she scrutinized her. Satisfied, she told the teenager that she wanted her to meet Dahl-Wolfe. "We're having a sitting tomorrow—could you come to the studio? It won't take long."[8]

Bacall showed up the next day and met the photographer, "a

rather short, stocky woman whose sandy hair was pulled up tight in a bun or braid on the top of her head." She put the high schooler at ease by chatting to her as she worked. "There was no real posing, she just caught me as I fell and as she wanted it," Bacall said. "It was much less painful than any other modeling I had done." Vreeland would step in with minor adjustments. She "knew just how to tie [a scarf], a little off center." The test shots were a success, and the following week Bacall was on her first "sitting," as fashion shoots were called in the 1940s, for which she would be paid ten dollars an hour—a princely sum. "I loved being with Louise and Diana—[I] felt comfortable," she remembered. "They worked perfectly together."[9]

Under Vreeland and Dahl-Wolfe's ministrations, Bacall appeared in the pages of *Bazaar* looking just as Slim Hawks described her: wholesome yet sexy. She was photographed standing bare-legged on a Florida beach, windblown and sun-kissed in a light summer dress;[10] tucked up on a sofa in a cozy Claire McCardell jumpsuit, head bent in concentration over her mending (a thrifty habit everyone was encouraged to take up in wartime);[11] standing by Carmel Snow's tall living room window in her slip, looking pensively into a hand mirror;[12] and perched on the edge of a marble bathtub in her underwear, one hand reaching to turn the tap as she looks over her shoulder to see who—from the knowing half smile on her face, we presume he's a man—has walked in.[13]

These sittings, she later recalled, were notable for their light-heartedness. "I'd say anything that came into my head . . . a lot of it made them laugh—through all of it, Dahl-Wolfe never looked up from the camera, never really took her mind off what she was doing. A total professional."[14] The photos are infused with vitality, a vignette in the life of a woman who seems real and relatable. With her soap-and-water sparkle and feline grace, Bacall plays the part of the American girl with a taste for clean lines whom McCardell had in mind every time she picked up her sketch pad. It was the relaxed atmosphere of the Dahl-Wolfe and Vreeland shoots that made this performance possible. When Bacall was subsequently sent to work with the photographer Baron George Hoyningen-Huene, whose aristocratic family had fled the Russian Revolution, he posed her like a statue and ordered her to hold still. She found him unfriendly and the experience so stressful she began to shake. The photos were a disaster.[15]

Although Vreeland and Dahl-Wolfe would hone her image, the idealized American woman was not new to fashion. She was most often described in contrast to another fashion stereotype, the Parisienne, her salient characteristics being her height, athleticism, and air of cheerful good health. Early in the twentieth century, the French writer Marcel Prévost declared that "through hygiene and sports . . . a real American type has been formed, tall and strong."[16] Her popular personification at the time was the statuesque Gibson Girl drawn by Charles Dana Gibson, who was often depicted as towering over the pip-squeak males in her wake. The American girl entered high fashion in 1924, via the couturier Jean Patou, an Americanophile who played jazz at his fashion shows and was known for his sportswear. Patou decided he needed American models to show clothes to American buyers so they would more clearly understand how his designs would look on their customers. That November, he placed an ad in *The New York Times* inviting aspiring models who could be ready to sail for France in three weeks' time to come to the *Vogue* offices on West 44th Street for an open casting call. Five hundred hopefuls showed up, and in the end six were chosen. Patou described them as "slender Dianas" in contrast to the "rounded French Venus."[17] In fact, the proportions of professional French and American models were not really that different, and the women he selected in New York were of all different heights and sizes: Patou's talent search was really a savvy marketing ploy. He got attention in both the United States, where stories were enthusiastic, and France, where they were indignant. For Patou's less sportswear-inclined peers, the advent of the athletic American type was a harbinger of change. Louise Boulanger, a couturier with ties to the art world whose clothes were deemed "super chic," lamented to Snow, "The day tennis came in, the demimondaine"—the kept women who were among the best customers of prewar haute couture—"went out, and fashion with her."[18]

The same year that Patou staged his model contest, John Robert Powers founded New York's first modeling agency. To distinguish his clients from showgirls, he dubbed them "Long-Stemmed American Beauties." "What I seek above all is a natural wholesomeness," he said.[19] Although Powers claimed to "invent" fashion modeling, it dated back to the nineteenth century.[20] Madame Worth, in the 1850s, modeled gowns for the customers of her husband's couture house. But it took longer for models to infiltrate fashion magazines. Baron Adolph de Meyer—the early twentieth century was the heyday of the (sometimes self-) titled fashion photographer—joined *Vogue*'s staff in 1913 but the women who sat for him during the early years of his career were society ladies, not professional models. Fashion photography gradually became distinct from portrait photography, and by the late 1920s the styled photo shoot, complete with model, was an established feature of fashion magazines. These shoots inevitably took place indoors, usually in the studio before a painted backdrop or seamless screen. Sometimes a room in a lavish apartment, like those belonging to Condé Nast or the cosmetics queen Helena Rubinstein, would be pressed into service. But when Snow suggested photographing a fashionable couple in their plane—the 1920s equivalent of the private jet, only far less common—she was told, to her annoyance, that *Vogue* didn't use outdoor shots.[21] Like de Meyer, who was still shooting under a black cotton shroud with a hairnet on his head to keep his coiffure from being disarranged when Snow fired him in 1932 (he had moved over to *Bazaar* in 1922), *Vogue* clung to the tried and true.[22]

Given these limitations, it was inevitable that, however skilled the photographer or appealing the subject, the results were a little stilted. Then, in the fall of 1933, Snow, who had by then decamped for *Harper's Bazaar*, was shown the work of a Hungarian photographer named Martin Munkácsi in the German magazine *Die Dame*. Munkácsi was a photojournalist in Europe, shooting everything from sporting events to Nazi rallies. His work was dynamic and edgy, a blend of expert composition and an on-the-fly shooting style that used unusual angles and cropping to convey the excitement of movement. The December issue had already gone to press, but upon learning that Munkácsi happened to be on a two-day visit to New York, Snow promptly decided to have him reshoot the issue's bathing suit story, which had been produced, per custom, in the studio. It was a stop-the-presses moment.[23]

On a frigid, cloudy November day, Munkácsi, Snow, and a model named Lucile Brokaw headed to the beach at Piping Rock, the exclusive Long Island country club where the Snows were members. Munkácsi, who spoke no English, made wild gestures with his arms. The two women shivered and stared at him, trying to decipher what he meant. Finally, Brokaw understood what he wanted and began to run down the beach, the long muscles in her thighs flexing and the cape she wore over her bathing suit flying behind her. Munkácsi clicked his shutter—and changed the course of fashion photography.[24]

He had caught "a typical American girl *in action*," Snow crowed years later, still thrilled at the innovation she had ushered into *Ba-*

zaar. William Randolph Hearst derided Snow's new find as "just a snapshot photographer," but she stood her ground—"Munky," as the *Bazaar* editors called him, became a regular contributor, bringing his irrepressible spirit to photos of models and celebrities who danced, whirled, and leapt across the magazine's pages.[25] Munkácsi flicked off Hearst's unenthusiastic assessment like a speck of dust on his lens. "Never pose your subjects," he wrote in an article for *Bazaar* in 1935. "Let them move about naturally. All great photographs today are snapshots." An accompanying image shows him floating on his back in the icy waters of Long Island Sound in October, his Speed Graphic camera held above the waves as he captures his shot, neither a shroud nor a hairnet in sight.[26]

Munkácsi's photos conveyed his models' physicality in a way that the frozen poses of earlier fashion photography simply could not. The women in his photographs had freedom and agency—they were modern, the quality that Snow was determined that *Bazaar* should reflect. When Edna Woolman Chase dismissed this style of photography as "farm girls jumping over fences," Snow was delighted.[27] The embrace of the new was what distinguished her magazine from *Vogue*. In this spirit, rather than continuing to edit solely for capital-S Society, Snow opened her pages up to a wider audience.

She began by hiring Brodovitch, a Russian émigré who had painted backdrops for the Ballets Russes in Paris before arriving in the United States in 1930, as her art director. Brodovitch's inventive use of type, unexpected cropping of photos, airy manipulation of negative space, and embrace of the double-page spread catapulted *Bazaar* into the front ranks of graphic design and made him a giant in his field. "Astonish me!" he would instruct his staff, a phrase he borrowed from Sergei Diaghilev, who had commanded the Ballets Russes to *"Étonnez-moi!"* Working first from sketches and then with mock-ups he spread out on the floor of his office, Brodovitch laid the magazine out cinematographically, pacing the reader's experience so that several pages in a row consisted of long-range views, followed by a zoomed-in close-up. He gave *Bazaar* a spare, clean style that was perfectly suited to the similarly spare, clean look of American sportswear.

Brodovitch's counterpart was Dr. Mehemed Fehmy Agha, a Turk who had come to *Vogue* via the short-lived German edition. Agha had his own elegant style but was kept from doing anything too daring by Chase. She had an especial aversion to negative space—or, as she called it, "waste space"—which she considered would be better filled with advice for her readers.[28]

The content that Brodovitch laid out was as innovative as his design. Snow defied Hearst's order that no Blacks were to appear in his publications by having Munkácsi take a series of portraits of the contralto Marian Anderson—you could argue these were action shots: she's singing in them—for the September 1937 issue. She sent Walker Evans to photograph public housing in New York City.[29] In 1944, Snow had her own maid, Mae Morrissy, write about the drudgery of being a domestic servant—it was "human slavery," Morrissy said.[30] Another story in this line was a profile of a model in Molyneux's postwar Paris salon, who was paid less than a secretary, lived in a cold-water flat, and subsisted on meager portions of noodles and turnips that left her malnourished and exhausted.[31] In 1942, she commissioned a story titled "I Had My First Baby When I Was Forty," a headline that could have been printed today (and one that doubtless resonated with Snow, who married at thirty-nine and had her three daughters between the ages of forty and forty-four).[32] She valued good writing, and paid the impressive array of mid-century writers who contributed to *Bazaar* higher fees than *The New Yorker*, which considered itself the most literary of American magazines. Snow even reconfigured the entire January 1946 issue to fit in a lengthy excerpt from Carson McCullers's *The Member of the Wedding.* No suggestion was too wild. When the beauty editor proposed an interactive palm-reading feature that involved having a reader press her hand onto a thermally sensitive page, Snow, who was equally devoted to the Catholic church and her psychic, gave it her enthusiastic approval. It never ran, however. Hearst lawyers objected on the grounds that fortune-telling through the post was illegal, and Snow reluctantly acquiesced to their demand to cut the piece.[33] But as a rule, if it was new and exciting, she wanted it for *Bazaar.*

When Kodachrome, the first color film for still cameras that offered reliably reproducible color saturation and sharpness, came onto the market in 1936, Snow was determined to get it into her pages.[34] Ninety years and billions of brightly hued images later, it's difficult to overstate the impact Kodachrome had on fashion magazines. Previously, the only color in their pages had been some underwhelming experiments with early color film and illustrations. Readers accustomed to having to imagine the color of a dress or coat in a photo, a vital detail that had to be explained in a caption, could suddenly see it for themselves. Almost overnight, color photography became the standard by which fashion magazines were judged. It was too expensive and time-consuming to use exclusively, but it was vital to have a few color images in every issue.

Fashion photographers who wanted to advance their careers were obliged to master this new technology, which came with a significant hitch: Kodachrome was fiendishly difficult to work with. In his memoir, Edward Steichen, who was then contributing to *Vogue*, described how in the early days, Eastman Kodak would send technicians to help photographers use the three one-shot cameras—one for each primary color—and powerful klieg lights that were required to get a usable shot.[35] But even with that assistance, some of the best black-and-white photographers struggled with color. The work of otherwise brilliant cameramen like Anton Bruehl and Hoyningen-Huene, who dabbled in color film, has an artificial look.

For a perfectionist like Dahl-Wolfe, that was never going to be good enough. "You have to study color like the scales of the piano," she maintained.[36] She brought several advantages to this challenge: First, she had studied color theory as an art student and trained herself to look at objects and analyze the value and intensity of their colors.[37] Second, she had worked as an interior designer, which gave her practical experience in how to harmonize and contrast color. With these skills as her foundation, she pushed herself to learn everything she could about Kodak's new product. When she wasn't on deadline, wrote *Bazaar*'s managing editor, Frances McFadden, Dahl-Wolfe "worked with her little camera on experiments with Kodachrome, experiments that were to set a new standard for color photography."[38]

By 1938, Dahl-Wolfe was able to successfully shoot color outdoors, a huge achievement for the time. Smaller cameras had replaced the cumbersome old one-shot ones, giving photographers greater mobility. And the light meter, invented in 1932, meant they no longer had to guess at f-stops and shutter speeds.[39] But even with these tools, shooting color in natural light was a gamble. It was a sign of Dahl-Wolfe's growing expertise that she was able to do so. One of the secrets, she maintained, was her ability to accurately gauge skin tones. Complexions with greeny-yellow undertones, she insisted, looked more natural in photos than those with the more obvious red ones.[40]

Given Dahl-Wolfe's boundary pushing, it was inevitable that Snow would want her for *Bazaar*, even before she had perfected her color technique. Prior to signing her contract, Dahl-Wolfe laid out her conditions. She would work in her own studio, not *Bazaar*'s, using her own assistants and retoucher (Josephine Landl, a woman so gifted Vreeland nicknamed her "Madame Rembrandt"), and she would have final say on all proofs.[41] At the time, each color proof required four separate etched copper plates: one cyan, one magenta, one yellow, and one black. When these colors were overlaid, endless variations of tone could be achieved. Once the desired effect was reached, that final proof would be used as a guide for the printers. Most photographers had to trust that the printers would do a reasonable job of getting the color right. Dahl-Wolfe insisted on supervising the process and would reject proof after proof in her pursuit of the correct balance of colors, a process that drove the printers mad. This was the kind of prima donna behavior that Snow understood and respected. She was a tough bargainer, but she agreed to all Dahl-Wolfe's demands. *Bazaar*'s editor in chief knew that color was the future of fashion photography, and she was determined that her magazine would surpass Edna Woolman Chase's *Vogue*, which had briefly surged ahead in the color-photography race (and also employed the top illustrators). "From the moment I first saw her color photographs I knew that the *Bazaar* was at last going to look the way I had instinctively wanted my magazine to look," Snow said.[42] Over the course of Dahl-Wolfe's twenty-two-year career with *Bazaar*, the magazine would publish six hundred of her color photos and thousands of black-and-white ones, and assign her the cover eighty-six times.[43]

The woman who would come to define the look of *Bazaar*'s fashion shoots was born in San Francisco in 1895 to Knut and Emma Dahl, immigrants from Norway. Her mother chose her names, Louise Emma Augusta Dahl, because she had heard it was good luck for a child's initials to spell a word; her selection, "LEAD," would prove prophetic.[44] Like Brodovitch, with whom she would work closely, Dahl-Wolfe had a connection with the Ballets Russes. Her mother had taken her to see the company when it came to San Francisco, an event that was one of the formative memories of her childhood. It was there, she later wrote, that she saw how different expressions of art—music, dance, sets, and costumes—could be, in her words, "magnificent together." [45]

She became interested in photography in 1919, after a chance visit to the studio of Anne Brigman. Brigman, along with Steichen, was a founding member of the Photo-Secession movement, which promoted the idea that photography was a fine art. It wasn't a philosophy that Dahl-Wolfe, who considered photography a craft, agreed with. But it was nevertheless a life-changing experience for the twenty-four-year-old, who was enchanted with both Brigman's bohemian decor and her lyrical nudes, which she posed against the backdrop of the California wilderness. After that one visit, Dahl-Wolfe said, "I had to get a camera!" She was soon spending all her money on photography.[46]

At first, Dahl-Wolfe imitated Brigman's work, posing her friends in the nude—and in turn posing for them—in various locales on the Monterey Peninsula. But while she was passionate about this new medium, Dahl-Wolfe did not yet consider it her life's vocation. She was working for the blue-chip San Francisco decorating firm of Armstrong, Carter, and Kenyon, and assumed that would be her career. Then, in 1926, her mother was killed in a car accident. Dahl-Wolfe, who had been in the car with her, was overcome with grief.

Her sister suggested she take a long trip abroad to assuage her sorrow. Traveling with a friend, Dahl-Wolfe went first to Europe and then North Africa. They were on a train in Kairouan, Tunisia, when Dahl-Wolfe spotted an artist from Tennessee named

Meyer "Mike" Wolfe and thought, "That's for me."[47] The couple married later that year. She hyphenated her name, she said, because she didn't want to be confused with another photographer named Wolfe, "but added Mike's because I loved him." [48] Theirs was a long and happy marriage. Dahl-Wolfe had the bigger career, something her husband never begrudged her. He helped her paint her sets, he made her laugh, and when she got irritable on the job, he soothed her.[49] His nickname for her was Queen Louise. For their twenty-ninth anniversary, he gave her a drawing he'd made that showed them both in the nude, with the words "I love you. No vessel can measure, no scales can weigh, no words can mouth how much."[50]

They spent the summer of 1932 in Gatlinburg, Tennessee, in a log cabin with no electricity. Wolfe painted and Dahl-Wolfe photographed every day, rigging up a darkroom with the battery from their Ford Model A so she could develop her film. It was then that she took her first published photograph, a portrait of a neighbor that appeared in *Vanity Fair* with the caption "Tennessee Mountain Woman." The summer spent focusing on their work seems to have acted as a catalyst—the couple moved to New York the following spring. They arrived in March 1933, during the weeklong bank holiday declared by President Roosevelt to try to stabilize the country's banking system. The miles of tin shacks they saw on the drive from New Jersey into Manhattan shocked them, as did the sight of well-dressed men selling apples on Fifth Avenue. But Dahl-Wolfe soon found work. From her studio on West 52nd Street, on a block of jazz clubs and speakeasies, she photographed still lifes for the recipe pages of *Woman's Home Companion* magazine.[51] She expanded into fashion at the suggestion of a friend, shooting campaigns for a rayon manufacturer and Saks Fifth Avenue. But the best training she got was photographing the models at Milgrim's, a dress shop on 57th Street. "Those girls were at least forty," she said.[52] She pulled out every trick she could think of, and invented more, to make them look fresh and appealing.

Vanity Fair's editor in chief, Frank Crowninshield, who'd published "Tennessee Mountain Woman," arranged for Dahl-Wolfe to see Dr. Agha at *Vogue*. She kept the appointment even though she was suffering from a severe case of the flu and looked and felt dreadful. The meeting turned out to be perfunctory. But on the strength of it, she sent him her portfolio to look at. It was returned with a note for Condé Nast that Agha had accidentally left inside. In it, he characterized her as "trying to learn photography" but too old—"about forty-eight," he estimated—to bother with.[53] Dahl-Wolfe, who was in her thirties at the time, was crushed—and furious. She took her portfolio to Brodovitch. Chase's loss was Snow's win.

Dahl-Wolfe began working with *Harper's Bazaar* in 1936, the same year her future partner, Diana Vreeland, did. Snow, who was always on the lookout for fresh talent, noticed Vreeland on the dance floor at New York's St. Regis Hotel. Vreeland was wearing a white lace Chanel evening gown with a matching bolero and roses in her blue-black hair. Although Vreeland had never worked for a magazine—indeed, had barely worked at all—Snow recognized a born fashion editor when she saw one. Most obviously, Vreeland had that undefinable quality known as style. She also had a vivid imagination and had grown up homely in a family of beauties, an experience that she translated into a keen understanding of how to capitalize on any woman's looks. Finally, although she looked like a lady of leisure, she needed the money.

As usual, Snow was right. The woman who first reported for work at the shabby Hearst magazine offices at 572 Madison Avenue was not yet the extraordinary caricature that she would become—"a combination of Madame de Sevigny and Falstaff," said her friend Cecil Beaton.[54] For that, she needed an outlet, and the supervision of a strong editor. At *Bazaar*, she found both. It was there that Diana Vreeland, society housewife, became Diana Vreeland, Fashion Editor. "She invented the profession," said the photographer Richard Avedon, who worked with her early in his career. "Before her, it was society ladies putting hats on other society ladies."[55] She is certainly the most quoted, and most referenced, fashion editor of the twentieth century.

Vreeland was born in 1903 in Paris to Emily Key Hoffman, a Gilded Age American debutante and avid big-game hunter, and her British stockbroker husband, Frederick Young Dalziel. After that, the facts are fuzzy. Vreeland preferred to transform plain or uncomfortable truths into heavily embroidered fantasies, which makes distinguishing the real from the fanciful events of her life a challenge. Whether or not she studied dance with Michel Fokine or was taught to ride by Buffalo Bill Cody, both highly improbable occurrences, she felt these anecdotes *should* be true. All her life, she would reflexively choose the brilliant over the banal.

The Dalziels returned to New York about eight months after she was born—not in 1914, as she later claimed—and settled into a house on East 77th Street. It was there that the teenage Vreeland began crafting the persona she would inhabit as an adult. She was always on the lookout for girls to idealize, she confided to her diary. When they didn't turn up, she vowed, *"I shall be that girl."*[56] Although she would later describe her childhood in rosy tones, her relationship with her mother was difficult. Vreeland found her mother's flamboyant and flirtatious manner embarrassing, and her mother found constant fault with her older daughter's looks, which she compared unfavorably to those of her younger child, Alexandra. Alexandra was petite and conventionally pretty, while Diana looked like her father, down to his substantial nose. "It's too bad you have such a beautiful sister and that you are so extremely ugly and so jealous of this," her mother once told her. "This is, of course, why you are so impossible to deal with."[57] (Coincidentally, the same dynamic played out in Elsa Schiaparelli's family—as a child, the designer felt so unsightly that she once crammed flower seeds into her nose and ears, thinking the ensuing blooms would mask her unprepossessing features).[58]

By sixteen, Vreeland was experimenting with what would become her signature "Kabuki" makeup, a theatrical affectation that made her Easter Island profile even more startling: skin powdered gardenia white, a slash of red lipstick, and emphatically applied rouge on her cheeks, forehead, and ears. She claimed to have studied dance rather than completing high school, training that informed her distinctive, loping walk: She kept her head and neck on a backward incline and led with her pelvis, swinging her legs out from the hips. A frequent prop was the standard fashion-editor-issue cigarette holder with which she stabbed the air to make a point or gripped between her teeth as she adjusted a model's hair or clothing.

She met her future husband, Thomas Reed Vreeland, at a Fourth of July party in 1924 and married him the following year. Reed Vreeland was always perfectly dressed, and had beautiful manners, a sweet disposition, and a fixation on surface detail that made him a worthy partner in artifice to his wife. His attitude toward his various jobs was diffident, his real milieu being the dinner party and the country house weekend. He was chronically unfaithful to Vreeland, which, characteristically, she refused to see.

The couple spent the first few years of their married life in Albany, where their older son was born, and Manhattan, where they welcomed their younger son. These sojourns Vreeland glossed over. Instead, she focused on their next move, to London, where Reed worked as a banker. In England, the lower cost of living allowed them to live grandly, although still beyond their means, a pattern they were to follow throughout their marriage. They bought and renovated a large house in Chelsea and kept a sizable staff, including a driver for the Bugatti in which they motored all over Europe. Vreeland was presented at court, an experience that nourished her aristocratic aspirations. With a friend, she opened a small lingerie shop. It was there, Vreeland recounted, that Wallis Simpson bought the nightgowns she wore for her first weekend with the Prince of Wales. This may have been true, or it may have been Vreeland's way of inserting herself into one of the major events in the history of the British monarchy—in her telling, this was the nightwear that sparked the affair that resulted in Edward VIII's abdication.

By 1935, the Vreelands were back in the United States. Shortly thereafter, the *Harper's Bazaar* chapter of Vreeland's life began. She was an immediate success, generating chatter and publicity with an utterly loopy column called "Why Don't You?" that has become part of magazine legend. It consisted of a series of fashion and lifestyle suggestions that, in the midst of the Depression, struck many as both ridiculous and out of touch. And yet they remained lodged in the minds of even the most skeptical of her readers. The most famous was "Why don't you wash your blonde child's hair in dead Champagne, as they do in France?" but every column included howlers, often larded with aristocratic names and allusions to history, art, and expensive jewelry.[59] Most were so specific in their references, notably in the shades of color that Vreeland relayed with a painter's eye, that they evoked an entire scenario in a single sentence. Why don't you . . . "bring back from Central Europe a huge white baroque porcelain stove to stand in your front hall, reflected in the parquet?"[60] . . . "wear, like the Duchess of Kent, three enormous diamond stars arranged in your hair in front?"[61] . . . "go serenely out in the snow in a court jester's hood of cherry cotton velvet?"[62]

Inevitably, they were lampooned, most memorably by S. J. Perelman of *The New Yorker*, who wrote, in response to Vreeland's suggestion regarding champagne and children's hair: "I decided to let my blonde child go to hell her own way, as they do in America." [63]

What Vreeland was really saying, in her singular fashion, was "Why don't you choose to make yourself more interesting?" It was the quality she valued above everything. Some of her suggestions, however, were indefensible, as when she asked, "Why don't you wear bare knees and long knitted socks, as Unity Mitford does when she takes tea with Hitler at the Carlton in Munich?" [64] So far as we know, Vreeland didn't approve of the Nazis. But she could be curiously aloof about right and wrong—in the Vreeland universe, mystique trumped morality.

By 1939, she had become *Bazaar*'s fashion editor, a job of which she said, "I was *the* fashion editor. I judged everything that went into the magazine whether it was a buckle or a girdle or a piece of fabric or a length of a sweater or anything." [65] This wasn't exactly true. Vreeland was not *Bazaar*'s sole fashion editor. And while Snow understood the value of Vreeland's brio, she kept it in check. If Vreeland announced that an entire issue should be magenta, Snow would allow her a couple of pages. When she came up with a plan to banish handbags in favor of pockets, Snow crisply vetoed the idea. "Listen, Diana, I think you've lost your mind," Vreeland reported her as saying. "Do you realize that our income from handbag advertising is God knows how many millions a year?" [66]

Nor would Snow allow Vreeland to cover Paris—she kept that prize for herself. In its place, Vreeland was left with what she initially considered second best: the American market. While this was a disappointment to her, it turned out to be an advantage. Because Snow was more interested in Paris than she was in New York, she was less exacting about the way American fashion was portrayed, which gave Vreeland greater leeway than she would have enjoyed if she'd been planning haute couture shoots.[67] Still, Manhattan's Garment District was certainly not where Vreeland's heart was. For a romantic, status-obsessed fantasist like her, only Paris could supply the requisite allure she craved in clothing—when war broke out in 1939 and other Americans scrambled to get berths on a ship headed for New York, Vreeland stayed behind to wrap up her couture fittings. She handled this disappointment in typical Vreeland fashion, by reshaping reality to her will. Her forays into the utilitarian lofts of Seventh Avenue she turned into adventures. "I tramped the streets. I covered the waterfront . . . I was always going up rusty staircases with old newspapers lying all over the place and ghastly looking characters hanging around . . . but *nothing* was frightening to me," she cried.[68]

She reimagined the clothes she found there, too. Vreeland took the shoulder pads out of suits, lowered hemlines, ordered red bows to be swapped out for purple ones, rejected platform shoes for the ballet slippers both she and Claire McCardell preferred, zhuzhed up bathing suits with wide leather belts, paired evening dresses with sandals, and when necessary crafted accessories out of thin air, like the silk scarf she twisted into a medieval-style liripipe headdress and adorned with flower-shaped pins for one shoot.[69] She literally edited Seventh Avenue, making the clothes she found there simpler, sleeker, and less cluttered (her models got the same treatment: Vreeland directed them to keep their makeup to a schoolgirlish minimum and brushed, braided, and coiled their hair to head-hugging sleekness). If she couldn't find the look she sought in an existing collection, she would jolly a designer into creating it for her, sometimes overnight. If she had to shoot an advertiser's clothing and couldn't find anything in its collection that met her standards, she'd design something herself, usually a copy of the Mainbocher suits that she favored in those years. That these garments never appeared in stores didn't faze her—she was a dream merchant, not an actual one.[70]

In fact, Vreeland was more than that: "She was a tremendous inspiration to American sportswear," one *Bazaar* colleague told *Vanity Fair*.[71] Bettina Wilson, Vreeland's counterpart at *Vogue*, said that her approach to fashion editing was not to report, but "to create . . . to motivate."[72] In 1946, on vacation in Saint-Tropez, Vreeland was galvanized by the sight of her first bikini.[73] Back in New York, she pushed the sportswear designer Carolyn Schnurer to create one of her own, the first ever seen in the US. "She kept telling me, 'Less of it! *Less* of it!'" Schnurer remembered.[74] Toni Frissell photographed Schnurer's bikini, a green polka-dot rayon suit of breathtaking smallness, for the May 1947 issue of *Bazaar*. It was worn by the model Dovima, who sprawled by the water with the straps of her top undone so that a strong breeze might carry it off. When Vreeland's scandalized colleagues expressed alarm over the overt sexiness of the shot, she announced that an attitude like that set civilization back a thousand years. Not every designer had Schnurer's tolerance for Vreeland's meddling. She once asked a *Bazaar* colleague, "Who is that Seventh Avenue designer who hates me so?" "Legion," he replied.[75]

Vreeland's soaring imagination, which often manifested as dottiness, was underpinned with discipline. Avedon, who first encountered her at the very beginning of his career, described her as "without exception, the hardest working person I've ever known."[76] Her work uniform consisted of dark wool separates. Her desk was obsessively tidy, and her daily diet was unvarying: porridge and tea for breakfast and a peanut-butter-and-marmalade sandwich with, depending on the source, a slug of whisky or a half-melted bowl of vanilla ice cream for lunch (another Vreelandism: "Peanut butter is the greatest invention since Christianity").[77] While not exactly nutrient-rich, these frugal repasts kept her lean and springy; as Cecil Beaton once remarked, Vreeland looked like she was made of cooked asparagus.[78]

Had Vreeland been *Bazaar*'s fashion editor in a different era, her influence might not have been quite so striking. But in the months after Paris fell, it was generally acknowledged that one of the problems facing American fashion was that it had no equivalent to the style leaders who inspired the couturiers and for whom they created their collections. There was little concept of fashion rising up from the street in those days; instead, it trickled down from the top. In the prewar years, fashion was "led" by the "Famous Forty," wealthy European women (and their Europeanized Americans counterparts) who bought their clothes in Paris and divided the year between the approved watering holes and sporting locales of the elite, all activities that were covered extensively in magazines like *Vogue* and *Harper's Bazaar.* These were the women Elizabeth Hawes described in *Fashion Is Spinach*, the couture clients whose lady's maids kept their expensive wardrobes in tip-top shape. (Vreeland, of course, had a lady's maid, Yvonne, whose duties included polishing the soles of her shoes—with a rhinoceros horn.)[79]

In a piece about New York's newfound importance, published in August 1940, Virginia Pope explained that designers created fashion, but these faultlessly groomed women *made* fashion—what they wore was news, and their preferences and way of life informed every couture collection. In comparison, she added, "no comparable stars light the horizons of our country."[80] Pope was making an observation. Others voiced real concern. Frances Corey, the fashion director of Bloomingdale's, believed that American designers needed to find their own Famous Forty. The country's designers were "some of the best in the world," she conceded, but they were overly concerned with the "mass of the people"—a remark that suggests she understood little about what made American designers great. She thought the country needed to build up its social life so as to provide designers with the types of "personalities" that the couturiers had.[81] It was an attitude rooted in the past.

Neither Vreeland nor Dahl-Wolfe had any interest in doing things the old way. Vreeland, in particular, liked to emphasize her fearlessness by reminding people of the Dalziel—her maiden name—motto: "I dare." More to the point, the first line of her memoir is "I loathe nostalgia."[82] Dahl-Wolfe was less flamboyant, but she was feisty, and she knew her worth. Her long relationship with *Bazaar* worked because it preserved her independence. Even when she was first starting out, she refused every job offer that stipulated she work in someone else's studio.

The combination of two such strong personalities had the potential for disaster, but Vreeland and Dahl-Wolfe's mutual respect allowed them to collaborate seamlessly. Neither was easy to work with. Vreeland rarely communicated directly with her underlings, preferring to issue vague, koan-like statements that she expected them to interpret to her satisfaction. She might send a junior editor in search of the perfect red, giving no more direction than that it should match the color of a child's cap in a Renaissance painting. Dahl-Wolfe could be huffy and thin-skinned, especially if she thought another photographer was impinging on her territory, and her temper was volcanic (one friend, the painter Pavel Tchelitchew, another of Snow's finds, called her "Vesuvius").[83] There were times when she refused for weeks on end to shoot for *Bazaar*, citing some imagined slight. Both women were demanding. But they saw much to admire in each other. Very few fashion editors had Vreeland's "outstanding creativity," Dahl-Wolfe said. "She was tops on a sitting."[84] In Dahl-Wolfe, Vreeland recognized an equal, someone who was as committed to perfection as she was. "Louise was passionate, more ignited by her métier than anyone I have ever known," she said. "She was . . . a pioneer in color and daylight."[85]

As the fashion editor, Vreeland determined the theme of the shoot and chose the clothes. She began by envisioning the page as she wanted it to look. She'd then act out her idea to her assistants, draping dresses and jackets over her body, describing how these garments felt and moved, striking poses, and giving a running commentary on the narrative she had constructed in her mind, throwing in allusions to art, history, culture, and dance. "Diana has never been content to simply present a costume," said Bettina Wilson. "She must create the type of woman who might wear the costume, consider where she might wear it, possibly stop to ponder on the life story of the imaginary woman in the ready-made suit in front of her."[86]

Vreeland grasped instinctively how to put clothes in a context that drew out their meaning, as when she had Dahl-Wolfe shoot a short-legged wool jersey bodysuit by Claire McCardell, the mother of athleisurewear, on a model doing yoga, a discipline that was almost unknown in the West in 1948.[87] For a self-professed high school dropout, she knew her stuff. And if she didn't, she made it up. When a young Avedon sought her assistance in photographing a dress he found dull, worn by a model he found dull, Vreeland half closed her eyes and began to speak in a hypnotic tone: "Just imagine Cleopatra . . . that young girl . . . everyone around her is so old . . ."[88]

In Dahl-Wolfe, who had a similarly deep well of material to draw on, Vreeland found her ideal partner. Dahl-Wolfe balanced Vreeland's oracular statements with wry juxtapositions and humorous touches, such as posing sylphlike models in lingerie next to blowsy Old Master nudes. She once photographed a model in a Hattie Carnegie hat with a ruffled crest before a large sculpture of an Etruscan warrior's head, the plume of his helmet a super-sized echo of the whimsical millinery. For another photo, taken on the balcony of the Museum of Modern Art, she played around with geometry, posing a model in a checked suit before the windowed grid of Manhattan office buildings. None of this was accidental. Dahl-Wolfe carefully plotted out every composition, even insisting on seeing what page would appear opposite each of her photos so she could plan for continuity.[89]

Her diminutive stature—yet another of her seemingly endless nicknames was Kewpie Dahl—meant that she almost always stood on a step ladder to photograph.[90] "Higher, get me higher" was her constant refrain in the studio. For color photography, she worked with a hulking eight-by-ten-inch view camera. She also used a Rolleiflex and a 3¼-by-4¼-inch Graflex, hanging its seven-pound bulk from her neck until she was diagnosed with three displaced vertebrae and had to start using a tripod.[91] While Vreeland could be remote and formal, Dahl-Wolfe was down-to-earth. Once work was done for the day, she would encourage the models to enact parodies of high-fashion poses while she snapped away, trying not to laugh so hard that she couldn't look though her viewfinder.[92]

Rather than trying to re-create the old fashion system by casting about for the "personalities" that Bloomingdale's fashion director advocated, Dahl-Wolfe and Vreeland opted for a more conceptual muse: the modern American woman whom Snow edited her magazine for. In their interpretation, she was independent, athletic, curious, comfortable in both wide-open landscapes and urbane settings like art exhibitions. She was well but never overly groomed. She was confident. She worked. She traveled. She liked practical clothes that didn't get in the way, but she demanded they have personality. She was equally at home in the city as she was in the country. American designers cited the lifestyle of their customers as their inspiration—Dahl-Wolfe and Vreeland showed what it looked like. This approach began to take shape as early as 1938, and reached its first apotheosis in a January 1942 shoot called "Flight to the Valley of the Sun."

Like most magazine shoots, it took place about two months before it appeared in print. In the late fall of 1941, Dahl-Wolfe, Vreeland, Dahl-Wolfe's assistant Hazel Kingsbury, and two models, Wanda Delafield and Bijou Barrington, left New York's Pennsylvania Station on a westbound train. Their destination was Arizona, then still terra incognita for much of the country and a relatively novel destination for fashion photographers. *Bazaar* had shot on location in the Southwest a few months previously, and its editors came back raving about a marvelous new dish they'd tried: "avocado mushed up with tomatoes and onion"—i.e., guacamole, something very few Americans of the era had ever eaten.[93]

Packed in Vreeland's trunks were the resort clothes that she intended to put on the models: a short plaid romper suit with elasticated legs by Claire McCardell, slim cropped trousers in tobacco brown and white-and-fuchsia stripes, bra tops and skinny black jerseys, dresses with swingy skirts and butterfly appliqués, and espadrilles and thong sandals, the latter of which she had copied from "the pornographic museum at Pompeii."[94] With Vreeland, a shoe was never just a shoe; it had a backstory and a lineage, in this case a torrid affair she imagined between a Roman aristocrat and her enslaved lover. The clothes and accessories she chose were young and casual, "clothes with breezes running through their seams," as she once characterized American sportswear, selected to harmonize with the desert landscape.[95] They correspond not even remotely with the resort fashions in the advertising carried by *Harper's Bazaar* that month. In page after page of ads, models pose in puff-sleeved, wide-shouldered tropical-print shirtwaist dresses worn with stockings and open-toe platform shoes, getups that read as stereotypically 1940s—the Betty Grable–Ginger Rogers paradigm again. Vreeland's choices and her styling are, in contrast, timeless.

The locations chosen for the shoot included an abandoned Western film set, a ranch, an old Spanish mission, and the Rose Pauson House, a striking Frank Lloyd Wright residence on the outskirts of Tucson that burned to the ground the following year (Dahl-Wolfe's photos are some of the best images of the exterior extant). Of the sixteen pages of photographs that the shoot yielded, the most striking were taken at the Pauson House. In one, Delafield stands in front of one of the cantilevered wooden structures that project from it like the prow of a ship that's run aground in the desert. Dahl-Wolfe shot her from below so that she looks heroic against the crystalline sky. She's wearing a mid-calf black linen skirt and a wool challis scarf that Vreeland had folded into a halter top. Her skin glistens, and her clothing is so minimal that we can see the shadow on her bare flank that's created by her bent arm. Everything in this photo shimmers with a bronze gleam.

The seamlessness of Dahl-Wolfe's partnership with Vreeland was on full display during this shoot. When Delafield came down with heat stroke, Vreeland, who was neither young nor beautiful, stepped in front of the camera. She models in two photographs: one taken at the Pauson House, in which she wears the narrow brown trousers and a fringed black shawl draped over a bra top and turns a sunglass-covered gaze to the sun, and another from the film set. In the latter, she stands in profile in front of an ersatz stagecoach depot, her luggage by her side. She wears a pale gray jacket and black skirt. One hand rests atop a leopard bag; the other brandishes a cigarette. Dahl-Wolfe has shaded the grays of the jacket and the black of the skirt to harmonize with the weathered boards of the building Vreeland is leaning against. The slatted wood awning overhead casts shadows that she has lined up with the horizontal planes of the building's plank construction. The two points of color are the mint jabot at Vreeland's throat, which is echoed in the pale greenish blue of the sky, and her red gloves, a hue that also appears in the rusty lettering of the building's sign. The harmonious colors and the exquisite balance of the composition suggest an Impressionist painting, but the subject is pure Americana. Across from this photo, an introductory paragraph describes Arizona as a place where "every phrase, every gesture, has color. It's a land not only to bring things to, but to brings things back from . . . this is the way all fashion is born."[96] There's no byline, but the sentiment is Vreeland through and through.

The behind-the-scenes photos that Dahl-Wolfe and her assistant took in Arizona show something of how the shoot came together. There's one of Vreeland dressing for the film set shot with the help of Barrington, who's wearing shorts and a bandeau top fashioned from a scarf, a concession to the high temperatures they were working in. In another, Vreeland, her plaid trousers rolled up above her knees, adjusts Barrington's scarf-draped head while Dahl-Wolfe, her back to the camera, gestures at them. She was taking the cover shot. In reality, the scarf and oversized sunglasses Barrington wore, which are the only items of clothing visible in the final crop, were a pale sky blue. But during the printing process, Dahl-Wolfe changed the color of the accessories to a gray-tinged cream and made the sky a deep indigo, an amped-up contrast that magnified the dramatic impact of the image. This and Barrington's pose—she's clutching the scarf under her chin with both hands, which emphasizes the size and shape of the bug-eyed sunglasses—give this photo an undercurrent of strangeness that is pure high fashion. The accompanying caption provides context: "She gazes straight into the sun through her smoked lenses. No makeup, no artifice, just a dash of bonfire red across her lips."[97] If it isn't quite true to life, it's true to the feeling that Dahl-Wolfe and Vreeland sought to convey.

Although they continued to work together, "Flight to the Valley of the Sun" was the last shoot of its kind that Dahl-Wolfe and Vreeland collaborated on for several years. Shortly after it was completed, Japan attacked Pearl Harbor and the United States entered the war. *Bazaar*, like other magazines, had to trim its budget and shift its content to suit the tenor of the times. But whether the two were shooting in Brazil (where they traveled in 1946), in Dahl-Wolfe's New York studio, or at her country house in Frenchtown, New Jersey, they remained constant to their vision of the American Look. Their depictions of ready-to-wear, a category of fashion that had previously been regarded as inferior to haute couture, gave it historic and cultural context and set a new standard for uncontrived elegance. Before them, Avedon said, "American style, as we know it, did not exist."[98]

Photos that Dahl-Wolfe and Vreeland took of Bacall continued to appear in *Bazaar* even after she left for Hollywood, underlining the role the magazine had played in her success. Bacall had become known for "The Look," in which she lowered her chin and gazed seductively upward, a variation on the sultry expression she wore on the Red Cross cover (although she always maintained she did it to keep her head from trembling with nervousness during her first scenes with Bogart). Grateful for the incredible career boost *Bazaar* had given her, Bacall returned to pose for Vreeland and Dahl-Wolfe even after she was well-known enough to have her name in the photo caption, or even the headline. For the April 1945 issue, the pair photographed her wearing two very understated evening looks, both consisting of a long, sarong-style patterned silk skirt and a sweater "plain as an undershirt."[99] In these ensembles, Sally Kirkland of *Life* magazine wrote four decades after the photos were taken, the actress was "the fashion editor's choice for the American Look of the '40s which still looks right today as Bacall does."[100]

By the time Bacall made this appearance in *Bazaar*, Paris had been liberated. In New York's fashion industry, as in the rest of the world, the joy felt on Liberation Day, August 25, 1944, was immense. Lord & Taylor hung a sign in its windows exulting, "Paris Is Free!" *The New York Times* wrote that American designers expressed "fervent hope" that the city would soon be back to normal.[101] But the delight and relief were tempered by the knowledge that New York designers would soon have to compete directly with their Paris colleagues for the attention of both the press and consumers. Many in the American fashion industry wondered if all the gains of the past five years would be lost. By October, *The New York Times* was reporting that the French were eager to resume the transatlantic fashion trade and were waiting only for reliable transportation to do so. Had the dresses, hats, suits, and gloves started arriving in the port of New York that month, their value would have amounted to $400 million, a significant sum for a country emerging from a lengthy and debilitating occupation.[102] In the absence of Paris, one writer observed, "Seventh Avenue's garment district became 'Seventh Heaven' for the designers. But how long can heaven last?"[103] The American Look was about to come up against the French Legend.

9

Sportswear Is Universal

New York and Paris

The position we've acquired as the fashion center we intend
to hold, and not even a peace treaty can take it away from us.

—FIORELLO LA GUARDIA[1]

Paris, December 23, 1944

The employees of the Hôtel Westminster regarded the tiny, frail-
looking woman who stood before them with astonishment. Coal
shortages meant that the hotel's electrical supply had been cut off
for the night, but even in the gloom of the lobby, Carmel Snow was
an unmistakable sight. Clad in a tailored suit, a hat perched on her
blue-tinted curls, the editor in chief of *Harper's Bazaar* looked as
though she had just alighted from a chauffeur-driven car. In fact,
she had walked through the dark, silent streets from the Métro, her
first ever foray into public transportation, in the last leg of an epic,
multi-week journey. Snow had been a frequent guest in the days
before the German occupation, but the idea that she might appear

at the front desk while the Allies were still fighting their way across France was so fantastic that even if a transatlantic cable had reached the hotel with the news of her arrival—telegrams between North America and Europe remained highly erratic—it would have been disregarded as fiction. The staff were deeply moved that she had risked her life to come to Paris. Each had the same tearful greeting for their new guest: "Permit me to embrace you."[2] The Westminster had, appropriately enough, been commandeered by the British military, and Snow was obliged to make do with a room in the annex rather than her usual suite.[3] But she was back in the city that had always felt like home.

Snow had begun plotting her return practically the moment Paris was liberated. She was determined not to let *Vogue*, which had boots on the ground in the form of a Paris edition and a French staff, scoop her on what she was certain was the biggest story of her career: the first comprehensive reporting on Paris fashion since 1940. She'd managed to get Lee Carson, a war correspondent for Hearst's International News Service (which was run by Eleanor Lambert's husband, Seymour Berkson) to write a piece for the October issue—given the printing schedules of monthly publications, this was the earliest it could be slotted in—but despite the story's optimistic title, "Preview of Paris Collections," it didn't contain a single photograph.[4] Edna Woolman Chase, meanwhile, had access to the work of Lee Miller, the American model turned photographer turned war correspondent who worked for British *Vogue*. Miller's reportage on the liberation of Paris had been published in American *Vogue*'s October 15 issue, and included a few street-style photos, one of the only glimpses its readers had seen of what Parisiennes were wearing for four years.[5] Along with Alison Settle of the London paper *The Observer*, Miller was the first foreign fashion journalist to enter Paris.[6] But Miller was embedded with the

American military and Settle had only to cross the Channel—Snow traveled thousands of miles to get her story.

Both Snow and Chase expanded their Paris coverage in their November issues. *Bazaar* had a wider array of photos, but *Vogue* had gotten hold of a Schiaparelli hat that an American army officer bought in Paris and sent to his wife in Philadelphia, who altruistically passed it on to a local boutique for copying. Modeling the striped pink turban in *Vogue* was Elsa Schiaparelli herself. Although her Paris couture house continued to function under the leadership of one of her staff, Schiaparelli had returned to New York in the spring of 1941.[7] "First Hat from Free Paris" expressed all the pent-up excitement that *Vogue*'s editors felt at the prospect of reengaging with their favorite couturiers. Despite the enormous gains made by American designers during the four preceding years, Snow and Chase, along with many other top fashion journalists, still regarded Paris as fashion's standard-bearer. Like addicts who'd been forced to quit cold turkey, proximity to the opiate of the haute couture rendered them powerless. Both women were impatient to know what the couturiers had been up to in their long imprisonment—and each was maneuvering to get the scoop first.

Snow, however, had an ace up her well-tailored sleeve: a former employee who was married to President Franklin Roosevelt's closest adviser, Harry Hopkins. This was Louise "Louie" Macy, the *Bazaar* editor who had distributed medical supplies and food to the refugees who flooded into Paris in May 1940 before escorting nineteen-year-old Gogo Schiaparelli, Elsa's daughter, to safety in New York. Macy was just the sort of glamorous staff member Snow loved. She was vivacious and charismatic, and she followed up a string of distinguished "beaux" with what her former boss would have called a "good" marriage. When she left *Bazaar* to wed Hopkins in July 1942, *Bazaar* ran a portrait of the bride and her new stepdaughter.[8] The marriage dropped Macy into the very center of the executive branch: Hopkins was judged so important by Roosevelt that the couple actually lived in the Lincoln Bedroom, just steps from the Oval Office. But despite her new status and her job as what *Bazaar* deemed "probably the country's most famous nurse's aide"[9]—Louise Dahl-Wolfe had photographed her for the Red Cross recruiting poster—Macy remained a devoted style hound.[10] When Hopkins had all his decaying teeth pulled out, she reportedly took the gold fillings to Fulco di Verdura, the Italian jeweler who designed Chanel's Maltese cross cuffs, and had them turned into earrings.[11] One of the few people immune to Macy's charms was Winston Churchill, who considered her a bad influence on FDR because she encouraged his love of martinis.[12]

Within days of Paris's liberation, Snow had tracked Macy down at Maine Chance, Elizabeth Arden's pioneering beauty resort in Prescott, Maine, where wealthy women of the era went to indulge in treatments like the Ardena bath, in which a guest's body was encased in several pounds of melted paraffin wax, a procedure that promised to "reach down to the very roots of your nerves to free them from tenseness and fatigue."[13] Snow's letter explained that she had applied to the Immigration and Naturalization Service (INS) to go to France as a war correspondent—an image that deserves a moment of contemplation—and begged Macy to prevail on Hopkins to fast-track her request. She cautioned Macy to be discreet, lest *Vogue* hear what she was up to and try to get there before her. Macy scribbled "What do you think Honey" across the top of the letter and passed it along to Hopkins.[14]

Snow had hoped to be on her way by October 1, but Roosevelt was running for reelection, and Hopkins was reluctant to assist with a frivolous-sounding appeal that might reflect badly on the president. She nevertheless continued to badger the couple, at one point even forwarding Macy a copy of an ad *Vogue* was running in various publications trumpeting the reopening of its Paris office, a development that was gall and wormwood to Snow.[15] When Hopkins wrote that he'd like to give Macy bound copies of all the issues of *Bazaar* she had worked on for Christmas, Snow assured him it would be "a joy" to collect them for him.[16] All through the fall of 1944, Snow kept up the flattery and pressure. Finally, Roosevelt was safely elected, and Snow received her clearance to go.

She left New York on December 7, 1944. At that point in the war, anyone who could possibly avoid flying over the North Atlantic did so; it was simply too dangerous. Instead, Snow took a remarkably circuitous route that, in the days of prop planes and frequent crashes, was still notable for its danger. She called it her "greatest adventure."[17] From New York she flew to Miami, where she climbed on board a plane bound for Trinidad. From Trinidad she took off for Caracas, then winged her way across the South Atlantic to Dakar. In Dakar, she boarded a flight to Lisbon, and then journeyed on to Madrid, where she arrived on December 16, the first day of the Ardennes Offensive. In Madrid, Snow paused for a few days to sleep in a real bed, attend Mass, and see Cristóbal Balenciaga, who gave her a box of chocolates and escorted her on a shopping expedition to the flea market.[18] Spiritually refreshed, she then boarded a train to Bordeaux, ensuring she had a seat by slipping a hundred-franc note to the French conductor who joined the train after it crossed through the Pyrenees and into France. In Bordeaux, she transferred to another train, again bribing a railway official, this time for a seat in a second-class carriage. The train was so full that, as on her last trip to Paris in January 1940, it was impossible to reach either the toilet or the dining car.[19] Unperturbed, Snow pulled out Balenciaga's present and encouraged her traveling companions to help themselves. They didn't need to be asked twice—it was the first taste of chocolate they'd had in four years. Finally, twenty-four hours after she'd left Madrid and sixteen days after she'd left New York, Snow's train pulled into the Gare de Lyon. A Citroën worker she'd befriended on the journey carried her bags and escorted her to the Métro. The famous lights were dimmed, and it was raining and eerily quiet, Snow noted, "but the smell of Paris!"[20]

Although she was overjoyed to be back, it was immediately clear to Snow that the city she loved had suffered. Food, previously a highlight of any sojourn in Paris, was scarce and unappealing. Snow was awakened by roosters crowing—enterprising Parisians had taken to keeping chickens in their apartments to supplement their scanty rations.[21] When her breakfast tray arrived, she was horrified by the coffee, which "tasted like nothing I ever drank before."[22] (She must have missed the WWD story published a few days before she left that advised visitors to Paris to bring their own coffee, as well as soap and cigarettes).[23] The grayish bread, served with no butter but a daub of jam, she left for visitors like Janet Flanner, the New Yorker correspondent who moonlighted for Bazaar. Flanner headed straight to the tray when she arrived in the morning and polished off every morsel. In wartime, hunger trumped good manners.

Parisians weren't just hungry in the winter of 1944; they were cold. Homes, shops, and offices were unheated. Hotels provided hot water for bathing only on Friday and Saturday mornings and switched their electricity off between five P.M. and eight thirty A.M.[24] When Snow went to order a suit that she called "my one splurge" at Balenciaga, her fitter's hands were so swollen by chilblains that she kept dropping the pins. Finally, she apologized, "I regret, Madame, my hands used to be so quick, but now, you understand, they don't seem to work as they used to."[25] Parisians looked poor and shabby, Snow thought, but she saw moments of levity, too. One day she watched the young seamstresses from Schiaparelli having a snowball fight with American GIs in the Place Vendôme, "all of them laughing, flirting, singing . . . a delightful scene."[26]

Although Snow had come to Paris to report on fashion, almost the first thing she did after arriving was get back on a train. She was bound for Sarrebourg in Lorraine, as close to the front lines as one could get at the time, with the photographer Henri Cartier-Bresson, whom she had hired to shoot a story on the Red Cross. It was an important project for Snow, who had worked for the Red Cross in Paris during World War I, and whose niece and name-sake, Carmel White, was doing the same in the current conflict. Cartier-Bresson's photos, accompanied by text written by Flanner from Snow's notes, appeared in the March 1945 issue of *Bazaar*, and showed American soldiers at the front.[27] The May issue featured more of Cartier-Bresson's photos, these showing the high-stakes evacuation of British soldiers following Operation Market Garden, the Allied plan to capture bridges in the German-occupied Netherlands. The plan failed, and the British suffered terrible losses.[28]

Although it seems incongruous for a fashion magazine to report from combat zones, World War II was such an all-encompassing event that it touched almost everyone on the planet. In this context, no publication could ignore what was happening. *Vogue*, too, printed its share of war photography and commentary, including Miller's shots of the newly liberated Buchenwald, a scene she described with white-hot rage.[29] Chase hesitated before publishing Miller's photos, but in the end, reasoning that the wealthy and sophisticated were as bereft as everyone else, she did. "Anguish knows no barriers," she wrote.[30]

Five New York–based *Vogue* editors saw the war up close, as Red Cross workers and war correspondents, including Bettina Wilson and Sally Kirkland. For the *Vogue* Paris staff, World War II was horrific. The sons of both the editor in chief, Michel de Brunhoff, and the fashion editor, Solange d'Ayen, were killed, the former murdered by the Gestapo and the latter in an accident as he tried to join the Resistance. D'Ayen herself was taken prisoner by the Gestapo and held in solitary confinement for three months in the notorious Fresnes Prison.[31] She was released, but her husband, who, unbeknownst to her, had been held in the same prison, later died in Bergen-Belsen. D'Ayen emerged from prison malnourished, "blown up like a balloon," and disfigured by sores on her face and legs. But ever the fashion editor, she told Bettina Wilson that the beige jersey Balenciaga dress she wore throughout "looked very well" after it was cleaned.[32] As terrifying as d'Ayen's ordeal had been, she herself came through relatively unscathed. Many others suffered far worse. Élisabeth de Rothschild, the estranged wife of a scion of the French banking family, changed her seat at a Schiaparelli fashion show rather than sit next to Madame Otto Abetz, the wife of the German ambassador to Vichy. She was deported and sent to Ravensbrück, where she died of typhoid.[33]

Wilson reached Paris on December 26, 1944, just days after Snow made her dramatic arrival at the Westminster. She was on leave from her job running Red Cross rest camps for officers in Cannes and felt that involving herself in *Vogue* activities would be unethical, but upon learning that Snow was also in town, "spreading good will for *Harper's Bazaar* as she proclaimed her faith in French fashion," tribal loyalty kicked in, and she was soon reporting to Chase about goings-on around town.[34] *Bazaar* and *Vogue* were once again in direct competition to cover Paris.

In some ways, Wilson reflected, nothing in fashion had changed. Her friends still wanted to talk about hats and clothes and exchange fashion-world gossip, and would travel any distance for a party, although they were now obliged to take the Métro or ride their bikes—there was no fuel for private cars.[35] But although a copy of the luxury magazine *Album de la Mode du Figaro* (edited by *Vogue*'s de Brunhoff and produced secretly in Monte Carlo) had been smuggled out of Europe the year previously and had given Wilson and Snow an inkling of what was going on in Paris fashion, neither was prepared for the clothes that were being worn that winter in Paris.[36]

Unlike the sleek, trim aesthetic of the nascent American Look, Paris fashion had evolved during the occupation into an uneasy mix of unwieldy proportions and spurious detail. Rounded shoulders were enlarged to gigantic widths, with shoulder pads that the French called "les americains"; huge sleeves were gathered into tight wristbands; dresses were liberally strewn with asymmetrical draping, pleating, and bows; jackets had long peplums; and skirts were short and swingy. Among the tiny minority who could afford it (i.e., less than 1 percent of Frenchwomen), this look came straight from the diminished output of the haute couture workshops. Everyone else cobbled together facsimiles from worn-out men's suits and coats or old curtains, the only material available. In the winter, women piled on everything they owned in an often futile attempt to keep warm. Mending had become a minor art form—Snow noted that Parisians' clothes were "exquisitely darned."[37] And of course, as in every country the Nazis conquered, Jews were forced to wear a yellow star on their left breast pockets, sewn on tightly enough, *Vogue* reported, that an SS man would be unable to poke a pencil between the stitches.[38]

Most noticeable to the Americans visiting wartime Paris were the enormous, elaborate hats that fashion journalists struggled to align with their cherished notions of Gallic good taste. Snow told milliners point-blank that their designs, some of which soared a foot in the air and relied on wood bases for support, were "dread-ful," although she excused them on the grounds that they "re-flected the confusion of the mind and spirit that the French had been through."[39] For Schiaparelli, the "incredible horror" of these hats represented a Paris that had retained a sense of humor despite all that it had suffered and was purposely putting up a provocative front. She interpreted preposterous millinery as a political state-ment, something akin to the pink pussy hats of 2017 or the *poufs* of the eighteenth century. As one fashion worker later said, she and her friends were prepared to suffer any indignity, to go without food and soap, but "we wouldn't look shabby and worn out. After all, we were *parisiennes*."[40]

Almost equally startling were the vertiginous clogs that were a common sight on Paris streets, a consequence of the near disap-pearance of leather. In 1939, France had produced approximately eight to ten million pairs of leather shoes; in 1941, six million of these pairs were requisitioned by the Germans.[41] When electric-ity was switched off every evening in shops and offices and work-ers started for home, Snow wrote, the air filled with the sound of wooden soles striking paving stones.[42] During the winter, those who could afford it had their clogs lined with either rabbit or cat fur, the only varieties available. Everyone else made do with straw.

A few examples of Paris haute couture had trickled into the United States during the war, notably when the actress wife of the famed French aviator Dieudonné Costes arrived in New York in the summer of 1943. Madame Costes's clothes, designed by cou-turiers such as Maggy Rouff and Madame Grès, were disparaged as showing vulgar "Berlin taste" and were unfavorably contrasted with the fashions of American designers.[43] But this was nothing compared with the outcry that followed when photos of postlib-eration Paris began appearing in newspapers and magazines in the

United States and elsewhere in August and September of 1944. Amid punishing wartime rations, readers were flabbergasted by the excessive use of fabric—and angry. The British, who had been fighting the Nazis since 1939 and had endured relentless civilian bombing, were especially outraged; *Picture Post*, the UK equivalent of *Life*, described them as "Fashions for Traitors."[44] Virginia Pope was less hyperbolic, but her restrained criticism is all the more chilling: The French, she wrote, were out of step with the times.[45]

The story took on such momentum that at the October meeting of the Fashion Group in New York City—themed "Fashion at International Crossroads"—Mildred Smolze of the *Tobe Report* expressed dismay at how negatively Paris fashions were being portrayed in the popular press. The public had been given the false impression that the French were not taking the war seriously, she argued, something that American women with husbands, sons, and fathers fighting in Europe would understandably resent. Furthermore, it was unfair to judge the French, who had lived through the harrowing experience of the occupation. "It is almost an insult," Smolze continued, "to offer fashions conceived under these circumstances to the very fashion-conscious American public."[46]

The profound divergence of French and Allied fashions was due to the very different attitudes from which they emerged. In countries with a less entrenched fashion tradition, utility—the name the British gave their government-decreed clothing—superseded flair. Americans, like the citizens of other Allied nations, proudly conserved fabric to aid the war effort, and regarded waste as unpatriotic. Despite the entreaties of her colleagues in France, Edna Woolman Chase had refused to publish images of the haute couture during the war. For her, anything produced under Nazi rule was tainted.[47] Meanwhile, the French perspective was that to continue to be flagrantly fashionable was to continue to be French—it demonstrated defiance, not capitulation. A national calamity was not an excuse for abandoning style. They interpreted extravagance as both a strike against the hated occupiers—a yard of fabric used by the couturiers was one denied to the Germans—and a point of pride. As for what defined fashion, that was their purview; it was one area in which France remained undefeated. The top-heavy shoulders, garish embellishments, and ludicrous hats were intended to make the wives of Nazi officials look ridiculous, explained Lucien Lelong, the head of the couturiers' union. The Germans, he told Wilson, had such an inferiority complex "that almost anything could be put over on them." [48]

In fact, the situation was more nuanced than that. Less than 1 percent of couture clients during the occupation were German.[49] Some were newly enriched collaborators or black marketeers— "the most dreadful woman in the world," said Snow—while many others were longtime customers who had remained in Paris.[50] And while a subset of couturiers were staunchly opposed to the occupation—like Madame Grès, who presented a collection in the colors of the French flag that led to the shutdown of her house— others were acquiescent. Jacques Fath and his wife, for example, were photographed attending Nazi receptions.[51] Most notoriously, Chanel, whose views had always been right-wing, closed her *maison de couture* in 1940, and took a German lover, the diplomat and possible spy Hans von Dincklage. She attempted to use anti-Jewish laws to take control of her financially successful perfume business from Pierre and Paul Wertheimer, brothers who had run it since the mid-1920s, and was even involved in a plot to persuade Churchill to come to a peace agreement with Hitler, a mad scheme that was named Operation Modellhut by the Nazis.[52] In September 1944, a few weeks after Paris was freed, she packed her bags and had her chauffeur drive her to Lausanne, Switzerland, where she remained in self-imposed exile until 1952.[53]

With the fall of the Vichy government, a united France was once again fully on the side of the Allies, and American authorities were anxious to promote positive relations between the two countries. They attempted to censor news about the startling new fashions, but the images leaked out. Via his contacts in the American press, Lelong was given the opportunity to defend himself and his peers. In its November 15 issue, *Vogue*, which was just as eager to resolve the issue as the couturiers, published an open letter from Lelong in which he explained that the French had no idea that citizens of the Allied countries were subject to clothes rationing. He had fought to keep the haute couture alive, and its workers employed so that they would not be sent as forced laborers to Germany. The couturiers were now designing mainly simple, practical clothes, he continued, and only indulged their whims for evening dresses to prove they hadn't lost their touch (furthermore, these gowns, Lelong hastened to add, would be sold only to the wives of diplomats from the neutral countries of Spain, Portugal, Switzerland, and Sweden). His wish, he told *Vogue* readers, was to "preserve for La Haute Couture Parisienne the place it has always had in the eyes of the world."[54] He concluded by saying that he hoped the friendly business relationships that had been so helpful to both France and the United States would soon resume. Lelong had cast himself as the preserver of the French Legend.

When the Germans captured Paris in 1940, they, too, believed in the French Legend (though they also had their nationalist detractors who protested against the "diktat" of Paris).[55] One of the first things that German soldiers, who benefited from the favorable exchange rate instituted by the new military government, did was go shopping for their wives and girlfriends. To the annoyance of Parisians, they cleared the shops of silk stockings, lingerie, perfume, shoes, warm sweaters—anything with a Paris label. Some even brought photos of the intended recipient so that saleswomen could estimate sizes.[56]

The true extent of the Nazi preoccupation with the French Legend became clear a few weeks later. Like the *New York Times* correspondent who wrote the impassioned acclamation of Paris, the invading Germans revered the city's cultural heritage—so much so that they planned to claim it for themselves. In late July 1940, five German officers showed up at 102 rue du Faubourg Saint-Honoré, the headquarters of the Chambre Syndicale de la Couture Parisienne. This visit was polite. A few days later, they returned, forced their way in, and carried off all the records pertaining to overseas buyers.[57] Lelong had assumed the Nazis would shut the haute couture down—and indeed, many couturiers, having reached the same conclusion, had already fled the city. Instead, Lelong learned that their intention was quite different: The Nazis wanted to move the haute couture to Berlin and Vienna. Their plan was to establish a school in Berlin where skilled French workers would train students in all the roles necessary to staff a couture house. When he refused to assist with this scheme, Lelong was ordered to the German capital to meet with officials there, the first of fourteen meetings he would have with them.

There, Lelong argued that fashion was an expression of national culture. If the Germans wanted a fashion industry of their own, they would have to nurture it themselves. The Parisian haute couture, Lelong insisted, could not be uprooted; either it remained in situ or it died. "It is not within the power of any nation to steal fashion creativity," he told his German hosts.[58]

The Nazis backed down from their demand that the haute couture be relocated, but they continued to harass Lelong. Materials were curtailed, and those who wished to purchase couture had to register with the military government (on the other hand, couture customers had to give up only fifteen of their one hundred annual clothing ration points to buy an entire seasonal wardrobe; those on more limited budgets had to spend thirty points to buy one new suit and were required to turn in a used one).[59] On four separate occasions, the Nazis announced that all couture houses would be shut down, and once, they even demanded that 80 percent of haute couture workers be reemployed in war industries that benefited the Reich.[60] Using delays and obfuscations, Lelong repeatedly put the Nazis off. In the end, only 3 percent of workers were reemployed; the remaining 12,000 continued to work for the one hundred or so couture houses that were still in operation in August 1944.[61]

In saving the haute couture, Lelong was not just preserving French culture, but ensuring his country's postwar recovery. Fashion was central to the French economy: The export of one haute couture dress generated enough money to buy ten tons of coal; a single liter of perfume, two tons of petrol.[62] For France to flourish again, it was imperative that the French Legend remained intact.

Back in New York, the fashion press had begun reporting on the liberation of Paris even before it happened. On August 11, *WWD* described how in the Garment District people were watching "mile by mile" as the Allies advanced on the French capital. The writer of the piece was Winifred Ovitte, the same journalist who had rallied the industry behind American designers in 1940. Now she was describing how "all are eager to pass into a cycle where the inspiration that is Paris will animate design and stimulate business."[63] For the die-hard Francophiles, that was certainly the case. But many had warmed to the idea of New York as an international fashion center. The riposte to Ovitte's piece, first published in the official magazine of the International Ladies Garment Workers Union in August and then quoted in *The New York Times* on September 2, articulated the countervailing desire to move on from the old ways. While "we have a lot to learn from the way Paris worked," the writer acknowledged, American designers "have little need for its antiquated inspirations, resorts, racetracks, fashion magazine vignettes, salons, and their chit-chat of the 100 leading families." [64]

Still, both *Vogue* and *Harper's Bazaar* resumed their coverage of Paris. In January 1945, *Vogue* put the extreme fashions of the French in the context of the "bravado" with which "German restrictions" and "Kraut regulations" were met. Readers were assured that this fashion cycle was over, and the new one would be more suitable. [65] Writing about the spring 1946 collections, Snow reminded readers of the challenges that the French people continued to face. "Everything is so difficult—the shops aren't heated, the workers are undernourished, the political situation is very tense." But Paris was beginning to turn the corner, she said, and "the tradition of French dressmaking is in full bloom." [66]

Snow finally returned to New York in mid-March 1945. She had been in France for three months, walking miles every day to do the rounds of the couture houses and assure them of *Bazaar*'s continued support. At night, she fell into bed so tired that for the first time in years she slept without the need of pills. [67] Her route home was less circuitous than her continent-hopping outbound journey, but still perilous. She took the train to Cherbourg, then a passenger ship across the North Atlantic, an undertaking then slightly safer than it had been a few weeks previously. Snow described the crossing as calm to her family, mentioning only in passing the frequent detonation of depth bombs that were aimed by Allied destroyers at German submarines. She was far more bothered by the cockroaches that skittered out of the drawer she was allotted in the crowded stateroom she shared with five other women and opted not to unpack her bags.[68]

Wilson was discharged from the Red Cross in the summer of 1945. Chase had been pestering the organization's head for weeks, asking him to release Wilson from duty so she could return to her position at *Vogue*. She hitched a ride back home in a B-17 bomber that was stippled with flak holes, arriving in Washington, DC, just two days before the Nazis surrendered. When she appeared at the *Vogue* tea party that had been organized to welcome her back a few days later, Chase's first words to her were "Now, Bettina, dear, why do you wear your hair so long? It really doesn't suit your long, thin face."[69]

Although Wilson initially returned to *Vogue*'s French office, she found postwar Paris discouraging. Everyone seemed to want to reconstruct their frivolous prewar lifestyles, a prospect that no longer captivated her. After a summer in Paris, she transferred to the New York office, where she covered the American market. Although she thought sportswear designers made "charming casual clothes," Wilson disliked what she called the "covered wagon" quality of American fashion, which she considered an overblown story.[70] At the same time, she conceded, "Paris fashion was not at its most brilliant after the war. There was a certain lethargy about the couture, and none of the prewar stars were showing great leadership."[71]

Couturiers had moved away from the style of the occupation years, and a sense of unease about these fashions, and what they represented, lingered for decades. It was still a touchy subject in 1971, when Yves Saint Laurent, who had been a child during the war years, created a collection he called "Libération" inspired by the clothes he remembered his mother wearing during that period. It's now considered one of his seminal collections, and helped kick off an interest in vintage clothing that persists to this day. But the reaction in France was harsh—no one wanted to be reminded of that time in the country's history. The impression lingered that even if the couturiers had protected their employees, they had been, as the fashion historian Lou Taylor commented, fiddlers at work while Rome burned.[72] Lelong, who had been the public face of the couture during the occupation and the immediate postwar period and had undeniably ensured its survival, was never regarded in the same way again. He was accused of collaboration—in fact, he had hidden Jewish workers—and although he was acquitted, his health was shattered by his wartime experiences. In 1948, on the advice of his doctor, he closed his *maison de couture* down permanently. Although many couture names have been resurrected in the past two decades, the House of Lelong remains buried in the past.

Postliberation, the haute couture faced both practical and aesthetic challenges. The most fundamental tool of their trade, fabric, remained vanishingly scarce: French textile production in 1944 was just 14 percent of prewar totals, and much of what was made was of poor quality.[73] The lethargy Wilson described resulted in aimless collections that earned lackluster reviews.[74] And postwar inflation drove prices up to three times their prewar levels.[75]

In desperation, the couturiers organized a traveling exhibition, the Théâtre de la Mode, or the Fashion Theater. Well-known artists, including the fashion illustrator Bébé Bérard, created twelve sets representing scenes from Paris life. These were inhabited by more than two hundred quarter-sized wire dolls dressed in exquisitely stitched, scaled-down versions of haute couture fashions. Like the fashion dolls of the seventeenth century, they were sent abroad as ambassadors for French fashion, with all profits from the exhibition going to charity.[76] The tactic worked: After the Théâtre de la Mode made its American debut in 1946, buyers resumed placing orders.

But it wasn't until 1947 that the haute couture was able to inspire the thrill that journalists and buyers remembered from the prewar years. On February 12 of that year, Christian Dior, whose couture house had recently opened, showed his first collection. Insiders had been aware of him as an up-and-coming talent: In a 1946 report to the Fashion Group, Snow had urged her audience to go to Paris to see Dior's work at the House of Lelong, where he was employed as a designer.[77] Wilson also encountered Dior chez Lelong and was treated to an illicit preview of the 1947 collection by Dior's friend Bérard, who sketched it for her on a bistro tablecloth.[78] Sitting in her front-row seat a few days later waiting for his show to begin, Wilson felt an "electric tension." When the first model stepped out, swirling a skirt so long and heavy that she sent the ashtrays on the tables by the runway clattering to the floor, Wilson knew that the future of the haute couture was assured.[79] Word got around that women in the audience that day were tugging their skirts down over their knees; the opulence of Dior's designs made them feel suddenly underdressed. It was "the collection that knocked out the entire world," exclaimed the new French magazine *Elle*.[80] "God help the buyers who bought before they saw this," a fashion pundit told *Life*. "It changes everything."[81]

But it was Snow who gave Dior's collection the name by which it would be known: the New Look.[82] When she got back to the office wearing the suit she had ordered from Dior, the first garment from his new couture house that any of the staff had seen in person, her editors mobbed her. "Carmel, it's divine!" Diana Vreeland rhapsodized as she examined Snow's tightly fitted, slope-shouldered jacket and full skirt. "It makes you look drowned."[83] Summarizing Dior's collection for the Fashion Group a few weeks later, Snow was no less hyperbolic. "Dior saved Paris as Paris was saved in the Battle of the Marne," she announced.[84] He had safeguarded not just Paris, but the French Legend. The New Look would dominate fashion well into the next decade.

For those who could read the signs, the New Look—with its hyperfeminine combination of rigidly tailored bodices, tightly fitted waists, padded hips, and enormous skirts that ate up yards of fabric (Dior was backed by Marcel Boussac, the textile king of France, so he could use as much material as he needed)—had been a considerable time in the making. After seven years of padded shoulders and shortish skirts, it was past time for the fashion pendulum to swing. Dior, who fondly remembered the clothes his mother and grandmother had worn during his Edwardian childhood, had been experimenting with elements of the New Look since before the war, when he had worked for the couturier Robert Piguet. In November 1941, *Bazaar* had published a photo of a longer skirt, the kind Diana Vreeland was partial to, with the caption "If it looks right to you . . . you're a woman of the future."[85] And for the past few years, Snow had observed her daughters and their friends pulling their belts to the very last hole to achieve a wasp waist, an effect that she experienced herself at a couture fitting in 1946, when the fitter pulled the measuring tape around her waist so tightly that she apologized, "Forgive me, Madame, if it martyrizes you."[86] But for the general public, the New Look was an abrupt rupture. Dior had swept away the wide-shouldered, short-skirted silhouette of the war years and replaced it with one that recalled the corseted hourglass form of the nineteenth century—the term "New Look" was more of a misnomer than an accurate description, one that led *Time* to observe a few years later that Paris still designed for lives of "Veblenesque leisure."[87]

Indeed, it required formidable foundation garments of the sort Lois Long had scoffed at in 1939. She was one of the few fashion journalists to regard Dior, a shy, sensitive man who was uncomfortable in the spotlight, with a jaded eye. To most he was, as one fashion expert told *Time* magazine, the "Atlas holding up the entire French fashion industry."[88] Long described her colleagues' infatuation with this "new darling" as "schoolgirl crushes," and although she was sympathetic to Dior's position, writing that she was sure he must feel terrific pressure to follow up the unprecedented success of his debut, she was skeptical of the New Look.[89] To Long, it was backward-looking, the antithesis of the fashions that had emerged in the United States during the war years. American women, she wrote, did not lead the "static life" of the clotheshorses that the haute couture was still designing for—they needed clothes they could move in, and she urged the country's designers to stick to creating the unfussy attire that they excelled at.[90]

Long was not alone in her suspicion of the New Look. In Dallas, a housewife named Mrs. Warren J. Woodward founded the Little Below the Knee Club. "I don't feel like throwing out my entire wardrobe and I thought a lot of women might feel the same way," she told *WWD*.[91] She was correct: Membership swelled to three hundred thousand women who picketed dress shops around the country.[92] Sometimes they were joined by the League of Broke Husbands.[93] But the protests fizzled out after about a year—the New Look was a sartorial juggernaut.[94] Most American designers created some version of it, albeit with an easier fit than the original. Despite Dior's observation that "I know very well the women," not many Americans were prepared to suffer the rigors of a boned corselet, no matter how often *Vogue* and *Harper's Bazaar* breezily touted their benefits. Sophie Gimbel, the in-house designer at Saks Fifth Avenue, tried one on and almost immediately took it off again, saying, "I've never been so uncomfortable in my life."[95]

Before the war, the leading Paris couturiers had been women. But because so many couture houses, including that of Madeleine

Vionnet, closed during the occupation, this dynamic was upended: Postwar, the successful couturiers were almost all men. The clothes they designed, while beautiful, were not created with the same intimate understanding of fit and comfort that a woman designing for other women brought to her work. Christian Dior did not just change the fashionable silhouette of the day; he reinvigorated the model of the male couturier as omnipotent dictator that Worth had patented and, with it, the tired old trope that women fell into step with whatever designers told them to do. The American press supported this perception, publishing stories with titles like "That Friend of Your Wife's Called Dior."[96]

But in New York, female designers continued to play an important role in the industry, creating clothes that allowed for freedom of movement and an independent lifestyle. Foremost among them was Claire McCardell, who ignored the New Look altogether (Betty Friedan's profile of her, published when McCardell was at the height of her fame, was titled "The Gal Who Defied Dior").[97] She thought the New Look's rigid fit contrary to her form-meets-function creed, and carried on designing the clothes she thought women really wanted. Her skirts were calf-length but light, and she continued to leave it up to her customers to decide how tightly they wanted to cinch their waists. But she resented the assumption that the success of the New Look meant that Paris was once again in control. After hearing a radio broadcast that questioned the ability of American designers to compete with the newly revived haute couture, she fumed in her private journal, "Are we returning to the dark ages when American designers were not allowed to think for themselves?"[98]

McCardell had articulated the fear that was uppermost in the minds of American designers and their supporters. But unlike earlier champions of American design, they now had proof, in the form of four years of sales and accolades, that Paris wasn't necessary to create good fashion. In the same talk in which she defended the couturiers against negative press coverage, Mildred Smolze of the *Tobe Report* acknowledged that there would be a postwar rush to see what was going on in Paris. But she doubted that Americans would find anything in Paris that they couldn't find at home. Of the city's protracted reign as the center of fashion, she said, only half was due to actual design talent—the other half was the allure of Paris.[99] The latter was no longer a given—the war had blown up the political and social factors that had made the city the global capital of culture and recast the United States as a much bigger player on the international stage. Moreover, air travel would soon make the world more accessible. Instead of one fashion capital, Smolze predicted, there would be many, including London and New York. There was no reason to squander the leadership position American fashion had achieved. New York had everything Paris used to have "except antiquity of culture," Smolze argued. "We have political prestige, money, international playgrounds, the best music, and more famous artists, writers and musicians than have ever congregated in one country before."[100] It was a perceptive dismantling of the French Legend.

What mattered now, Smolze concluded, was that retailers and the press continued to support American designers. Even Valentina, who had never been much of a team player, gave this notion her support. Although she was unable to attend that meeting of the Fashion Group, she sent a statement. American magazines, she wrote, needed to cover American designers the same way they did the French, by acknowledging that they had the same power to create trends.[101] The New York fashion world would always have its Paris acolytes. But Smolze and Valentina made their entreaties to an audience whose perception of American fashion had been radically transformed in a relatively brief time. By 1944, even die-hard Francophiles recognized that it was no longer a given that Paris was the leader and New York the follower; a new paradigm had emerged, of partner fashion centers, each with their own set of skills. Designers who worked for large brands were still often anonymous, but there was a growing group who enjoyed brand-name recognition.

Even *Vogue* and *Bazaar*, whose editors still pined for Paris, agreed that American designers could now stand shoulder to shoulder with the couturiers. The spring 1944 fashions were so self-assured, observed one *Vogue* writer, that she interpreted them as "a hopeful sign for American fashion independence after the war."[102] For a magazine that had once expressed the opinion that American fashion was a concept beyond the pale, this was a dizzying concession.

When Snow traveled to Paris in December 1944, she took with her six months' worth of *Harper's Bazaar*, which she proudly showed to the couturiers she met with and was gratified to hear their praise of the fashion they saw in them.[103] And although she had vowed to "do my best to help revive the fashion industry in France," Snow published a robust defense of American fashion in the October 1944 issue of *Bazaar*, the same one that had carried the first style news from postliberation Paris.[104] *Bazaar*'s argument echoed that of the rationale Lelong used to keep the haute couture going—that the "frugal modesty and dignity" of American fashion reflected the country in which it was made. Referencing pioneer women, the Old West, workmen's overalls, and the futuristic garb of superheroes, the magazine's writer contended that these were the clothes that best suited "the modern American girl."[105]

New York fashion emerged from World War II with a much clearer sense of its strengths than it had in 1940. For one thing, the

sizing issues that had exasperated Elizabeth Hawes had largely been
resolved, thanks to the War Production Board, which had sponsored the measuring of one hundred thousand American women.
The resulting standardized measurements gave ready-to-wear designers the ability to create clothes in graduated sizes for a variety
of body types and provided them with such detailed information
that the exactness of their fits approached that of made-to-order.[106]
This made it possible to produce ready-to-wear that impressed even
the French. When a delegation of French retailers visited Saks Fifth
Avenue in 1947, they marveled at the quality and variety of the
ready-to-wear merchandise and pronounced the store "a temple of
smartness." The accuracy of the sizing was wonderful, they told
WWD, as was the possibility of offering a woman everything she
needed in one store, something that did not exist in France.[107] Production values were so high that by the late 1940s, Paris couturiers
were following the lead of American made-to-order designers and
launching their own ready-to-wear lines. Dior founded Christian
Dior–New York in 1948, a ready-to-wear collection that, in a tacit
acknowledgment of the excellence of American mass manufacturing, was produced in Manhattan's Garment District.[108]

New York had produced stylish, well-made clothing before the
war. What the absence of Paris had done was make this evident.
Now, even with Paris once again ascendant, American designers
continued to create the types of clothes that their customers had
grown to consider indispensable. "America's love for separates grew
even more in this time as 'do-it-yourself' types eschewed French
copies in favor of buying one or two longer skirts and playing
around with various tops and accessories for their own New Look,
easy to manage and vary with the occasion," observed Sally Kirkland.[109] American women now had their choice of what style to em-
ulate: the prescribed look of Paris or the DIY ethos of sportswear.

Although the change didn't happen overnight, in the end separates just made more sense.

It was not just the French who were enthusiastic about American fashion. In 1945, the Australian-British journalist Madge Garland wrote a piece for the British edition of *Harper's Bazaar* in which she extolled the "beautiful and interesting" clothes she found in the United States.[110] No one made better casual clothing, she added. Garland mentioned no designer by name, explaining they would be meaningless to British readers, but the fashions used to illustrate her article, photographed by Louise Dahl-Wolfe, include designs by McCardell and Potter.

Gazing out from one photo is Slim Hawks, a half smile on her face, her hands tucked into the pockets of her knee-length shorts. Garland did not use Dorothy Shaver's term "American Look," but it was essentially what she was talking about. Hawks, along with her protégée Lauren Bacall, exemplified it, but it was embodied by women all over the United States. The American girl had become a type, just like the chic Parisienne. And in doing so, she gave American fashion another means of creating a distinct identity.

The idea of the American Look and the American girl, which had been launched by Shaver's 1945 promotional campaign for Lord & Taylor and given a major boost by *Life*'s coverage, were well-established concepts by the second half of the decade, used by advertisers to sell everything from cosmetics[111] and shoes[112] to motor oil.[113] *Look* magazine, a rival to *Life*, published an American Look diet and exercise plan booklet that readers could order. *Look*'s editors compared the American Look's influence to the Marshall Plan, the initiative to provide foreign aid to postwar Western Europe, and claimed that "the whole world" wanted to copy it.[114] After touring Europe in 1949, Lambert reached a similar conclusion, telling a journalist that it was now the French who copied American fashions, and that in Britain, where clothes rationing had ended just one year previously, women couldn't get enough American pullovers and skirts.[115]

Fashion journalists spent the war years patriotically boosting American design. But once Paris was liberated and the French were no longer *hors de combat*, it became necessary to define what set a New York– or California-designed dress apart from one that originated in a couture salon. The obvious answer was that the former was (usually) mass-produced while the latter was made-to-order. Concealed in this self-evident assessment was the answer: American fashion was modern. As Smolze had pointed out in her Fashion Group talk in 1944, New York had everything required to be a fashion center except a tradition of cultural leadership—a handicap she suggested was quickly changing. Why not, then, capitalize on what the city *did* have, and position it as a positive? Couture was slow and conservative. It was the past. Mass production was innovative and bold. It was the future.

"Modern" was used to describe not just the way American fashion was produced, but its attitude and its customer, the "modern American girl" identified by *Harper's Bazaar* in 1943. In a February 1946 piece titled "American Modern," *Vogue* laid out its tenets: a sophisticated use of humble fabrics, the pairing of high and low elements, and a preponderance of separates that a customer could personalize. Wool jersey was modern, as was wearing thong sandals with gold jewelry and a sweater and pulling a look together from a selection of separates.[116] In a *Bazaar* piece from June 1945, modern was identified as a machine that could cut out thousands of identical dresses that a thousand different women would each make her own.[117] Designers claimed the label for themselves. Sydney Wragge, a sportswear leader who designed as B. H. Wragge, titled an ad for his fall 1946 collection "American Modern," and designated himself the "maestro of the coordinated wardrobe."[118] By 1959, this style of dressing—mixing and matching from a selection of separates—was described as "universal" by Vera Maxwell, a celebrated sportswear designer and contemporary of McCardell's, in an interview she gave to *WWD*. It could be worn anywhere in the world, Maxwell said, for almost any daytime activity.[119] It was the backbone of the modern wardrobe.

In Europe, the seeds of this fashion coup had been sown even before the war was over. Starting in 1943, American factories turned out simple, streamlined clothes for the newly liberated people of Europe. Designed to be made quickly and fit anyone who needed it, this clothing would, said *Life*, "make [Europeans] look like Americans."[120] Italy had been the cradle of the Renaissance and the birthplace of fashion and had long been known as a center of textile and leather goods production. But it had no real status as a fashion center. Before World War II, it had couturiers—who, like couturiers everywhere, copied Paris—but no industrial manufacturing of clothing. Moreover, the country's economy had been crushed by the war. That changed when money and aid from the Marshall Plan began to pour into the country. Using the American template of progressive manufacturing techniques, Italy reinvented itself as fashion center in an amazingly short space of time.[121] Italian fashion was eagerly snapped up by American consumers, who identified with its ease and admired its cultural bona fides. Within just a few decades, Milan, like New York, was regarded as one of the world's fashion capitals. The reputation of both cities rests on ready-to-wear.

Parisian couture continued to make headlines—Dior, in particular received the sort of coverage that heads of state or wars did—and the years 1947 to 1957 are referred to as "the Golden Age of couture."[122] The dates reference the launch of the New Look and

Dior's death, of a sudden heart attack, at the age of fifty-two. The House of Dior was taken over by his assistant, twenty-one-year-old Yves Saint Laurent, who was then still known as Yves Mathieu-Saint-Laurent. In his brief tenure at Dior, Saint Laurent introduced such non-couture references as black leather jackets inspired by the students of the Left Bank, an innovation that horrified the *maison*'s conservative clientele.

Saint Laurent launched his own couture house in 1962, to which he added Rive Gauche, his ready-to-wear line, in 1966. Named for the Left Bank of the Seine, the student quarter where he first saw the casual attire that inspired him, Rive Gauche marked the first time a couturier successfully launched a full ready-to-wear line in France (in fact, Lucien Lelong had dabbled in ready-to-wear in the 1930s, with a capsule collection he called Édition, a fact that might be better known were his *maison* ever to be revived). The boutique looked nothing like Saint Laurent's couture house in a former *hôtel particulier*, which was painted stark white and furnished in a restrained modernist style. Rive Gauche was housed in an old bakery and had an Orientalist, haute bohemian vibe: The walls and ceiling were lacquer red, the lighting was low, and clothes were hung casually on the walls. The ambiance was more nightclub than dress shop.[123] Within a few weeks of the September 19 opening, it had become a center of French youth culture.[124] When Saint Laurent opened stores in New York in 1968 and London in 1969, he was greeted like a star, with mobs clamoring for a glimpse of him. Bacall came to the New York opening, posing for the paparazzi in one of Saint Laurent's black jersey jumpsuits (when she was asked by one photographer who had designed it, she retorted, "Of course it's Saint Laurent. When it's pants, it's Yves's").[125] The New York and London boutiques were followed by one in Milan. Miuccia

Prada, who was then a student, remembers rushing as soon as it opened and buying a pink, puff-sleeved dress.[126]

The generally held view is that Rive Gauche was a watered-down version of Saint Laurent's couture collection. In fact, the opposite was true. With Rive Gauche, Saint Laurent was free of the traditional expectations of haute couture; he could experiment. And his audience was more receptive to new ideas: Although women were still barred from wearing trousers in most jobs and many public spaces in 1966, one of the best-selling items in the first Rive Gauche collection was a pantsuit—which Catherine Deneuve bought on the boutique's opening day. Saint Laurent had shown a few in his previous couture collection, but they had not made much of an impression. Emboldened by the ready-to-wear success, he sent pantsuits back down his couture runway for his spring 1967 show, this time playing up their masculine associations by having the models wear ties and fedoras, which were counterbalanced with high heels, seductive makeup, and masses of jewelry. He called the new jackets he designed for these suits "*les smokings*," the French term for a tuxedo.[127] The *smoking* became a symbol of the new freedoms women were claiming, and an instantly recognizable—and much copied—Saint Laurent signature.

Although he continued to produce haute couture collections, Rive Gauche became Saint Laurent's creative workshop. In 1971, the designer made his position clear when he told a French television journalist, "I have chosen to present my fashion through my ready-to-wear collection rather than through my haute couture."[128]

Two years after this interview was broadcast, it would become clear just how influential ready-to-wear could be.

10

The Battle of Versailles

Ready-to-Wear and Haute Couture

It was a five-star war. And Eleanor Lambert won.

—JOE EULA[1]

Versailles was crumbling. Louis XIV's preferred residence, from which his ambition to transform France into the world's preeminent luxury brand was disseminated, had begun to decline after the revolution, when its contents were sold at auction and the buildings allowed to slide into disrepair. By the time Gérald Van der Kemp arrived at Versailles to take a job as an assistant curator just after World War II, the rooms were bare, the staircases were near collapse, and rain poured through the roof and into the basements through rotted-out floors.[2] He tackled his work with such zeal that by 1953, he was appointed the palace's chief curator-cum-restorer.

Van der Kemp had already proven himself a dedicated protector of France's national treasures. He had been an assistant curator at the Louvre, which he joined in 1936. When World War II began, he served in the army, was captured at Dunkirk, and escaped, walking 125 miles in two days, a feat that left him with a permanent limp. He was then sent to the Château de Valençay in central France, where the Louvre had secreted away its valuables, including the *Mona Lisa*, for safekeeping. Van der Kemp became the painting's personal guardian; he even slept next to it. When a German officer, seeking retaliation after a number of his men were killed by the Resistance, threatened to burn the château to the ground with the *Mona Lisa* inside and shoot Van der Kemp, the young curator dissuaded him. Hitler, he told the officer, would never forgive the man who committed such an egregious act of cultural vandalism.[3] At the war's end, Van der Kemp personally carried Leonardo da Vinci's masterpiece back into the Louvre.[4]

By 1973, Van der Kemp had managed to rid the palace of its large rat population and had led a global hunt to identify and purchase the palace's lost treasures. What couldn't be bought he had reproduced, often at considerable expense. At the time, the French government, still ambivalent about the country's royalist past, contributed the equivalent of a few thousand dollars a year toward the upkeep of this symbol of the Ancien Régime.[5] This meant that Van der Kemp, with the aid of his American second wife, Florence Harris, a former Washington, DC, society columnist, was obliged to tap private citizens for funds. They occupied the same twenty-one-room apartment at Versailles that Jean-Baptiste Colbert had lived in—in a sense, Van der Kemp was once again sleeping with the valuables entrusted to him. "His theory is that you must always be hitting the small nail on the head if you want to accomplish anything," explained Harris.[6] The couple often hosted dinner parties at which they courted prospective donors, many of them wealthy Americans. The latter were invariably impressed by Van der Kemp, a tall, cultivated man with an aquiline nose who always sported a fresh boutonniere and identified strongly with Louis XIV.[7] Harris complemented his patrician charm with her American warmth and casualness; she sometimes used one of the palace's antique chamber pots as a gravy boat.[8]

In the summer of 1973, the Van der Kemps found themselves lounging poolside with Eleanor Lambert at La Fiorentina, the Riviera estate of the Australian-born Lady Kenmare.[9] Lambert knew of the restoration efforts at Versailles, and casually announced that she had an idea. It was a crazy idea, she warned, but she thought it might raise the kind of money Van der Kemp needed. Still in search of another $60 million to address issues like the termites that had colonized Versailles's woodwork, he readily took the bait.[10] What was it, he asked?

Lambert proposed that Van der Kemp host a fashion show at Versailles—but with an unexpected twist. Instead of having only French designers present their collections, she proposed that an equal number of American designers also participate. They could bill it as an evening of fun for deep-pocketed patrons of the arts and sell tickets. She'd be happy to handle the publicity, and she suggested that Baroness Marie-Hélène de Rothschild, the queen of Paris hostesses, organize the festivities.

Van der Kemp responded enthusiastically.[11] He offered the Royal Opera, also known as the Théâtre Gabriel, which had been built by the master architect Ange-Jacques Gabriel in 1770 for the wedding celebrations of the future Louis XVI and Marie Antoinette, as the venue, a suggestion that French president Georges Pompidou quickly agreed to.[12] The evening of November 28, 1973, was selected for what was christened, using the French word for entertainment, the Grand Divertissement à Versailles. But in New

York, it became known by the name given to it by *WWD*: the Battle of Versailles.[13]

To Lambert, it was the biggest opportunity of her career. Since her earliest days as a fashion publicist, she had been determined to show the world that American designers were just as worthy of acclaim as Parisian couturiers. Every one of her achievements had been calculated to enhance their status. The New York Dress Institute, the International Best-Dressed List, and National Press Week were merely the early stages of this quest. Beginning in the 1950s, Lambert had organized American fashion shows all over the world, even traveling to Moscow in 1959 for an American exhibition at the behest of President Dwight Eisenhower.[14] In 1962, she had created the Council of Fashion Designers of America (CFDA), which, unlike the old manufacturer-oriented NYDI, put the needs of designers first. The following year, she testified before the US Senate, successfully arguing that fashion should be recognized as an art form, an accomplishment that meant that the CFDA would receive financial support from the recently created National Endowment for the Arts.[15] In 1968, she staged the only fashion show ever held at the White House, a red, white, and blue extravaganza called "How to Discover America in Style."[16]

Lambert had taken American designers out of the back rooms where they had been confined and given them recognition—her client Bill Blass, who had once told people that he was in advertising rather than admit to being in fashion, was now a celebrity who appeared in his own ads and chummed around with his upper-class clients.[17] But she had hesitated to put them into direct competition with their French counterparts. The timing and the occasion, she knew, must be perfect. As the 1960s gave way to the 1970s, she judged that the moment had arrived.

A number of factors had aligned to support Lambert's decision. Most important, haute couture had been in decline for years, a victim of more casual lifestyles and a viable alternative in the form of upscale ready-to-wear. The numbers were telling: Just after World War II, there had been approximately fifteen thousand haute couture customers; by the early 1970s, only three thousand remained.[18] The tipping point came when Cristóbal Balenciaga closed his house down in 1968 without naming a successor. The man whom Christian Dior had called "the master of us all" recognized that his trade had become irrelevant. When he died in 1972, *WWD* covered the news under the headline "The King Is Dead."[19]

To the young, however, Balenciaga had been passé for years. As an art student in the 1950s, Barbara Hulanicki, who would go on to found London's era-defining fashion retailer Biba, remembered wondering when she would be old enough "to cope with all that elegance." Her generation considered Balenciaga's dresses too structured and stiff to have any appeal. He lacked humor, Hulanicki thought—"but I suppose Paris fashion has no humor."[20] Her designs for Biba were deliberately tongue-in-cheek, inspired by children's clothing and the vintage fashion popularized by films such as *Bonnie and Clyde* (1967) and *The Garden of the Finzi-Continis* (1970), and executed in the moody plums, greens, and browns of a fresh bruise. With its low prices, willowy fits, and tiny sizes, Biba, like much of 1960s fashion, was for teenagers and women in their early twenties, a skyrocketing demographic that had little interest in costly, made-to-order clothing.

A cruel dismissal of haute couture and the women who wore it was emblematic of the new emphasis on youth. Couture was for "face-lifted old hags," the author of an advice book sniped, adding, "When you're over seventy you need props."[21] Even the French had lost their respect for the work of the *grands couturiers*. When Coco

Chanel offered to dress Brigitte Bardot, the actress demurred with a bored "Couture is for grannies." By the early 1970s, an economic downturn and a tense political climate further depressed haute couture sales: Oil prices were sky-high globally, Watergate and antiwar protests roiled the United States, strikes and work stoppages ground industry to a halt in Britain, and terrorism and kidnappings across Europe all made the rich leery of displaying their wealth too ostentatiously.

Few designers understood this better than Roy Halston Frowick, who dropped his first and last names and became simply Halston. Originally from Indiana, he had begun his career as a milliner in Chicago before taking a job at Bergdorf Goodman, where he created the pillbox hat Jackie Kennedy wore to her husband's inauguration. When hat sales declined, he switched to clothing. After showing his first made-to-order collection in 1968, he told *WWD* that he couldn't imagine doing anything as old-fashioned as beads and ball gowns, adding, "I really don't want the collection to look like couture."[22] Instead, he created soft, unlined, easy-to-wear pieces in luxurious fabrics that felt like a caress on the skin, a concept he expanded to ready-to-wear the following year. Today, we would call it "stealth wealth." At the time, Halston's combination of sensuousness and practicality, coupled with his fondness for trousers, was hailed as the modern way to dress. By 1970, *Vogue* was calling him a "super source of fashion," a designer who knew "what we want, and should have, to wear."[23]

Lambert, who had been following his career since his pillbox days, regarded Halston as a unique talent, not unlike Claire McCardell, whose streamlined aesthetic and "revolutionary" tag he shared.[24] As the nickname that *WWD* bestowed on him, Mr. Clean, implied, he was the purest example of the uncomplicated American approach to fashion. Moreover, just as McCardell had been, he was tapped into the culture, translating the unfettered, anything-goes mood of the times into clothes that were unabashedly sensual yet simple (or at least simple-seeming—like McCardell, Halston was a master technician). This lack of pretense, Lambert recognized, was the great strength of American fashion. Halston, an original talent who was uninfluenced by Paris, was its ablest practitioner, but there was a critical mass of others who were also creating inventive, modern, well-made ready-to-wear. With Halston as her anchor, Lambert decided it was finally time to go head-to-head with the haute couture.

In contrast to the pared-back approach of the Americans, the French, she was confident, would veer toward their default lavishness, an outcome she all but guaranteed by suggesting that de Rothschild organize the event. A stylish blonde who was imposing rather than beautiful, the former Marie-Hélène van Zuylen had married into one of the largest family fortunes ever amassed. She and her husband, Baron Guy de Rothschild, were famous for hedonistic gatherings like their mauve-tinted Proust Ball of 1971 and their Surrealist Ball of 1972. Held at their sumptuous home outside Paris, the eighty-bedroom Château de Ferrières, the latter featured fur-clad servants pretending to be cats, an interactive maze, and tables decorated with taxidermized tortoises and disassembled dolls. As the queen of the evening, Marie-Hélène wore an enormous stag's-head mask designed by Salvador Dalí complete with antlers and real diamond teardrops.[25] Rather like Marie Antoinette, the de Rothschilds knew no limits. If you gave Marie-Hélène de Rothschild $1 million, Lambert believed, she would spend $2 million.[26]

France had a number of strong prêt-à-porter designers in 1973, many of them women, like the press favorites Sonia Rykiel, Gaby Aghion of Chloé, and Emmanuelle Khanh. They catered to a young, fashion-forward clientele who couldn't have afforded haute couture even if they had any interest in it. But ready-to-wear was still considered second-class to couture. De Rothschild, an haute couture client, insisted that only couturiers be allowed to participate in the Battle of Versailles, a decision that effectively made the French team entirely male. As it happened, every one of the anointed five— Yves Saint Laurent, Marc Bohan of Dior, Hubert de Givenchy, Pierre Cardin, and Emanuel Ungaro—had successful ready-to-wear lines. For Versailles, however, they would exclusively show haute couture.

Accompanying Halston to Paris were Anne Klein, Bill Blass, Oscar de la Renta, and Stephen Burrows; all five were Lambert clients. A graduate of the Traphagen School, Klein had started working as a freelance sketcher on Seventh Avenue when she was just fifteen.[27] Small and slender herself, she had shaken up the petites market, which had previously assumed all short women were stout, with sleek designs scaled to fit smaller frames. In 1968, she and her second husband, Chip Rubinstein, had founded Anne Klein Inc., which specialized in smart but lighthearted clothes for working women. She focused on separates and encouraged her customers to buy different sizes in tops and bottoms if they needed to—a groundbreaking concept at the time.[28] She was accompanied to Versailles by her husband and her young assistant, a six-months-pregnant Donna Karan. Unbeknownst to anyone but Rubinstein, Klein was ill with the breast cancer that would kill her four months later.

Blass had also started his career as a sketcher, arriving in Manhattan's Garment District fresh from Indiana in 1939, when he was seventeen. Blond, handsome, and perma-tanned, he immersed himself fully in the role of American sophisticate. Both his conversation and his designs had the jaunty flair of a Cole Porter lyric: He liked sharp tailoring, upscale interpretations of WASPy stalwarts like twin sets, and Golden Age of Hollywood glamour. His society clients adored him. In 1970, he had bought out the Seventh Avenue manufacturer where he'd worked since 1959 and renamed it Bill Blass Limited.[29]

The debonair Oscar de le Renta was born in the Dominican Republic in 1932, trained under Balenciaga in Spain (he also began as a sketcher) and Antonio del Castillo at Lanvin-Castillo in Paris, and was renowned for his pretty, ladylike clothes, often rendered in bright, zesty colors. His aim, he often said, was to make a woman feel beautiful. He and his French-born wife, Françoise, were a modish couple who entertained constantly. Like Blass, de la Renta bought the manufacturer he worked for, and renamed it for himself, in 1965.

At thirty, Stephen Burrows was both the youngest participant, and the only Black one. Earlier that year he had won a Coty Award, the first Black designer to do so, but was so new to mainstream fashion that when Lambert invited him to Versailles he wasn't even her client yet, an omission she soon rectified. His pieced jersey dresses, tops, and skirts were cut to fit like a second skin. Burrows's signature flourish was a curly "lettuce" hem—the name came courtesy of Diana Vreeland—a production error that he turned into an asset.[30]

Behind the scenes there was the inevitable drama. Halston had recently sold his company to Norton Simon Inc. and was enjoying the perks of sudden wealth. His already healthy ego had ballooned—he had begun referring to himself in the third person, a trait he had in common with Elsa Schiaparelli—and he was reluctant to share billing with his competitors. When Lambert first approached him, he turned her down. But as the press around Versailles began to heat up, he changed his mind, telling *WWD* that while he was, of course, extremely busy, it had turned into such a big deal that he'd decided to go.[31]

Klein, on the other hand, was enthusiastic from the beginning—in her estimation, she more than deserved her spot—but was rejected by the French, who objected to her "commercial" aesthetic. Lambert was adamant that a woman designer be included and considered Klein the ideal choice. She refused to back down. In the end, it was de la Renta, whose wife had once been editor in chief of Paris *Vogue*, who persuaded the French to agree to her participation. "We're *all* ready-to-wear," he told Pierre Bergé, Saint Laurent's business partner. "She's an important part of our industry."[32]

As November approached, de Rothschild briskly took charge of drumming up donations, asking that guests give in units of $10,000. Tickets were priced at $235, a detail that the press seized on as emblematic of the frivolousness of hosting a fashion show in the middle of an energy crisis caused by the OPEC oil embargo.[33] The French committee, headed by the Duchesse de Brissac, included such luminaries as André Malraux, the former minister of culture—a sign of the seriousness with which fashion was regarded in France. The American committee, headed by the socialite C. Z. Guest after Jackie Onassis bowed out, citing the conflict of her daughter's birthday, consisted almost entirely of ladies who lunched.[34]

As Lambert had predicted, the French were intent on creating a maximalist splash. Jean-Louis Barrault, the famed actor, director, and—cue French joke—mime, had been hired to direct. A headliner at the Comédie-Française in the 1940s, and one of the stars of *Les Enfants du Paradis*, a World War II–era film that is often cited as one of the greatest ever made, Barrault had impeccable credentials. But his references were creaky, and his vision sounded like a parody of Gallic hauteur: a reenactment of one of the court spectacles that had been staged during the time of Marie Antoinette, complete with floats, one for each French designer's segment. When he learned of this detail, Joe Eula, who designed the American set, responded, "Floats? You mean horses making a mess on stage?"[35]

The couturiers were not particularly impressed, either. Bohan, who was given a Cinderella-style pumpkin to build his scene around, muttered, "What the hell am I going to do with a pumpkin?" when he heard the news. Saint Laurent was assigned a 1930s-style elongated roadster float; Givenchy, a flower basket that would descend from the rafters; Ungaro, a gypsy circus cart; and Cardin, a rocket ship.[36] A plethora of celebrities had been invited to share the stage with the couturiers: Josephine Baker, the actresses Danielle Darrieux and Capucine, Jane Birkin, Louis Jourdan, and Rudolf Nureyev. Also in the mix were the nude dancers from the Crazy Horse, the burlesque revue on the avenue Georges V. Music would be provided by a live forty-person orchestra.[37]

The Americans, meanwhile, had Liza Minnelli, fresh from her success as Sally Bowles in the film version of *Cabaret*. For their music, they would use a tape that included prerecorded silences for set changes, which meant that everyone would have to keep time perfectly or what was happening on stage would not align with the soundtrack, a risky strategy that was driven by financial constraints.[38]

The burden of meeting these expectations was borne by the thirty-six models who traveled to France with the American contingent. Ten of them were Black: Billie Blair, Jennifer Brice, Alva Chinn, Pat Cleveland, Norma Jean Darden, Charlene Dash, Bethann Hardison, Barbara Jackson, Ramona Saunders, and Amina Warsuma.[39] Although Lambert had cast Black models as early as the 1940s, women of color were just beginning to gain a foothold in the industry, which meant that their rates were lower than those of well-known white models like Lauren Hutton. The bare-bones budget of the American production worked in their favor. Although there was no variation in body type—all the girls were rail-thin—their presence reflected changing American racial dynamics and the emergence of the Black Is Beautiful movement. The contrast with the overwhelmingly white French models was pointed.

The Americans' single biggest expense was Kay Thompson. She was and is best known as the author of the *Eloise* books, but she'd had a storied career as a vocal coach and choreographer—and, like Lambert, she was also Minnelli's godmother.[40] For a fee of $10,000, she agreed to choreograph the American segment. The entire New York contingent segment cost $50,000, with each designer pitching in between $5,000 and $10,000.[41] Each French designer spent about $30,000 on their portion of the show.[42]

The American set was so simple—just a series of painted fabric panels—that Eula carried it to France in a duffel bag. But when he arrived at Versailles for the rehearsal on November 27, the day before the show, he discovered the panels were much too short—he'd been working in feet instead of meters. With no time to re-create the work he'd done in New York, he unfurled a length of black velvet in the Hall of Mirrors and sketched in a hasty likeness of the Eiffel Tower. In the cavernous Théâtre Gabriel, that was all the Americans had.[43]

Once Thompson and company arrived at Versailles, any preconceptions they had about the refinement and sophistication of France disappeared. The workrooms were primitive. There was no toilet paper, no food, no heating, and seemingly no plan. The French, without consulting their guests, rehearsed first. This left the Americans to wait around, bemused and nervous, as their hosts practiced their convoluted routines.[44] The tension was broken slightly by the arrival of the pixieish Zizi Jeanmaire, one of the most beloved entertainers in France. At that point she was best known for her saucy rendition of a song called "Mon Truc en Plumes," in which she was backed by a bevy of young men wielding large pink ostrich-feather fans.[45] Jeanmaire was dressed both onstage and off by Saint Laurent and was appearing at his request.

For the Americans, however, it was the entrance of Baker that caused the most excitement. For the young Black models in particular, Baker was a powerful symbol. She had left the United States for Paris fifty years earlier to escape racism and had become an international superstar. Now sixty-six, she wore a flesh-colored bodysuit studded with crystals that showed off a figure almost as lithe as it had been in the 1920s. That she was there on behalf of the French designers was an irony not lost on anyone. During a break in the interminable French rehearsal, de la Renta approached Baker and asked if she would join him and the ten Black models for lunch. That meal, said Warsuma, was "the highlight of my life."[46]

The French had so many complicated cues to master and artistic temperaments to manage that by the time they were ready to hand things over to the Americans, it was ten in the evening. Tempers flared when Klein, who was scheduled to go on first and was worried that her unostentatious clothes would be lost in the considerable depths of the Théâtre Gabriel's stage, monopolized Thompson's time with endless questions. Halston, unable to control himself any longer, got into a screaming match with Thompson, who promptly quit. By the time tempers had been soothed, Thompson was reinstated, and Blass's team stepped onto the stage, the electricians announced they were leaving for the night and switched off the lights. Everyone stumbled around in the dark until Rubinstein managed to get Van der Kemp on the phone and begged him to have them turned on again.[47] It was not an auspicious start.

The next evening, Wednesday, November 28, a full moon lit Versailles with a regal glow. The corridor outside the Théâtre Gabriel was illuminated by torches held aloft by helmeted members of the Garde Républicaine.[48] Marie-Hélène de Rothschild, in a low-cut ostrich-feather-trimmed pale green gown by Saint Laurent, diamonds glittering in her thick tresses, greeted the guests as they made their way into the auditorium. She wasn't the only one, in those pre-animal-rights days, who chose to accessorize with feathers— *Vogue* counted so many that "we wondered how the birds were doing."[49] The men wore black tie, and the women were in evening dresses, many made by one of the couturiers presenting a collection that night. One of the most prominent attendees, Princess Grace of Monaco, arrived in a cream-colored Madame Grès gown and red mantle with a ruby-and-diamond necklace around her throat and a matching tiara on her head. Had all the jewelry on display been on the premises the previous night, its collected firepower might have lit up the darkened theater. The sables, minks, and ermines deposited at the coat check could have carpeted the palace's entire ballroom floor, noted one journalist.[50] Keeping a vigilant eye on all the loot were a phalanx of walkie-talkie-carrying plainclothes guards and one hundred footmen in eighteenth-century livery.[51]

The audience of 720 settled into its seats, most of which were not very comfortable—the 1770s version of stadium seating—and a hush fell over the auditorium. De Rothschild stepped out from behind the fleur-de-lis-spangled curtain and announced that the Grand Divertissement had raised $280,000, or the equivalent of almost $2 million today.[52]

The curtain rose, Bohan's unwieldy pumpkin coach was trundled onto the stage, and the French portion of the evening began. Events unfolded at a stately pace. Each designer's segment was interspersed with musical interludes and dramatic readings. The Crazy Horse dancers revolved around the fourteen stripper poles that had been erected for them on stage and flashed glittery G-strings.

"Whether they were couture or not, no one said," deadpanned Enid Nemy of *The New York Times*.[53] Baker sang "J'ai Deux Amours." Two hours after it began, it finally drew to a close.[54] The audience rushed out to the lobby for a drink.

In contemporary reports of Versailles, actual descriptions of the fashion tended to be cursory—the couturiers' clothes, although undoubtedly beautiful, were generally judged a little passé compared with the streamlined simplicity of the ready-to-wear shown by the Americans, much of which just slipped onto the body, without the hooks and myriad buttons of the French. Details were glossed over. Instead, many chroniclers concentrated on the chasm that existed between what Eugenia Sheppard, a widely syndicated columnist and the doyenne of the American fashion press, called the "funereal" French first act and the explosive American second one.[55]

Minnelli ran out onstage in head-to-toe Halston: gray flannel trousers and a camel turtleneck with a contrasting red cardigan draped around her shoulders and a fedora on her head. Behind her, all thirty-six models, wearing shades of beige that ranged from vanilla to brown, pantomimed tourists reacting to their first sight of the Eiffel Tower. Minnelli began to belt out "Bonjour, Paris" from the 1957 film *Funny Face*, in which Thompson had played a delirious fashion editor based on Vreeland ("Never to be discussed," the real Vreeland had told a young editor who accompanied her to a screening).[56] Instantly, the mood in the audience switched from bored to electrified. A chorus of "bravos" began that continued until long after the Americans had left the stage.

Minnelli was followed in quick succession by the segments choreographed by Klein, Burrows, Blass, Halston, and de la Renta. Each designer sent out a zippy twenty looks. The music was loud: rock 'n' roll, soul, Cole Porter, and the soundtrack to Visconti's 1969 film, *The Damned* (still a fashion favorite more than five decades after its release). But it was the models who stole the show. Unlike the elegant but rather static couture mannequins, these girls were trained to really *sell* clothes. Many of the Black models had started out with the Ebony Fashion Fair, a traveling fashion show founded in 1958 by Eunice Johnson, the wife of *Ebony* magazine publisher John H. Johnson. A fashion lover from an early age, Mrs. Johnson regarded dress as a form of Black self-empowerment. She outfitted her models in the most spectacular ensembles she could find, including haute couture, and she encouraged them to be more than just clothes hangers—whether they were in a small-town high school gym or the Kennedy Center, they were exuberant performers who *worked* the runway.[57]

On the Théâtre Gabriel stage, these same models twirled, sashayed, and strutted. At Thompson's insistence, they kept up a relentless pace.[58] For Klein, Barbara Jackson ran toward the audience and kicked up her leg like a Rockette. In the Burrows segment, Pat Cleveland whirled like a top, spinning so fast that it seemed she would career right over the edge of the stage. She stopped just short, hitting her mark perfectly, just as the nonstop soundtrack required. Behind her, a row of models advanced, strode to the edge of the stage, struck a pose, and froze. For Blass, Billie Blair, lit by a single spot on the darkened stage, her hair marcelled so that she looked uncannily like Baker in her Jazz Age heyday, threw back her head and spun with such intensity that, just as planned, the fur coat she wore slid right off her shoulders in one voluptuous slither. Halston, the only one of the designers to have well-known models—Schiaparelli's granddaughter Marisa Berenson, and the "Halstonettes" who accompanied him everywhere—had a more subdued presentation. The models, dressed in sexy, sequined evening gowns, stood stock-still in the pitch dark, came to life as the spotlight hit them, and then froze again. Finally, it was time for de la Renta. For him, Blair played the part of a magician, pulling colored scarves out of her sleeve as models in gossamer confections in matching hues appeared behind her.[59]

Minnelli emerged again for the finale, this time in a 1920s-style beaded black cocktail dress by Halston. She sang the title song from *Cabaret*. Then the models reemerged, wearing black dresses from all the designers, and everyone sang "Au Revoir, Paris," which Thompson had written especially for Versailles.

Thirty-five minutes after Minnelli had first set foot on the stage, the American segment was over.[60] The audience, composed mainly of the cream of French society, a group that had until that evening considered haute couture the only way to dress, roared its approval. Programs flew up into the air. The Americans had come to the birthplace of the French Legend, and they had won. It was the fashion smackdown of the century.

Jacqueline de Ribes, one of the most soignée women in France, rushed backstage to place an order with de la Renta. A French singing star made a beeline for the rack of Blass designs, holding them up against her body to gauge their fit. The French were good, said the Duchesse de la Rochefoucauld, "but the Americans were sensational."[61] Baker, who had lived in France for decades, told a reporter that she was proud to be an American. She sought out Blair, made up to be her double, and put her hand to the young model's face. "I came to Paris in 1925," Baker told her. "And you came to Paris tonight."[62]

Even the dazed couturiers were uncharacteristically enthusiastic. Bohan judged the New Yorkers "perfect." The American clothes "had soul," pronounced Ungaro. "Fabulous," echoed Saint Laurent.[63] They were not praising the clothes, however, as much as they were applauding the performance. Ready-to-wear can never replicate the intricacy and technical wizardry of haute couture, which despite its plummeting clientele remained the barometer by which they judged all fashion. But by 1973, haute couture was old hat. The French had put on a show loaded with allusions to past glories, and it had fallen flat—the only time the audience perked up was when Baker was onstage.[64] The couturiers, Sheppard remarked, had done "everything in their power to confirm that made-to-order fashion is going out of date."[65]

The showmanship of the Americans made an indelible impression on the French designers, not just because it was more energetic and powerful than their own, but because it was so contemporary—it reflected popular culture, not the Ancien Régime. Moreover, the effervescence of the models and their joyous, unfettered movements had perfectly conveyed the comfort and freedom of the best American design. And the mass-produced clothes they wore confirmed the promise of the American industry: that everyone can be beautifully dressed.

It's this promise that made the Americans the victors that night, not the clothes they made. Haute couture is a rarefied craft created for the pleasure of the elite—the woman with the lady's maid whom Elizabeth Hawes expressed such frustration with. Hawes wanted women to break free of the tyranny of perfect chic that haute couture demanded because she knew it was both unnecessary and at odds with modern life. Versailles confirmed what the women who pushed American fashion onto the world stage in the 1940s had known: The French Legend exists only if you accept its premise.

Versailles gave Klein, Burrows, Blass, Halston, and de la Renta a huge boost of confidence. For decades, Paris had overshadowed their industry and their achievements. But that evening they had been the Davids who bested Goliath—they returned home triumphant. Subsequent generations of American designers, who began their careers after haute couture had relinquished its grip on fashion, have not been measured against its standards, nor does anyone expect them to be copyists. Today, ready-to-wear is a $3 trillion business, an amount that is equal to 2 percent of the world's gross domestic product.[66] The tenets that got designers like McCardell labeled as revolutionaries—comfort, ease, practicality—now describe the way we all dress.

Haute couture remains a revered part of France's heritage, but the cultural impact it once had has fizzled. Even its definition is hazy; to many people, "haute couture" simply means expensive designer clothing. There are now only a fraction of the couture clients that existed in 1973, perhaps a couple of hundred, who pay upward of $20,000 for a dress.[67] No one would describe them as fashion leaders—in fact, almost no one outside their circle could identify them. The most interest anyone takes in an haute couture gown is when it appears on a red carpet, worn by a celebrity who was loaned it for the evening.

The global fashion capitals that Mildred Smolze of the *Tobe Report* predicted in 1944 have proliferated. Some have the components—a skilled labor force, a populace interested in fashion, a vibrant art scene, stylish restaurants and nightclubs—that made Paris such a powerful locus of style. But when designers want to prove themselves, they still go to Paris. The French Legend is no longer common currency, though it is by no means vanquished. Bernard Arnault and François-Henri Pinault, the chief executives of LVMH and the Kering Group, the world's two largest luxury conglomerates, use marketing techniques that rely on the same clichés of French taste and savoir faire that have been in circulation for centuries to push their brands, which include Christian Dior, Yves Saint Laurent, and Balenciaga. As long as we continue to believe in them, they'll work.

But what the American designers foresaw at Versailles is now evident to everyone: Fashion is intimately entwined with popular culture, permeating everything from music and film to politics and sports. Contemporaneously, and expedited by social media, it has become far more diverse and welcoming than it once was. In the first installation of a two-part exhibition on American fashion presented by the Costume Institute in 2021 and 2022, *In America: A Lexicon of Fashion*, half of the designers represented were contemporary ones, a cohort that included a greater range of racial and gender identities than any previous Costume Institute show (the second part—the more historic *In America: An Anthology of Fashion*—drew parallels between McCardell and Shaker crafts, underscored the interconnectedness of Hawes's fashion design and her writing, and imagined a literal Battle of Versailles, in which mannequins wearing couture dresses brawled with opponents in mass-made garb).[68]

None of this would have happened without the dissemination of ready-to-wear that began during the 1930s and accelerated during World War II. The democratic vernacular of American fashion—its insistence that comfort coexist with style, its understanding that one item of clothing can perform multiple functions, its trust in the consumer to make her own choices—informs the way we all dress today.

The temporary disappearance of haute couture during the war years was an emergency for the American fashion industry. But it was also an opportunity. The women who ruled Seventh Avenue recognized that opportunity and turned it into a revolution.

AFTERWORD

In the mid-twentieth century, fashion was one of the only industries that offered women the chance to be more than a wife and mother. Although few rose to the heights that Dorothy Shaver, Claire McCardell, or Carmel Snow attained, many found both professional satisfaction and good salaries working as buyers or copywriters for department stores, as clothing or textile designers, or as journalists. Grace Mirabella, who later became editor in chief of *Vogue*, was thrilled to be chosen from thousands of applicants as one of Macy's twenty-five executive trainees after she graduated from Skidmore College in 1950. "I would wear a white flower on my blouse, ride in the executive elevator, and be called 'Miss Mirabella' by salesclerks decades older than I was. I would be paid fifty-seven dollars a week. I was golden," she wrote in her autobiography.[1]

Women like Shaver, McCardell, and Snow were giants in their fields. They wielded enormous influence and commanded respect everywhere they went. And yet they are almost entirely forgotten, their accomplishments lost to history. It's a wrong that I hope this book can begin to redress.

Snow hung on as editor in chief of *Harper's Bazaar* until 1958. During her twenty-four-year reign, she transformed it from a dowdy runner-up to *Vogue* into the most cosmopolitan fashion magazine of its time. Her risky journey to a newly liberated Paris burnished her reputation as an editor who would go to any length to get her story. Under her stewardship, the *Bazaar* of the 1940s and early 1950s was at the peak of excellence. Snow continued to promote new talent, including Richard Avedon, who came to be as important to *Bazaar* as Louise Dahl-Wolfe.

By the mid-1950s, Snow's alcoholism was impairing her ability to do her job. Her fiercely protective staff covered for her. But although she remained at the top of the masthead, a replacement was brought in to take over the day-to-day running of the magazine. The editor selected by Hearst management to take over from Snow was her niece, Nancy White, of whom Vreeland said, "We needed an artist, and they sent us a housepainter." Others were more direct. White, said one outraged editor, was a philistine and a boob.[2] Far more commercially minded than her aunt, White, who'd been the editor in chief of *Good Housekeeping*, which Snow dismissively referred to as "*Good House-cooking*," faced a stony wall of resistance from her new staff.

In 1957, on her last trip to Paris as *Bazaar*'s editor, Snow was demanding and insulting, showing none of the charm that had previously softened her sometimes caustic tongue. At a party at one of the de Rothschild mansions, the still immaculately turned-out Snow was so inebriated that she urinated on the stairs and had to be taken home.[3] December 1957 was the final issue of *Bazaar* in which her name appeared as editor in chief. Shortly thereafter, the magazine began a downward slide.

White's handling of a contretemps involving Truman Capote's novella, *Breakfast at Tiffany's*, illustrated the reality of the new *Bazaar*. Capote, whom Snow had first published in 1945, had expected his latest work to appear in the May 1958 issue.[4] Under Snow's leadership, no one from the business side of the magazine had ever dared to question an editorial decision. White, however, didn't have her aunt's authority. The publishers complained about Capote's use of four-letter words and the lax morals of his heroine, which made White waver. She decided to canvass other retailers regarding their thoughts on Capote's title; predictably, they objected. Capote was pressured to change his manuscript. In the end, *Breakfast at Tiffany's* was cut, and *Bazaar* ended its distinguished history as a publisher of quality fiction.[5] The fashion, too, suffered from White's pedestrian point of view. Snow had published Dahl-Wolfe's sensual photos of Claire McCardell's skin-baring bathing suits; her niece was suspicious if a model in a trench coat had her hands too close to her body.[6]

After Snow left *Bazaar*, "she shrank," said one of her former editors.[7] She tried retiring to Ireland, but she'd outgrown the country of her birth—a local doctor, paying a house call, was outraged by her lacy Paris nightgown and demanded she change into something decent. The friends she thought would stop for a weekend on their way to Paris never materialized.[8] Snow returned to New York, where she and her husband—who had begun drifting apart years earlier—lived almost totally separate lives. She still went to Paris, but without the weight of *Bazaar* behind her, she was ignored, a wrenching experience for a woman who had once reigned supreme over her profession. Her health declined. One of the few things that buoyed Snow's spirits in her final years was working on her memoir with a former *Bazaar* colleague, Mary Louise Aswell. Exactly one week after Aswell had finished interviewing her, on May 7, 1961, Snow died.[9] She was seventy-three. Aswell completed Snow's memoir, *The World of Carmel Snow*, on her own. Her funeral, held at New York's St. Patrick's Cathedral, was attended by every manufacturer in the city's garment industry.[10] A tribute to her, by Janet Flanner, appeared in the July 1961 issue of *Bazaar*. All the legends about Snow, Flanner wrote, were true.[11] In a review of

Penelope Rowlands's 2005 biography of Snow, the fashion critic Cathy Horyn wrote that her version of *Bazaar* "remains a lucid example of what a fashion magazine can be."[12]

Snow outlived her archrival, Edna Woolman Chase, by four years. Chase remained at the helm of *Vogue* until 1952. She, too, wrote her memoirs, titled *Always in Vogue*, working with her daughter, Ilka Chase. It was published three years before Chase died, on March 20, 1957. Although Bettina Wilson, who by then appeared on the masthead as Bettina Ballard, had hoped to succeed her, it was Jessica Daves who was appointed *Vogue*'s new editor. But, like Snow, Chase found it difficult to relinquish the job that had defined three-quarters of her life. She undermined Daves's authority by continuing to attend meetings and voicing endless suggestions and stretched her retirement out until 1954. It was just one of the burdens that the new editor had to contend with. Fatally, Daves had no chic whatsoever. This meant, among other things, that she failed to command the respect of the couturiers, who frequently failed to recognize her and condescended to her when they did. Had anyone ever dared disrespect Chase, she would have frozen the offender with one of her formidable glares. But as fierce as she was, Chase never got over the loss of Snow. In 1945, thirteen years after Snow had left *Vogue* for *Harper's Bazaar*, to the confusion of the recently hired young editor Chase was lunching with, tears poured unchecked down Chase's face as she spoke of her former protégée.[13]

After completing her lecture tour in December 1940, Elsa Schiaparelli had returned to Paris, taking with her one suitcase and thirteen thousand vitamin capsules intended for distribution to the children of France. The latter caused a fracas when her ship docked in Bermuda, where British officials, ignoring the navicert she had obtained, confiscated the vitamins. The issue was resolved, but it established an unlucky precedent. Once in Paris, Schiaparelli faced pressure from all sides: The Germans and Italians mistrusted her because of earlier comments she had made opposing fascism, and the French questioned her loyalty. With some help from American friends in the diplomatic service, she left for New York again in May 1941. Before departing, she had herself legally named president director of her couture business, which continued to operate during the war under the creative direction of Irene Dana. This was a precaution: Her two biggest shareholders were Jewish, and Nazi law stated that Jewish businesses could be seized. When her ship reached Bermuda, she was again questioned by British officials, who wanted to know about her relationship with the Germans and her contacts in the United States. Schiaparelli was free to go, but this incident marked the start of a dossier kept on her by the British Ministry of Economic Warfare that lasted through October 1944. Her reputation sustained further damage a few months later, when she was denounced as a German sympathizer who had used the vitamin incident to stir up anti-British feeling.[14]

The upshot was that Schiaparelli was blacklisted by the British. Payments from her UK perfume business were blocked, and when she applied to do war charity work in Britain, her visa requests were always denied. She never knew the cause of these problems. Compounding her distress was the fact that despite her attempts to safeguard it, her Paris couture house was placed under a German administrator in February 1942.[15]

Schiaparelli returned to Paris in July 1945 and retook control of her business, but she never regained the influence and prestige she had once enjoyed. Her brand of highly individual chic, which had been such a pivotal force in the 1930s, was no longer in demand. In December 1954, she filed for bankruptcy and closed her salon down for good.[16] Earlier that year, her onetime rival, Coco Chanel, had made her return to couture after an absence of fifteen years with a collection of trim cardigan suits that defied the trussed-up silhouette of the New Look. American women were the first fans of what is still considered the signature Chanel statement.

Schiaparelli died in her sleep at her home in Paris on November 13, 1973—just fifteen days before the Battle of Versailles, where the haute couture that she had so valiantly defended was shown to be a relic of an earlier age.

Elizabeth Hawes, who had brought her collection to France four decades earlier, should have been an inspiration for the American designers at Versailles, but she had been so thoroughly banished from the fashion world by 1973 that it's doubtful that any of them had ever heard of her. In fact, Hawes was never able to revive her fashion career after closing her business in 1940. In retrospect, this was a ruinous decision. Had she remained in business, she might be rightly remembered as a seminal American designer. Hawes's forthright opinions had labeled her as a troublemaker, a reputation that became even more entrenched after she stopped designing. She continued to write, even working for the left-leaning daily paper *PM* from 1940 to 1942, where she sprinkled her fashion pages with reminders that the industry was built on the labor of poorly paid workers.[17]

Working as a couturier had made Hawes increasingly conscious that the gulf between her political beliefs and her life experience was vast. Much of the work she did after closing her business was an attempt to rectify this. After leaving *PM*, she took an unskilled job at Wright Aeronautical, the biggest aircraft manufacturer in the world, where she worked the graveyard shift, grinding and polishing engine parts for sixty cents an hour. The job opened her eyes to the realities of working mothers who didn't have maids and nannies and prompted her to question the feminist ideology that she'd imbibed at Vassar, which professed to speak for all women.[18] The book she wrote based on that experience, *Why Women Cry, or Wenches with Wrenches*, published in 1943, concluded that cooperative childcare would benefit everyone,[19] and called for government funding to study women's reproductive health, a topic considered far beyond the pale of polite conversation at the time.[20]

Hawes's time at Wright also gave her an appreciation of the power of unions, which led her to move to Detroit—her marriage to Joseph Losey was over at this point—to work as a United Auto Workers union organizer. The rampant sexism and sexual harassment she saw there were the subject of her next book, *Hurry Up Please It's Time*, whose title she borrowed from T. S. Eliot's *The Waste Land*. Her opinions, on everything from gender relations to childcare, were radical, at least by the standards of the 1940s. She believed that only economically independent women could have equal relationships with men and suggested that if men weren't willing to commit to thirty hours of childcare per week, they shouldn't become fathers.

These views, her stint at *PM*, and her suspected involvement with the Communist Party prompted the FBI to open a file on Hawes in 1940. That J. Edgar Hoover considered a fashion designer worthy of surveillance was not that surprising—the FBI kept files on many Americans with leftist political beliefs—but Hawes's case was particularly tragic. She was conflated with another, even more radical Elizabeth Hawes: Elizabeth Day Hawes, a fellow Vassar alum, who was a labor organizer in the notoriously union-resistant Southern textile mills.[21] It's just one of the many errors in the dossier; even the name of Hawes's first best-selling book was mangled— it's referred to as *Fashion and Spinach*. Friends, acquaintances, and professional connections were interviewed about their association with Hawes, and though their statements were innocuous (one man whose business she patronized, who wisely refused to divulge his name, described her as "a very nice lady"), and the bulk of the file contained only hearsay and rumors, its mere existence in that red-baiting era was disastrous.[22] Hawes opened another dress business in New York in 1948, but even though old customers were still bringing her their suits from the 1930s to remake, she was never able to replicate the success she had known before the war.[23]

She spent the remainder of her life working odd jobs—including, at one point, designing for the bridal firm Priscilla of Boston, one of the worst mismatches in fashion history—and writing more books. She ping-ponged between New York and Saint Croix, in the US Virgin Islands, for several years, which resulted in her 1951 book, *But Say It Politely*, about racism and the hypocrisy of white liberals. She returned to the theme of fashion with her 1954 book, *It's Still Spinach*, but her voice had curdled, becoming more bitter and less funny.[24]

Hawes lived in California for much of the 1960s, designing bright knits with naughty messages encoded in them. There, she befriended Rudi Gernreich, the designer who created the topless "monokini." Gernreich was a generation younger than Hawes, but the two had a lot in common: They both disdained conventional ideas about dress and liked to shake up the status quo. These similarities resulted in the two being paired in a retrospective runway show at the Fashion Institute of Technology in 1967 called *Two Modern Artists of Dress*. An audience of six hundred people who had paid fifteen dollars apiece for their tickets applauded almost continuously during Hawes's portion.[25] *WWD*'s coverage of the show characterized her as "the great rebel of the thirties." The piece ended with an observation that sums up Hawes's life and career: "Rebels are rebels only in their time."[26] But that recognition came too late to make much difference to Hawes. She was by then living in New York's Hotel Chelsea and drinking heavily. She died there on September 6, 1971, never having learned of the FBI file that derailed her life.[27]

In 1953, twenty-one years after Claire McCardell took over as head designer at Townley Frocks, the modern art dealer Frank Perls organized an exhibition of her work at his gallery in Beverly Hills. Instead of showing McCardell's clothes on mannequins, Perls hung them on wire forms suspended from the ceiling—like Calder mobiles, said Sally Kirkland. Perls had first seen one of McCardell's gowns on a woman in his gallery and had been struck by its purity. It looked, he thought, like it came "straight from the Acropolis." It was only after he inquired about it that he learned it was an inexpensive dress designed by an American.[28]

Today, fashion retrospectives are a staple of museum programming, but at the time, it was unheard of—*Look* magazine described it as probably the first one-person show where clothing was exhibited as a work of art.[29] To be acknowledged in this way was an indication of the singular esteem that McCardell inspired. Not to be outdone, both Neiman Marcus and Lord & Taylor, two of her biggest retail accounts, also organized exhibitions in her honor. Two years later, McCardell earned another distinction when she was invited to create a collection using textiles created by the most important artists in the world, including Pablo Picasso and Marc Chagall.[30] In 1956, she published a book, *What Shall I Wear? The What, Where, When, and How Much of Fashion*, in which she outlined her clothes philosophy (one tip: you can't have too many fun coats).[31] For a time, it seemed that her star was endlessly ascendant. Townley made plans to launch a McCardell perfume and, in a move that would have brought her full circle, a line of paper dolls.[32]

Then, in 1957, with no warning, she was diagnosed with cancer. Despite treatment, she became increasingly weak and sick. True to her quietly rebellious nature, she defied doctors' orders and kept going in to Townley. When she became confined to her hospital bed, Adolph Klein asked her old friend Mildred Orrick to assist McCardell with completing what would be her last collection. By January 1958, McCardell could barely stand up by herself. But with Orrick's help, she put on her favorite red denim suit, snuck past the nurses' station, and made her way to the Pierre Hotel in Manhattan for her runway show. The audience of journalists and buyers gave her a standing ovation.[33]

Two months later, on March 22, 1958, at the age of fifty-two, McCardell died. No one was appointed to replace her—there just wasn't anyone else like McCardell. In her memory, Klein gave ten of McCardell's dresses to the Costume Institute and donated her sketches to her alma mater, Parsons.[34] Her family gave her personal wardrobe to the Fashion Institute of Technology. These donations continue to inspire both students and designers.

Marjorie Griswold never stopped championing designers she believed in. By the time she retired from Lord & Taylor in 1970, she had helped to make Gernreich, Bonnie Cashin, Emilio Pucci, and Lilly Pulitzer household names.[35] She died on February 23, 1991, at eighty-four.[36]

Griswold's boss, Dorothy Shaver, continued her policy of innovation at Lord & Taylor, opening five new stores before dying of a stroke on June 28, 1959, at the age of sixty-six. She was working up until the very end: In September 1958, she initiated a "British Fortnight" event at all six branches, thereby anticipating the British Invasion by six years. At the time of her death, she was planning the opening of a seventh Lord & Taylor location, in Washington, DC. News of her demise appeared on the front pages of *The New York Times* and *WWD*, both of which described how she challenged Paris's domination of fashion with her American Fashions campaign.[37]

In an interview with the latter, the display director of Saks Fifth Avenue compared Shaver to Madame Pompadour, another patron of artisans, craftspeople, and writers. Her pallbearers were young Lord & Taylor executives whose careers she had nurtured.[38]

Shaver died before department stores began their extended decline into irrelevancy. As of this writing, the landmark Lord & Taylor building on Fifth Avenue at 38th Street is owned by Amazon, a retailer that has none of the warmth or humanity of the store she led.

Lois Long remained at *The New Yorker* until 1970, forty-five years after her first column was published. No matter what was in vogue, be it the New Look, miniskirts, or jeans, she held fast to her definition of good fashion, insisting on flattering cuts, comfort, and practicality. Her favorite designer of the 1960s was Saint Laurent, whom she dubbed "the Maestro." She was years older than his target customer, but she sensed the timeliness of his designs. When he opened the Rive Gauche boutique on Madison Avenue in 1969, she pronounced it "superb."[39]

A few months after the Rive Gauche column was published, Long had dinner with William Shawn, who had become editor in chief of *The New Yorker* after Harold Ross died in December 1951, and Kennedy Fraser, one of the magazine's up-and-coming writers. They met at the Algonquin Hotel, where, decades earlier, Lambert had encountered Dorothy Parker before they set out for a tattoo parlor on the Bowery. In 1925, Long had been hired to bring a youthful voice to *The New Yorker*. Now sixty-nine, she was being supplanted by a twenty-two-year-old. Her replacement, Fraser, who admitted that her only qualification was her age, favored velvet hot pants and boots. Long still dressed formally, wearing a Lilly Daché hat to type her column. Fraser described her as no longer glamorous; she was an old lady "with pebble glasses and an absurdly large wig" who repeated herself and drank too much.[40]

Shawn cavalierly let Long think that Fraser would consult with her during the handover, while stressing to the younger woman that she should do no such thing.[41] For a magazine renowned for its old-fashioned good manners, it was a harsh dismissal. Joseph Mitchell, a colleague of Long's who had what was perhaps the world's longest case of writer's block, didn't publish a word after 1965, yet drew a *New Yorker* salary until his death in 1996.[42] But Long wrote about fashion, not generally considered a worthy topic for a serious writer. Under Fraser, *The New Yorker*'s fashion coverage became chillier. She regarded it from the slightly perplexed, judgmental distance of one who doesn't like it very much, a stance that made her writing seem weightier than Long's.

Long died four years after leaving *The New Yorker*, on July 29, 1974. With her obituary, *The New York Times* ran a photo of the wrong Lois Long, a fashion designer whom *The New Yorker*'s Long had not cared for.[43] At the party that was held, at Long's request, in lieu of a funeral, the guests agreed that she would have milked that gaffe for all it was worth.[44]

Virginia Pope left *The New York Times* in 1955. She could often be seen at the Metropolitan Opera with a group of her students from the Fashion Institute of Technology—she believed that exposure to culture was as important to fashion design as the ability to drape or intuit trends. She died on January 16, 1978. Her obituary in the *Times* quoted the designer Pauline Trigère, who described Pope as the first journalist to treat fashion as news. Of Pope's *Fashions of the Times* show, the last one of which had been held in 1952, Trigère said, "I was damn proud of being in it. We all were." [45]

Diana Vreeland had hoped to be named Snow's successor at *Bazaar*. But Snow, who had worked with Vreeland for more than a quarter century, was convinced that she could neither stick to a budget nor handle a publishing executive and didn't recommend her (to be fair to Snow, this was not an unusual opinion—Vreeland was famous for her eye, not her business sense). She swallowed the humiliation and stayed on at *Bazaar* until late 1962, when she got the job offer that she had dreamed of: editor in chief of *Vogue*. By January 1963, the dumpy Daves had retired, and Vreeland was in control, with free rein to indulge the wildest excesses of her imagination.

The *Vogue* of the 1960s was a fashion fever dream, a riotous pastiche of royalty, Beautiful People, Dynel hair extensions, haute couture, go-go boots, and face paint—what Vreeland called "the myth of the next reality." [46] The location shoots that she had pioneered with Dahl-Wolfe were now supersized: Like a fashionable offshoot of *National Geographic*, *Vogue* roamed the globe in search of dramatic, difficult-to-reach locales, which were then splashed over twenty-four or more pages in a single issue.

Vreeland's profligacy, as Snow had foreseen, was epic. Discussions of money bored her. She kept drivers waiting for hours, ordered costly reshoots on a whim, and thought nothing of putting photographers, models, fashion editors, and trunks of clothes on long-haul flights to get a single image. Once, she sent the photographer David Bailey and the model Penelope Tree to England for a three-day shoot, only to reject all the photographs. When Bailey demanded to know why, she replied, "Because there's no languor in the lips!" [47]

Vreeland's reign was incredibly glamorous, but it was nerve-racking for her staff. And eventually, it was ruinous. By the early 1970s, Vreeland's baroque vision, all flower children and lamé, was out of touch. In the first quarter of 1971, *Vogue* lost 38 percent of its advertising pages (it was a tough time to run a fashion magazine;

Bazaar's advertising declined almost as much during the same period). Circulation was dropping.[48] Someone had to take the blame. Vreeland was abruptly fired in early 1971, and Mirabella was promoted to editor in chief.

Vreeland was then sixty-eight years old, and no one would have blamed her for retiring. But she required a stage for her gigantic personality. Her beloved Reed had died five years earlier, a day she had marked in her datebook with a heart pierced by an arrow.[49] She was lonely. And she needed an income. In the summer of 1972, she embarked on a new career, as a consultant for the Costume Institute at the Metropolitan Museum of Art. Until this point, the Costume Institute had been something of a sleepy backwater. The twelve exhibitions Vreeland organized, beginning with a magisterial retrospective of Balenciaga's oeuvre in 1973, the year after his death, changed that. Using the pizzazz—a term she's credited with inventing—she'd perfected during her years in magazines, she created displays that, while light on historical accuracy, expertly conveyed the dream of fashion she believed everyone needed. Some transported visitors to a particular place—Imperial Russia, the Austro-Hungarian Empire—while others evoked a period of time, all filtered through Vreeland's rococo lens. The success of her fashion exhibitions spurred countless museums to mount their own.

By 1986, Vreeland's health was failing. She developed macular degeneration, and then emphysema.[50] Her world, which had once been so expansive, telescoped. She died on August 2, 1989. In 1993, the Costume Institute honored her memory with an exhibition of her own: *Diana Vreeland, Immoderate Style*. Her legend has grown with every passing year.

For twenty-two years, Louise Dahl-Wolfe said, *Bazaar* was "heaven." But after Snow and then Alexey Brodovitch resigned, the new art director had the presumption to show up on set and look through her lens, something that had never happened before. "Suddenly my enthusiasm vanished," she said.[51] She continued to work for a few more years, including a six-month stint at *Vogue*, but in 1960, she retired from fashion photography. The reason, she said, was that advertisers had gained too much influence over magazines.[52] She and her husband lived quietly, spending time in Tennessee and at their country house in Frenchtown, New Jersey, a converted creamery that had been the site of many *Bazaar* shoots.

Wolfe predeceased his wife, dying in 1985. Dahl-Wolfe's mourning was intense and tinged with anger. After almost six decades together, she couldn't understand why he had abandoned her. She died four years later, on December 11, 1989, at the age of ninety-four.

Until the advent of digital printing, it was impossible to reproduce prints from Dahl-Wolfe's Kodachrome negatives that resembled the images that had appeared in *Bazaar*—her eye had been so acute that no one else could approximate what she saw. An exhibition of her work was finally made into a coffee-table book in 2000. The curator explained that the shortcomings of technology up until this point were to blame for the delay—that, and the fact that Dahl-Wolfe would have thought such a publication was pretentious and vain.[53]

Eleanor Lambert outlived almost all of her contemporaries, dying on October 7, 2003, in the apartment she had lived in for six decades. Three months earlier, she had celebrated her one hundredth birthday. One month earlier, she had attended New York Fashion Week, an event that would not have existed without her.

At her memorial at the Metropolitan Museum of Art, her grandson Moses Berkson showed a short video he had made of her.

Lambert appeared in the tunic-and-trouser suit that had become her uniform in her later years, a turban on her head. In New York, she said, "every idea gets a hearing. Anything you want to do, you can find someone to listen to you. If no one agrees with you, then you had better get another idea."[54]

ACKNOWLEDGMENTS

Empresses of Seventh Avenue would not exist without the support of a small army of talented individuals.

I am tremendously grateful, as always, to my agent, Stéphanie Abou, and her colleagues at Massie McQuilkin. Thank you for making it possible for me to tell this story.

It has been a dream to work with everyone at St. Martin's Press. I would especially like to thank my editor, Sarah Cantin, who not only read chapters in what seemed like the blink of an eye, but unfailingly knew how to make them better. I truly could not have asked for a better partner. A huge thank-you to Drue VanDuker for remembering every detail and answering every question with patience and good humor. Heartfelt thanks are also due to Mary Beth Constant for her exemplary copy editing and to Michael Storrings for giving *Empresses* such an elegant cover and endpapers. I would be remiss if I didn't thank Jennifer Enderlin, Laura Clark, Lauren Riebs, John Morrone, Ginny Perrin, Diane Dilluvio, Omar Chapa, Katie Bassel, and Michelle Cashman.

Thank you to Lourdes Font for being so unstinting with her time and expertise. Patricia Mears, your encouragement means the world to me—thank you. Thank you also to Mary Gehlhar and Rebecca Matheson.

For their help with research, I would like to thank April Calahan, as well as the librarians at the Gladys Marcus Library at the Fashion Institute of Technology and the New York Public Library. Thank you to Frida McKeon Loyola. And thank you to John Tiffany for generously sharing his memories of working with the one and only Eleanor Lambert.

Tamara Beckwith, thank you for walking around Brooklyn on a decidedly brisk day to take my photo for the dust jacket. And thank you to Aimee, Brian, Pia, and Solenne for the use of their apartment.

Thank you to Kathleen Conkey for legal advice.

Finally, Euan and Francesca, thank you for every day.

NOTES

Introduction

1. Elizabeth Hawes, *Fashion Is Spinach* (New York: Random House, 1938), ix.
2. Jessica Daves, *Ready-Made Miracle: The Story of American Fashion for the Millions* (New York: G. P. Putnam's Sons, 1967).

1: Such Clothes Have Never Been Made in America Before

1. Edna Woolman Chase and Ilka Chase, *Always in Vogue* (Garden City, NY: Doubleday, 1954), 314.
2. Carmel Snow with Mary Louise Aswell, *The World of Carmel Snow* (New York: McGraw-Hill, 1962), 145.
3. "Month-by-Month History of the First Year of the War," *New York Times*, September 1, 1940, E5.
4. "Best-Dressed Women—and Why," *Vogue*, February 1, 1938, 87.
5. Sandra Stansbery Buckland, "New York and Paris Fashions During World War Two: A Competitive Love Affair," in *Paris Fashion and World War Two: Global Diffusion and Nazi Control*, ed. Lou Taylor and Marie McLoughlin (New York: Bloomsbury, 2020), 140.
6. "Normandie Packed in Mothballs," *New York Times*, October 8, 1939, 43.
7. "Media Monday: The S.S. Normandie Fire (1942)," Hudson River Maritime Museum History Blog, February 7, 2022, https://www.hrmm.org/history-blog/media-monday-the-ss-normandie-fire-1942.
8. Lou Taylor, "Paris Couture, 1940–1944," in *Chic Thrills: A Fashion Reader*, ed. Juliet Ash and Elizabeth Wilson (Berkeley: University of California Press, 1993), 127.
9. Bettina Ballard, *In My Fashion* (New York: David McKay, 1960), 144.

10. Ballard, *In My Fashion*, 81.

11. Snow, *The World of Carmel Snow*, 75.

12. Chase and Chase, *Always in Vogue*, 255.

13. Snow, *The World of Carmel Snow*, 78.

14. Snow, *The World of Carmel Snow*, 75.

15. Chase and Chase, *Always in Vogue*, 106.

16. Snow, *The World of Carmel Snow*, 81–82.

17. Diana Vreeland, *D.V.*, ed. George Plimpton and Christopher Hemphill (New York: Alfred A. Knopf, 1984), 47.

18. Ballard, *In My Fashion*, 302.

19. Snow, *The World of Carmel Snow*, 108.

20. "Arrived Safely, Good Crossing," *Harper's Bazaar*, March 15, 1940, 44–45.

21. Snow, *The World of Carmel Snow*, 136–37.

22. Snow, *The World of Carmel Snow*, 137.

23. "Paris Openings—As Usual," *Vogue*, March 1, 1940, 51.

24. Snow, *The World of Carmel Snow*, 137.

25. Elsa Schiaparelli, *Shocking Life: The Autobiography of Elsa Schiaparelli* (London: V & A Publications, 2007), 25.

26. "The Pulse of Fashion," *Harper's Bazaar*, March 1, 1940, 51.

27. Penelope Rowlands, *A Dash of Daring: Carmel Snow and Her Life in Fashion, Art, and Letters* (New York: Atria Books, 2005), 261.

28. Rowlands, *A Dash of Daring*, 261–62.

29. Rowlands, *A Dash of Daring*, 382.

30. Rowlands, *A Dash of Daring*, 262.

31. Taylor, "Paris Couture, 1940–1944," 128.

32. "Paris and London Fashion Editors Relate Recent Foreign Experiences," *Women's Wear Daily*, June 27, 1940, 35.

33. Rowlands, *A Dash of Daring*, 271.

34. B. J. Perkins, "War's Extension to Mediterranean Shuts Europe to U.S. Commerce," *WWD*, June 11, 1940, 1.

35. Ballard, *In My Fashion*, 182.

36. Ballard, *In My Fashion*, 156.

37. Chase and Chase, *Always in Vogue*, 320.

38. Alice K. Perkins, "Paris Designers Busy Making Models, Helping Refugees," *WWD*, June 11, 1940, 1.

39. Alice K. Perkins, "Paris Designers Busy," 1.

40. Alice K. Perkins, "Paris Designers Busy," 1.

41. "Fall of Paris Major Topic in Apparel Trade," *WWD*, June 14, 1940, 36.

42. "Fall of Paris Major Topic," 36.

43. B. J. Perkins, "Glimpses of Paris," *WWD*, May 14, 1940, 8.

44. "Great Recuperative Powers of France Expected to Bring About Re-emergence in Art and Industry," *WWD*, June 17, 1940, 1.

45. Lois Long, "On and Off the Avenue: Feminine Fashions," *New Yorker*, September 12, 1942, 53.

46. Winifred J. Ovitte, "The 'Spirit of Paris' Will Inspire Future of U.S. Fashion Industries," *WWD*, June 17, 1940, 1.

47. "Paris-Weaned Designers Spend August in U.S.A. Testing Their Ingenuity," *Life*, August 26, 1940, 64.

48. "New York Openings," *Harper's Bazaar*, September 1, 1940, 41.

49. "Vogue's Eye-View of the American Fashion Openings," *Vogue*, September 1, 1940, 41.

50. Long, "On and Off the Avenue: Feminine Fashions," *New Yorker*, September 14, 1940, 63.

51. "*Fiorello!* A Study Guide," Timeline Theatre Company, https://timelinetheatre.com/app/uploads/fio_study_guide.pdf, accessed October 10, 2022.

52. "Mayor Urges Dress Men to Give Designers a Break," *WWD*, March 21, 1940, 6.

53. "City to Call on Union, Mfrs, to Study Exodus," *WWD*, May 29, 1940, 1.

54. Virginia Pope, "Mayor Has Plan to Aid Fashion Bid," *New York Times*, August 22, 1940, 22.

55. "Best-Dressed Women—and Why," 87.

56. Samuel Feinberg, "Inferiority Complex Lifts—American Design to Fore," *WWD*, September 13, 1940, 26.

57. "Mainbocher, Inc. to Be at 6 East 57th St.," *WWD*, September 20, 1940, 2.

58. Chase and Chase, *Always in Vogue*, 325.

59. Dilys Blum, *Shocking! The Art and Fashion of Elsa Schiaparelli* (Philadelphia: Philadelphia Museum of Art, 2003), 223.

60. "None Can Displace Paris, Says Schiaparelli," *WWD*, September 24, 1940, 2.

61. "Named as President of Fashion Group," *New York Times*, February 28, 1940, 36.

62. "La Guardia Asks Individuality of Dress for Great Mass of Women," *WWD*, September 27, 1940, 1, 40.

63. "La Guardia Asks Individuality of Dress for Great Mass of Women," 1, 40.

2: The Birth of the French Legend

1. "The Paris That Did Not Fall," *New York Times*, June 15, 1940, 14.
2. Joan DeJean, *How Paris Became Paris: The Invention of the Modern City* (New York: Bloomsbury, 2015), 4.
3. Joan DeJean, *The Essence of Style: How the French Invented High Fashion, Fine Food, Chic Cafés, Style, Sophistication, and Glamour* (New York: Free Press, 2006), 162.
4. DeJean, *The Essence of Style*, 4.
5. DeJean, *The Essence of Style*, 9.
6. Colleen Hill, *Fairy Tale Fashion* (New Haven: Yale University Press, 2016), 16.
7. DeJean, *The Essence of Style*, 181.
8. DeJean, *The Essence of Style*, 181.
9. DeJean, *The Essence of Style*, 188.
10. Quoted in DeJean, *The Essence of Style*, 15.
11. DeJean, *The Essence of Style*, 15.
12. Elizabeth Mikosch, "The Manufacture and Trade of Luxury Textiles in the Age of Mercantilism," *Textile Society of America Symposium Proceedings* (1990), 54, https://digitalcommons.unl.edu/cgi/viewcontent.cgi?article=1611&context=tsaconf.
13. Joan DeJean, "When Women Ruled Fashion," *Lapham's Quarterly* 8, no. 4 (Fall 2015), https://www.laphamsquarterly.org/fashion/when-women-ruled-fashion.
14. DeJean, "When Women Ruled Fashion."
15. Lourdes Font and Beth McMahon, "Fashion: Origins and Development," Oxford Art Online, July 2, 2009, https://www.oxfordartonline.com/groveart/display/10.1093/gao/9781884446054.001.0001/oao-9781884446054-e-7002082669.
16. Quoted in DeJean, "When Women Ruled Fashion."
17. DeJean, *The Essence of Style*, 58.
18. DeJean, *The Essence of Style*, 63.
19. DeJean, *The Essence of Style*, 67.
20. DeJean, *The Essence of Style*, 79.
21. Joan DeJean, "Couched in History," *New York Times*, September 26,

2010, https://archive.nytimes.com/opinionator.blogs.nytimes.com/2010/09/26/why-is-a-sofa-like-a-writing-desk/.

22. Mikosch, "The Manufacture and Trade of Luxury Textiles," 58.

23. Valerie Steele, "Paris, 'Capital of Fashion,'" in *Paris, Capital of Fashion*, ed. Valerie Steele (London: Bloomsbury Visual Arts, 2019), 12.

24. DeJean, *The Essence of Style*, 68.

25. DeJean, *The Essence of Style*, 48.

26. DeJean, *The Essence of Style*, 17.

27. Judith G. Coffin, "Gender and the Guild Order: The Garment Trades in Eighteenth-Century Paris," *Journal of Economic History* 54, no. 4 (December 1994), 779.

28. Steele, "Paris, 'Capital of Fashion,'" 15.

29. Caroline Weber, *Queen of Fashion: What Marie Antoinette Wore to the Revolution* (New York: Picador, 2007), 26.

30. Weber, *Queen of Fashion*, 48.

31. Weber, *Queen of Fashion*, 26.

32. Weber, *Queen of Fashion*, 72.

33. Weber, *Queen of Fashion*, 103.

34. DeJean, *The Essence of Style*, 12.

35. Valerie Steele, *Women of Fashion: Twentieth-Century Designers* (New York: Rizzoli, 1991), 20.

36. Weber, *Queen of Fashion*, 107.

37. "Rose Bertin, 1747–1813," Château de Versailles, https://en.chateauversailles.fr/discover/history/great-characters/rose-bertin, accessed June 29, 2023.

38. DeJean, "When Women Ruled Fashion."

39. Olivier Courteaux, "Charles Frederick Worth, the Empress Eugénie, and the Invention of Haute-Couture," Napoleon.org (History Website of the Foundation Napoleon), https://www.napoleon.org/en/history-of-the-two-empires/articles/charles-frederick-worth-the-empress-eugenie-and-the-invention-of-haute-couture/, accessed August 12, 2022.

40. Rupert Christiansen, *City of Light: The Making of Modern Paris* (New York: Basic Books, 2018), 22.

41. Christiansen, *City of Light*, 86.

42. Lourdes Font, "Charles Frederick Worth," Grove Art Online, July 2, 2009, https://www.oxfordartonline.com/groveart/display/10.1093/gao/9781884446054.001.0001/oao-9781884446054-e-7002081277.

43. Edith Saunders, *The Age of Worth* (Bloomington: Indiana University Press, 1955), 62.

44. Saunders, *The Age of Worth*, 63.

45. Courteaux, "Charles Frederick Worth."

46. Courteaux, "Charles Frederick Worth."

47. Courteaux, "Charles Frederick Worth."

48. Saunders, *The Age of Worth*, 108.

49. Saunders, *The Age of Worth*, 109.

50. Font, "Charles Frederick Worth."

51. Edith Wharton, *The Age of Innocence* (New York: Charles Scribner & Sons, 1968), 197.

52. "Vanderbilt Ball—How a Costume Ball Changed New York Elite Society," Museum of the City of New York Blog: New York Stories, August 6, 2013, https://blog.mcny.org/2013/08/06/vanderbilt-ball-how-a-costume-ball-changed-new-york-elite-society/.

53. Caroline Rennolds Milbank, *New York Fashion: The Evolution of American Style* (New York: Harry N. Abrams, 1996), 16.

54. Marlis Schweitzer, "American Fashions for American Women: The Rise and Fall of Fashion Nationalism," in *Producing Fashion: Commerce, Culture, and Consumers*, ed. Regina Blaszczyk (Philadelphia: University of Pennsylvania Press, 2011), 133.

55. *Frank Leslie's Ladies Gazette of Fashion*, January 1854, 1.

56. Schweitzer, "American Fashions for American Women," 133.

57. Milbank, *New York Fashion*, 41.

58. Max Meyer records (1952 October–1953 February), Special Collections and College Archives, Fashion Institute of Technology, https://atom-sparc.fitnyc.edu/max-meyer-records, accessed August 31, 2022.

59. "The 'Paris' Fiction," *WWD*, October 31, 1912, 1.

60. Schweitzer, "American Fashions for American Women," 134.

61. Snow, *The World of Carmel Snow*, 27.

62. Edward Bok, "American Fashions for American Women," *Ladies' Home Journal*, September 1909, 1.

63. Edward Bok, "Are the Only Clever Women in the World in Paris?," *Ladies' Home Journal*, January 1910, 1.

64. Schweitzer, "American Fashions for American Women," 145.

65. Schweitzer, "American Fashions for American Women," 144.

66. "Prizes for American Fashion," *New York Times*, December 4, 1912, 12.

67. "The New York Times's Prize Contest Winners in American Fashion," *New York Times*, February 23, 1913, 84.

68. *The Traphagen School: Fostering American Fashion* exhibition (March 5, 2019–March 30, 2019), Museum at FIT, https://exhibitions.fitnyc.edu /traphagen-school/, accessed October 4, 2022.

69. "Purposes of the Fashion Fête," *WWD*, October 17, 1914.

70. "The Story of the Fashion Fête," *Vogue*, November 1, 1914, 36–37.

71. Chase and Chase, *Always in Vogue*, 126.

3: She's Barred from France!

1. Hawes, *Fashion Is Spinach*, 14.

2. Hawes, *Fashion Is Spinach*, 105.

3. "Le Vrai et le Faux Chic," written and illustrated by Georges Goursat (Sem), Metropolitan Museum of Art, https://www.metmuseum.org/art /collection/search/368003, accessed September 23, 2022.

4. Hawes, *Fashion Is Spinach*, 115.

5. Hawes, *Fashion Is Spinach*, 34.

6. Bettina Berch, *Radical by Design: The Life and Style of Elizabeth Hawes, Fashion Designer, Union Organizer, Best-Selling Author* (New York: E. P. Dutton, 1988), 14.

7. "Baroness Is Killed by Fall at the Ritz," *New York Times*, July 8, 1925, 1.

8. Hawes, *Fashion Is Spinach*, 36.

9. Janet Flanner, *Paris Was Yesterday, 1925–1936* (New York: Viking Press, 1972), xxi.

10. Flanner, *Paris Was Yesterday*, xx.

11. Hawes, *Fashion Is Spinach*, 37.

12. Flanner, *Paris Was Yesterday*, xxi.

13. Hawes, *Fashion Is Spinach*, 36.

14. Hawes, *Fashion Is Spinach*, 38.

15. Hawes, *Fashion Is Spinach*, 41–42.

16. Hawes, *Fashion Is Spinach*, 45.

17. Hawes, *Fashion Is Spinach*, 44.

18. Hawes, *Fashion Is Spinach*, 45.

19. Hawes, *Fashion Is Spinach*, 45.

20. Hawes, *Fashion Is Spinach*, 52.

21. Hawes, *Fashion Is Spinach*, 55.

22. Hawes, *Fashion Is Spinach*, 59.

23. Hawes, *Fashion Is Spinach*, 57.
24. Hawes, *Fashion Is Spinach*, 53.
25. Hawes, *Fashion Is Spinach*, 53.
26. Hawes, *Fashion Is Spinach*, 59.
27. Hawes, *Fashion Is Spinach*, 60.
28. Judith Thurman, "Scenes from a Marriage: The House of Chanel at the Met," *New Yorker*, May 23, 2005, 85.
29. Hawes, *Fashion Is Spinach*, 60.
30. Hawes, *Fashion Is Spinach*, 61.
31. Hawes, *Fashion Is Spinach*, 61.
32. Hawes, *Fashion Is Spinach*, 62.
33. Hawes, *Fashion Is Spinach*, 62.
34. Hawes, *Fashion Is Spinach*, 62.
35. Hawes, *Fashion Is Spinach*, 63.
36. Hawes, *Fashion Is Spinach*, 83.
37. Hawes, *Fashion Is Spinach*, 87–88.
38. Hawes, *Fashion Is Spinach*, 103.
39. Hawes, *Fashion Is Spinach*, 18.
40. Hawes, *Fashion Is Spinach*, 112.
41. Jan Glier Reeder, "Jessie Franklin Turner: An Intimate Affair," in *The Hidden History of American Fashion: Rediscovering 20th-Century American Designers*, ed. Nancy Diehl (London: Bloomsbury Academic, 2018), 7.
42. Bernadine Morris, "Valentina, a Designer of Clothes for Stars in the Theater, Dies at 90," *New York Times*, September 15, 1989, B5.
43. Hawes, *Fashion Is Spinach*, 230.
44. Reeder, "Jessie Franklin Turner," 16.
45. "Mrs. George Grant Mason," *Vogue*, May 15, 1932, 76.
46. Tom Davis, "American Woman," *Hatch*, January 16, 2019, https://www.hatchmag.com/articles/american-woman/7714756.
47. Adele Gilbert, "La West a Style Influence? No, Says Miss Hawes; Designer Breaks with Hepburn for Ban on Sequins," *The Record* (Hackensack, NJ), January 27, 1934, 13.
48. Berch, *Radical by Design*, 69.
49. Berch, *Radical by Design*, 69.
50. April Calahan and Cassidy Zachary, "Elizabeth Hawes: Fashion Rebel,"

Dressed: The History of Fashion podcast, RedCircle, March 27, 2018, https://redcircle.com/dressed-the-history-of-fashion/exclusive-content.

51. Berch, *Radical by Design*, 8.
52. Berch, *Radical by Design*, 10.
53. Berch, *Radical by Design*, 9.
54. Berch, *Radical by Design*, 8.
55. Hawes, *Fashion Is Spinach*, 33.
56. Schiaparelli, *Shocking Life*, 81, 83.
57. Berch, *Radical by Design*, 66.
58. Hawes, *Fashion Is Spinach*, 295.
59. Berch, *Radical by Design*, 81.
60. Berch, *Radical by Design*, 84.
61. Gavrik Losey, interview by Rebecca Arnold, September 12, 2016, Special Collections and College Archives, Fashion Institute of Technology.
62. "Pandora" (1936), Elizabeth Hawes, Metropolitan Museum of Art, https://www.metmuseum.org/art/collection/search/159390, accessed September 20, 2022.
63. Hawes, *Fashion Is Spinach*, 158.
64. Hawes, *Fashion Is Spinach*, 162–63.
65. Hawes, *Fashion Is Spinach*, 165.
66. Hawes, *Fashion Is Spinach*, 167.
67. Hawes, *Fashion Is Spinach*, 169.
68. Hawes, *Fashion Is Spinach*, 175.
69. Hawes, *Fashion Is Spinach*, 176.
70. "Elizabeth Hawes," Getty Images, https://www.gettyimages.com/detail/news-photo/miss-elizabeth-hawes-a-well-known-american-modiste-is-news-photo/515349878, accessed September 20, 2022.
71. "Paris Cold to Show of American Designer," *New York Times*, July 25, 1931, 2.
72. Phyllis McGinley, "A Fashion Designer at Work," *Redbook*, November 1937, 7.
73. W. A. Taylor and Co., "'A Dinner Without Apricot Liqueur Is No Dinner at All' Says Elizabeth Hawes" (advertisement), *Redbook*, December 1934, 96.
74. Lord & Taylor, "Two Lovable Frocks Whose Future Is Rosy If Washed with Ivory Flakes!" (advertisement), *Cosmopolitan*, June 1934, 18.

75. Camel, "Let Up—Light Up a Camel . . . a Grand Way to Rest the Nerves Says Famous American Designer Hawes" (advertisement), *Good Housekeeping*, May 1939, 74.

76. Simplicity Pattern, "How Healthful Doublemint Gum Makes You Doubly Lovely" (advertisement), *Cosmopolitan*, February 1938, 119.

77. Virginia Cotier, "Designers of Today and Tomorrow: Elizabeth Hawes," *WWD*, July 24, 1935, 3.

78. Losey, interview by Arnold; Hawes, *Fashion Is Spinach*, 185.

79. "In Tune with Our Times: A Fashion Designer at Work," *Redbook*, November 1937, 7.

80. Berch, *Radical by Design*, 71.

81. Hawes, *Fashion Is Spinach*, vii.

82. Hawes, *Fashion Is Spinach*, v.

83. Hawes, *Fashion Is Spinach*, 6.

84. "Elizabeth Hawes Says 'Fashion Is Spinach'—And Tries to Prove It," *WWD*, March 22, 1938, 30.

85. Long, "On and Off the Avenue: Feminine Fashions," *New Yorker*, April 16, 1938, 46.

86. Berch, *Radical by Design*, 76.

87. Hawes, *Fashion Is Spinach*, 191.

88. Hawes, *Fashion Is Spinach*, 247.

89. Hawes, *Fashion Is Spinach*, 265.

90. Hawes, *Fashion Is Spinach*, 253–54.

91. "Elizabeth Hawes to Open Wholesale Business Next Fall," *WWD*, December 21, 1937, 1.

92. Hawes Inc., "It Cannes Happen Here" (advertisement), *WWD*, November 4, 1938, 7.

4: The Dress That Revolutionized the Industry

1. Claire McCardell, *What Shall I Wear? The What, Where, When, and How Much of Fashion* (New York: Abrams Image, 2022), 150.

2. Betty Friedan, "The Gal Who Defied Dior," *Town Journal*, October 1955, 97.

3. Best & Co., "The New Woman Demands a New Type of Clothes" (advertisement), *New York Times*, September 25, 1938, 7.

4. Kohle Yohannan and Nancy Nolf, *Claire McCardell: Redefining Modernism* (New York: Harry N. Abrams, 1998), 41.

5. Friedan, "The Gal Who Defied Dior," 97.

6. Sally Kirkland, "McCardell," in *American Fashion: The Life and Lines of Adrian, Mainbocher, McCardell, Norell, and Trigère*, ed. Sarah Tomerlin Lee (New York: Quadrangle, 1975), 211.

7. Elizabeth Hawes, "I Choose a Monk's Robe," *Good Housekeeping*, February 1939, 54–55.

8. "Success Story of the Shift Dress," *Vogue*, December 1, 1938, 92.

9. Friedan, "The Gal Who Defied Dior," 97.

10. Friedan, "The Gal Who Defied Dior," 97.

11. Kirkland, "McCardell," 232.

12. "Best-Dressed Women—and Why," 87.

13. "Best-Dressed Women—and Why," 87.

14. Long, "On and Off the Avenue: Feminine Fashions," *New Yorker*, February 26, 1938, 50.

15. "Best-Dressed Women—and Why," 87.

16. "Best-Dressed Women—and Why," 87.

17. "American—Feet First," *Vogue*, February 1, 1938, 115.

18. Kirkland, "McCardell," 218.

19. "American—Feet First," 115.

20. Kirkland, "McCardell," 295.

21. McCardell, *What Shall I Wear?*, 150.

22. McCardell, *What Shall I Wear?*, 149.

23. "Women Designers Set New Fashions," *Life*, January 14, 1946, 87.

24. Eleanor Lambert, "As Appearing in Vogue" (press materials), Eleanor Lambert papers, Special Collections and College Archives, Fashion Institute of Technology.

25. Valerie Steele, "McCardell's American Look," in *Claire McCardell: Redefining Modernism* (New York: Harry N. Abrams, 1998), 8.

26. Yohannan and Nolf, *Claire McCardell*, 16.

27. Yohannan and Nolf, *Claire McCardell*, 16.

28. Kirkland, "McCardell," 216.

29. Yohannan and Nolf, *Claire McCardell*, 19.

30. Phyllis Lee Levin, *The Wheels of Fashion* (Garden City, NY: Doubleday, 1965), 224.

31. Kirkland, "McCardell," 218–19.

32. Quoted in Elizabeth Evitts Dickinson, "A Dress for Everyone," *Washington Post Magazine*, December 12, 2018, https://www.washingtonpost.com

/news/magazine/wp/2018/12/12/feature/the-designer-who-radically
-suggested-that-women-should-wear-whats-comfortable/.

33. Kirkland, "McCardell," 218.

34. McCardell, *What Shall I Wear?*, 30.

35. McCardell, *What Shall I Wear?*, 15.

36. Steele, "McCardell's American Look," 8.

37. Kirkland, "McCardell," 219.

38. Osborn Elliott, "The American Look," *Time*, May 2, 1955.

39. Kirkland, "McCardell," 226.

40. Yohannan and Nolf, *Claire McCardell*, 36.

41. Kirkland, "McCardell," 304.

42. Kirkland, "McCardell," 274.

43. "Week-End Snowbirds," *WWD*, February 2, 1937, 8.

44. "Designer Returns from Paris Wearing a Reindeer Coat," *WWD*,
November 9, 1937, 21.

45. Helen P. Wulbern, "Designers of Today and Tomorrow: Claire McCardell," *WWD*, November 14, 1940, 4.

46. Quoted in Dickinson, "A Dress for Everyone."

47. Dickinson, "A Dress for Everyone."

48. McCardell, *What Shall I Wear?*, 35.

49. Levin, *The Wheels of Fashion*, 227.

50. Russell Maloney, "Hattie Carnegie," *Life*, November 12, 1945, 68.

51. Maloney, "Hattie Carnegie," 66.

52. Kirkland, "McCardell," 232.

53. Kirkland, "McCardell," 232.

54. Yohannan and Nolf, *Claire McCardell*, 46.

55. Elliott, "The American Look."

56. Yohannan and Nolf, *Claire McCardell*, 49.

57. Elliott, "The American Look."

58. Yohannan and Nolf, *Claire McCardell*, 50.

59. Yohannan and Nolf, *Claire McCardell*, 50.

60. Yohannan and Nolf, *Claire McCardell*, 50.

61. Friedan, "The Gal Who Defied Dior," 97.

62. Kirkland, "McCardell," 239.

63. "I'm Doing My Own Work," *Harper's Bazaar*, November 1942, 54.

64. Kirkland, "McCardell," 254.

65. Kirkland, "McCardell," 258.

66. Kirkland, "McCardell," 258.

67. McCardell, *What Shall I Wear?*, 122.

68. Quoted in Steele, "McCardell's American Look," 13.

69. Kirkland, "McCardell," 292.

70. Michael Musto, "At the Costume Institute with Polly Mellen," *New York Times*, May 16, 1999, section 9, 2.

71. "Claire McCardell," *Vogue*, February 1, 1945, 125.

72. Patricia Mears, *American Beauty* (New Haven: Yale University Press, 2009), 38.

73. Kirkland, "McCardell," 245.

74. McCardell, *What Shall I Wear?*, 54.

75. McCardell, *What Shall I Wear?*, 11.

76. Friedan, "The Gal Who Defied Dior," 98.

5: The Most Exciting Store in the Country

1. Marylin Bender, "Store Buyer Enjoys Living a Double Life," *New York Times*, January 8, 1964, 44.

2. "'American Look' Ads Planned by Lord & Taylor," *WWD*, January 12, 1945, 1.

3. Émile Zola, *The Ladies' Paradise* (Oxford: Oxford University Press, 1998), 234.

4. Jan Whitaker, *Service and Style: How the American Department Store Fashioned the Middle Class* (New York: St. Martin's Press, 2006), 35.

5. Lester Gaba, "Lester Gaba Looks at Display," *WWD*, May 6, 1947, 85.

6. "Surrealism Inspires Newest Window Displays at Bonwit Teller," *WWD*, December 21, 1936, 1.

7. Gaba, "Lester Gaba Looks at Display," 85.

8. Donald L. Pratt, "Surrealist Bounces Through Window of Bonwit Teller Into Night Court," *WWD*, March 17, 1939, 40.

9. William Leach, *Land of Desire: Merchants, Power, and the Rise of a New American Culture* (New York: Pantheon Books, 1993), 8.

10. Whitaker, *Service and Style*, 2.

11. Bender, "Store Buyer Enjoys," 44.

12. Aaron D. Backes, "History of New York's Abraham & Straus Department Stores," Classic New York History, April 6, 2021, https://

classicnewyorkhistory.com/history-of-new-yorks-abraham-straus
-department-stores/.

13. Kirkland, "McCardell," 243.

14. Jeanne Perkins, "No. 1 Career Woman," *Life*, May 12, 1947, 125; Allene
    Talmey, "No Progress, No Fun," *Vogue*, February 1, 1946, 159.

15. Long, "On and Off the Avenue: Feminine Fashions," *New Yorker*,
    March 23, 1932, 52.

16. Kirkland, "McCardell," 243.

17. Bernice Fitz-Gibbon, *Macy's, Gimbel's, and Me* (New York: Simon &
    Schuster, 1967), 171.

18. Fitz-Gibbon, *Macy's, Gimbel's, and Me*, 171.

19. Kirkland, "McCardell," 240.

20. Jeanne Perkins, "No. 1 Career Woman," 122.

21. Bender, "Store Buyer Enjoys," 44.

22. Rebecca Jumper Matheson, "Sara Pennoyer: Twentieth-Century Retail
    Advertising Executive and Her Creation, *Polly Tucker: Merchant*," *Fashion Style & Popular Culture* 5, no. 1 (January 2018), 67.

23. "Good Housekeeping Finds Out What a Department Store Buyer
    Does," *Good Housekeeping*, July 1941, 24–26.

24. Friedan, "The Gal Who Defied Dior," 98.

25. Adrian, "Do American Women Want American Clothes?," *Harper's Bazaar*, February 1934, 37.

26. Jeanne Perkins, "No. 1 Career Woman," 117.

27. "Lord & Taylor Exhibition of Modern French Decorative Art," *WWD*,
    March 3, 1928, 18.

28. "Lord & Taylor French Art Exhibition Staged to Obtain Public Reaction
    to New Style," *WWD*, February 29, 1928.

29. Whitaker, *Service and Style*, 146.

30. Talmey, "No Progress, No Fun," 159.

31. Talmey, "No Progress, No Fun," 159.

32. Talmey, "No Progress, No Fun," 159, 196.

33. Jeanne Perkins, "No. 1 Career Woman," 117.

34. Talmey, "No Progress, No Fun," 196.

35. Jeanne Perkins, "No. 1 Career Woman," 117.

36. Jeanne Perkins, "No. 1 Career Woman," 117.

37. Jeanne Perkins, "No. 1 Career Woman," 118.

38. Jeanne Perkins, "No. 1 Career Woman," 118.

39. "Dorothy Shaver Is Dead at 66; Headed Lord & Taylor Since '45," *New York Times*, June 29, 1959, 1.

40. Jeanne Perkins, "No. 1 Career Woman," 122.

41. Jeanne Perkins, "No. 1 Career Woman," 117.

42. Jan Whitaker, "Lunching in the Bird Cage," *Restaurant-ing Through History*, August 7, 2008, https://restaurant-ingthroughhistory.com/2008/08/07/lunching-in-the-bird-cage/.

43. *Tobe Report*, August 8, 1946, 1.

44. Jeanne Perkins, "No. 1 Career Woman," 125.

45. Jeanne Perkins, "No. 1 Career Woman," 125.

46. "Lord & Taylor Has 24 Hour Telephone Service" (advertisement), *New York Times*, December 11, 1940, 11.

47. Whitaker, *Service and Style*, 116.

48. Talmey, "No Progress, No Fun," 159.

49. "American Designers Create Clothes for the Average American Woman," *Sumter Daily Item*, September 3, 1941, 8.

50. "American Designers Feted at Luncheon at Lord & Taylor," *WWD*, April 13, 1932, 2.

51. Quoted in Stephanie M. Amerian, "Fashioning and Selling the American Look: Dorothy Shaver and Modern Art," *Investigaciones de Historia Económica*, June 18, 2015, 105.

52. Milbank, *New York Fashion*, 98.

53. "Store Executive Stresses Merits of New York Designers," *New York American*, October 4, 1934.

54. Quoted in Amerian, "Fashioning and Selling," 105.

55. Amerian, "Fashioning and Selling," 106.

56. "Fashion: New York Couture," *Vogue*, April 15, 1933, 33.

57. Talmey, "No Progress, No Fun," 196.

58. Talmey, "No Progress, No Fun," 196.

59. "Design American Way, Advises Dorothy Shaver," *WWD*, July 30, 1940, 31.

60. "Govt. Aide to Continue Her Store Duties," *WWD*, May 15, 1942, 32.

61. "Finds Style Centre Here," *New York Times*, April 14, 1932, 18.

62. Text of remarks made at Fashion Group meeting, July 11, 1940, Special Collections and College Archives, Fashion Institute of Technology.

63. "Design American Way, Advises Dorothy Shaver," 31.

64. "Design American Way, Advises Dorothy Shaver," 31.

65. "Design American Way, Advises Dorothy Shaver," 31.

66. Beryl Williams Epstein, *Fashion Is Our Business* (New York: J. B. Lippincott, 1945), 123.

67. Kirkland, "McCardell," 243.

68. Kirkland, "McCardell," 250.

69. "Be Nifty—Be New—Be Interchangeable," *Harper's Bazaar*, September 1944, 82.

70. "What Is the American Look?," *Life*, May 21, 1945, 87.

71. "'American Look' Ads Planned by Lord & Taylor," *WWD*, January 12, 1945, 1.

72. "'American Look' Ads Planned by Lord & Taylor," 21.

73. "Style Leadership for America Seen," *New York Times*, January 12, 1945, 18.

74. "What Is the American Look?," 88.

75. "The French Look," *Life*, September 10, 1945, 91.

76. Lord & Taylor, "Let's Get This Question of American Designers Straightened Out Right Now!" (advertisement), *New York Times*, May 14, 1944, 13.

6: A Good Designer Need Not Breathe the Air of Paris

1. Long, "On and Off the Avenue: Feminine Fashions," *New Yorker*, September 7, 1940, 50.

2. Virginia Pope, "True U.S. Couture Emerges in Shows," *New York Times*, September 4, 1940, 25.

3. "For the First Time in History—AMERICA MAKES THE MODE" (advertisement), *New York Times*, September 5, 1940, 12.

4. Chase and Chase, *Always in Vogue*, 316.

5. Long, "On and Off the Avenue: Feminine Fashions," *New Yorker*, September 7, 1940, 50.

6. Long, "On and Off the Avenue: Feminine Fashions," *New Yorker*, October 31, 1936, 60.

7. Long, "On and Off the Avenue: Feminine Fashions," *New Yorker*, September 7, 1940, 50.

8. Long, "On and Off the Avenue: Feminine Fashions," *New Yorker*, September 14, 1940, 60.

9. Eleanor Lambert, interview by Phyllis Feldkamp, December 8, 1977, Oral History Project of the Fashion Industries, Gladys Marcus Library, Fashion Institute of Technology, New York, https://atom-sparc.fitnyc.edu/eleanor-lambert-interview-1977-december-8-2.

10. Virginia Pope, "The Fashion Capital Moves Across Seas," *New York Times*, August 18, 1940, 92.

11. Pope, "The Fashion Capital Moves," 92.

12. Sandra Stansbery Buckland and Gwendolyn S. O'Neal, "'We Publish Fashions Because They Are News': *The New York Times* 1940 Through 1945," *Dress* 25, no. 1, 33.

13. Pope, "The Fashion Capital Moves," 92.

14. Booton Herndon, *Bergdorf's on the Plaza: The Story of Bergdorf Goodman and a Half Century of American Fashion* (New York: Alfred A. Knopf, 1945), 159.

15. Brendan Gill, *Here at* The New Yorker (New York: Random House, 1975), 203.

16. Bill Cunningham, "Our Miss Pope," *New York Times*, October 24, 1993, Section 6, 82.

17. "Lois Long Is Dead; Fashion Editor, Writer on *New Yorker* Staff Since Founding," *New York Times*, July 31, 1974, 36.

18. Gill, *Here at* The New Yorker, 203.

19. Joshua Zeitz, *Flapper: A Madcap Story of Sex, Style, Celebrity, and the Women Who Made America Modern* (New York: Crown Publishers, 2006), 89.

20. George Eells, *Ginger, Loretta and Irene Who?* (New York: G. P. Putnam's Sons, 1976), 191–92.

21. Long, "The Talk of the Town: Mixtures Reported," *New Yorker*, March 26, 1927, 21.

22. Harrison Kinney, *James Thurber: His Life and Times* (New York: Henry Holt, 1996), 26.

23. Kinney, *James Thurber*, 379.

24. Kinney, *James Thurber*, 380.

25. Kinney, *James Thurber*, 378.

26. Kinney, *James Thurber*, 380.

27. Kinney, *James Thurber*, 379.

28. Kinney, *James Thurber*, 29.

29. Zeitz, *Flapper*, 99.

30. Long, "Tables for Two," *New Yorker*, September 12, 1925, 32.

31. Kinney, *James Thurber*, 380.

32. Dale Kramer, *Ross and* The New Yorker (Garden City, NY: Doubleday, 1951), 83, 101.

33. Jane Grant, *Ross, The New Yorker, and Me* (New York: Reynal in association with William Morrow, 1968), 213.

34. Gill, *Here at The New Yorker*, 206.

35. Kramer, *Ross and The New Yorker*, 34.

36. Long, "On and Off the Avenue: Feminine Furbelows," *New Yorker*, May 9, 1936, 74.

37. Long, "On and Off the Avenue: Feminine Fashions," *New Yorker*, January 1, 1927, 34.

38. Long, "On and Off the Avenue: Feminine Fashions," *New Yorker*, March 19, 1932, 66.

39. Long, "On and Off the Avenue: Feminine Fashions," *New Yorker*, April 4, 1936, 62.

40. Long, "On and Off the Avenue: Feminine Fashions," *New Yorker*, February 27, 1937, 60.

41. "New Colour in Your Life," *Vogue*, September 1, 1939, 76.

42. Long, "On and Off the Avenue: Feminine Fashions," *New Yorker*, September 25, 1937, 58.

43. Long, "On and Off the Avenue: Feminine Fashions," *New Yorker*, March 31, 1934, 56.

44. Long, "On and Off the Avenue: Feminine Fashions," *New Yorker*, April 22, 1939, 35.

45. Long, "On and Off the Avenue: Feminine Fashions," *New Yorker*, June 20, 1936, 44.

46. Long, "On and Off the Avenue: Feminine Fashions," *New Yorker*, February 26, 1938, 50.

47. Long, "On and Off the Avenue: Feminine Fashions," *New Yorker*, September 25, 1937, 59.

48. Long, "On and Off the Avenue: Feminine Fashions," *New Yorker*, October 31, 1936, 62.

49. Long, "On and Off the Avenue: Feminine Fashions," *New Yorker*, February 26, 1938, 50.

50. Lois Long, "This and That," *New Yorker*, March 12, 1938, 58.

51. Long, "On and Off the Avenue: Feminine Fashions," *New Yorker*, September 9, 1939, 57.

52. Long, "On and Off the Avenue: Feminine Fashions," *New Yorker*, September 28, 1940, 56.

53. Pope, "The Fashion Capital Moves," 92.

54. "Virginia Pope Talks on Fashion Trends in Paris, New York," *Vassar Miscellany News*, March 24, 1937, 8, https://newspaperarchives.vassar.edu/?a=d&d=miscellany19370324-01.2.28&e.

55. Cunningham, "Our Miss Pope," 82.

56. Virginia Pope, "Behind the Easter Parade," *New York Times*, April 21, 1935, SM8.

57. Cunningham, "Our Miss Pope," 82.

58. Virginia Pope, "They're Made to Order," *New York Times*, November 9, 1935, X10.

59. Long, "On and Off the Avenue: Feminine Fashions," *New Yorker*, April 30, 1938, 54.

60. Virginia Pope, "Style Show Lifts Prestige of U.S.: Designs by American Stylists That Are Aiding United States' Bid for Leadership in Fashion," *New York Times*, September 5, 1940, 27.

61. Buckland and O'Neal, "'We Publish Fashions,'" 37.

62. Virginia Pope, "There Are Frocks of Diaphanous Chiffon and Touches of Crisp Organdie," *New York Times*, January 22, 1933, X9.

63. Cunningham, "Our Miss Pope," 82.

64. Buckland and O'Neal, "'We Publish Fashions,'" 35.

65. "New York Becomes the Natural Center of the Fashion World," *Tobe Report*, October 3, 1940, 2.

66. Buckland and O'Neal, "'We Publish Fashions,'" 38.

67. Virginia Pope, "Fashion Forecasts," *New York Times*, September 13, 1942, SM17–SM52.

68. "Mayor to Attend New Fashion Show," *New York Times*, October 5, 1942, 10.

69. Deborah Needleman, "Celebrating 10 Years of T Magazine," *New York Times*, October 17, 2014, https://archive.nytimes.com/tmagazine.blogs.nytimes.com/2014/10/17/celebrating-10-years-of-t-magazine/.

70. Virginia Pope, "Fashions of Today . . . and Fashions of Tomorrow," *New York Times*, October 11, 1942, SM28.

71. Cunningham, "Our Miss Pope," 82.

72. Virginia Pope, "Showing Heralds Return to Luxury," *New York Times*, October 30, 1946, 30.

73. Cunningham, "Our Miss Pope," 82.

74. Cunningham, "Our Miss Pope," 82.

75. "Our History," Fashion Institute of Technology, https://www.fitnyc
.edu/about/history.php, accessed April 5, 2023.

76. "Clothing Designers Overjoyed at Liberation of Paris, Doubt City Will
Dominate Fashion," *New York Times*, August 24, 1944, 1.

77. "Clothing Designers Overjoyed at Liberation of Paris, Doubt City Will
Dominate Fashion," 16.

78. Lee Carson, "French Women Chic Despite War Curbs," *New York
Times*, August 29, 1944, 14.

79. Virginia Pope, "Accent on Youth Marks Styles for the Spring by Jo Copeland," *New York Times*, January 8, 1944, 16.

80. Long, "On and Off the Avenue: Feminine Fashions," *New Yorker*, September 23, 1944, 56.

81. "French Ready to Export Gowns As Soon as They Get Transport," *New
York Times*, October 21, 1944, 13.

82. Quoted in Buckland and O'Neal, "'We Publish Fashions,'" 39.

83. Long, "On and Off the Avenue: Feminine Fashions," *New Yorker*, September 23, 1944, 56.

84. Long, "On and Off the Avenue: Feminine Fashions," *New Yorker*, September 22, 1945, 70.

85. Long, "On and Off the Avenue: Feminine Fashions," *New Yorker*, September 22, 1945, 70.

7: The Godmother of American Fashion

1. *Eleanor: Godmother of American Fashion*, documentary film directed by
Moses Berkson (2013).

2. Babette, "Schiaparelli Arrives," *San Francisco Examiner*, November 1,
1940, 16.

3. "Schiaparelli Finds U.S. Too Cost-Minded," *WWD*, December 11, 1940,
32.

4. Kheel Center ILGWU Collection Timeline, Cornell University ILR
School, https://ilgwu.ilr.cornell.edu/timeline/#1930–1939, accessed April
24, 2023; Eleanor Pollock, "Paris, U.S.A.," *Saturday Evening Post*, July 8,
1944, 25.

5. "'Streamlined' Promotional Program Outlined," *WWD*, December 17,
1940, 18.

6. Pollock, "Paris, U.S.A.," 24.

7. "N.Y. Dress Promotion Plan Is Underway," *WWD*, March 10, 1941, 1; John Tiffany, interview by Nancy MacDonell, May 21, 2023, Brooklyn, NY.

8. Lambert, interview by Feldkamp; Pollock, "Paris, U.S.A.," 25.

9. "'New York Creation' Labels Will Identify 90% of Dresses Made in U.S. After July 1st," *WWD*, June 17, 1941.

10. New York Dress Institute, "Mrs. Roosevelt and Mayor La Guardia Launch 'New York Creation' Label" (advertisement), *WWD*, July 9, 1941, 18.

11. New York Dress Institute, "Start Today to Laugh at Beulah" (advertisement), *WWD*, October 15, 1941, 7.

12. Harry Berlefein, "Critic of N.Y. Label Brings Protest Before Dress Arbiter," *WWD*, October 21, 1941, 20.

13. New York Dress Institute, "Mrs. Washington at Valley Forge" (advertisement), *WWD*, January 21, 1942, 26.

14. "Hochman Lashes Out Against N.Y. Ad Fund Critics in Speech Here," *WWD*, November 14, 1941, 24.

15. Lambert, interview by Feldkamp.

16. Amy Fine Collins, "The Lady, the List, the Legacy," *Vanity Fair*, April 2004, https://www.vanityfair.com/news/2004/04/eleanor-lambert200404.

17. Bill Berkson, *Since When: A Memoir in Pieces* (Minneapolis: Coffee House Press, 2018), 14.

18. Amy Fine Collins, "The Lady, the List, the Legacy."

19. Lambert, interview by Feldkamp.

20. Tiffany, interview by MacDonell, May 21, 2023.

21. Amy Fine Collins, "The Lady, the List, the Legacy."

22. Lambert, interview by Feldkamp.

23. *Eleanor*, directed by Moses Berkson.

24. *Eleanor*, directed by Moses Berkson.

25. Amy Fine Collins, "The Lady, the List, the Legacy."

26. Jennifer Harbster, "Eleanor Lambert—Empress of Seventh Avenue," Library of Congress Blogs, January 19, 2012, https://blogs.loc.gov/inside_adams/2012/01/eleanor-lambert-empress-of-seventh-avenue/.

27. Lambert, interview by Feldkamp.

28. *Eleanor*, directed by Moses Berkson.

29. *Eleanor*, directed by Moses Berkson.

30. Amy Fine Collins, "The Lady, the List, the Legacy."

31. *Eleanor*, directed by Moses Berkson.

32. *Eleanor*, directed by Moses Berkson.

33. Bill Berkson, *Since When*, 14.

34. Lambert, interview by Feldkamp.

35. "1930s: Fashion Publicist Eleanor Lambert Recalls an Era of Scandalous Elegance," *Vogue*, November 1999, 458.

36. Lambert, interview by Feldkamp.

37. "In the Courts," *WWD*, January 12, 1937, 50.

38. Lambert, interview by Feldkamp.

39. Quoted in Amy Fine Collins, "The Lady, the List, the Legacy."

40. Bill Berkson, *Since When*, 11.

41. Tiffany, interview by MacDonell, May 21, 2023.

42. Amy Fine Collins, "The Lady, the List, the Legacy."

43. Lambert, "As Appearing in Vogue" (press materials).

44. Yohannan and Nolf, *Claire McCardell*, 115.

45. Amy Fine Collins, "The Lady, the List, the Legacy."

46. Alice Hughes, "A Woman's New York: Blond Eleanor Lambert No. 1 Fashion Instigator of U.S.," *Fort Worth Star-Telegram*, July 24, 1947, 10.

47. "1930s: Fashion Publicist Eleanor Lambert," 458, 534.

48. "1930s: Fashion Publicist Eleanor Lambert," 458.

49. Bill Berkson, *Since When*, 12.

50. Amy Fine Collins, "The Lady, the List, the Legacy."

51. Amy Fine Collins, "The Lady, the List, the Legacy."

52. Jay Day Dress Company: About, https://jaydaydressco.com/pages /about, accessed May 1, 2023.

53. Lambert, interview by Feldkamp.

54. "Where Fashion Gets Its Wings" (advertisement), *Vogue*, December 15, 1943, 2–3.

55. "Pattern for Leadership" (advertisement), *Vogue*, October 1, 1945.

56. "British Duchesses Are Best Dressed," *New York Times*, January 29, 1940, 13.

57. Amy Fine Collins, *The International Best-Dressed List: The Inside Story* (New York: Rizzoli, 2019), 33.

58. Amy Fine Collins, *The International Best-Dressed List*, 33.

59. "Mrs. Williams Tops Best-Dressed List," *New York Times*, December 27, 1940, 17.

60. "Mr. and Mrs. Harrison Williams's House in Palm Beach," *Vogue*, May 1, 1932, 43–44.

61. "Fashion: Mrs. Harrison Williams," *Vogue*, February 15, 1948, 82.
62. Amy Fine Collins, "The Lady, the List, the Legacy."
63. Amy Fine Collins, "The Lady, the List, the Legacy."
64. Amy Fine Collins, *The International Best-Dressed List*, 63.
65. Margaret Mara, "Top Fashion Publicist Stimulates Recognition of American Design," *Brooklyn Daily Eagle*, November 19, 1945, 13.
66. "The American Fashion Critics' Award Sponsored by Coty" (advertisement), *WWD*, January 16, 1942.
67. "Designer Honored by Fashion Critics," *New York Times*, January 23, 1943, 10.
68. Bernadine Morris, "Norman Norell, Designer, Dies; Made 7th Ave. the Rival of Paris," *New York Times*, October 26, 1972, 89.
69. Yohannan and Nolf, *Claire McCardell*, 69.
70. "3 Style Designers Win Awards As 'Tops in Their Field in 1943,'" *New York Times*, February 4, 1944, 18.
71. *Eleanor*, directed by Moses Berkson.
72. Lambert, interview by Feldkamp.
73. Claire Hampel, "Should We Say Goodbye to Fashion Week? A Breakdown of the Industry's Economic Impact," *Business Edge*, September 28, 2022.
74. Tiffany, interview by MacDonell, May 21, 2023.
75. Amy Fine Collins, "The Lady, the List, the Legacy."
76. Adelia Bird Ellis obituary, *New York Times*, March 11, 1975, 38.
77. *Eleanor*, directed by Moses Berkson.
78. Pollock, "Paris, U.S.A.," 25.
79. "How New York Fashion Week Created American Style," *Studio 360*, WNYC, June 2, 2016, https://www.wnycstudios.org/podcasts /studio/segments/how-new-york-fashion-week-created-american -style.
80. Pollock, "Paris, U.S.A.," 25.
81. Pollock, "Paris, U.S.A.," 25.
82. "Institute Missed Boat with Press Showings, But It's Not Too Late, Says Fashion Writer," *WWD*, July 28, 1943, 13.
83. Pollock, "Paris, U.S.A.," 25.
84. Lambert, interview by Feldkamp.
85. Pollock, "Paris, U.S.A.," 90.
86. Pollock, "Paris, U.S.A.," 90.

87. "Fashion: Wardrobe by Traina-Norell," *Vogue*, February 1, 1944, 89.

88. "1940s: Rosamond Bernier," *Vogue*, November 1999, 534.

89. Levin, *The Wheels of Fashion*, xvi.

90. Photo by John Rawlings, Getty Images, https://i.pinimg.com/originals
    /84/70/8c/84708cc0a481e0669d7933ec62378299.jpg.

91. "1940s: Rosamond Bernier," 534.

92. Ballard, *In My Fashion*, 157–58.

93. "Big Bags and Belts," *Life*, November 19, 1945, 85.

94. Ballard, *In My Fashion*, 158.

95. Ballard, *In My Fashion*, 158.

96. "Grandma Gets Lowdown on Trip of Nation's Fashion Press to N.Y.,"
    WWD, July 27, 1943, 16.

97. Laura O. Miller, "Grandma Rises to the Defense," *WWD*, August 12,
    1943, 18.

98. Michael Gross, *Model: The Ugly Business of Beautiful Women* (New York:
    Perennial, 2003), 237.

99. *Eleanor*, directed by Moses Berkson.

100. Hughes, "A Woman's New York," 10.

101. Mara, "Top Fashion Publicist Stimulates Recognition of American De-
     sign," 13.

102. Amy Fine Collins, "The Lady, the List, the Legacy."

103. Hughes, "A Woman's New York," 10.

8: The American Look

1. Diana Vreeland, *D.V.*, 47.

2. Louise Dahl-Wolfe, *A Photographer's Scrapbook* (New York: St. Martin's/Marek, 1984), 86.

3. Rowlands, *A Dash of Daring*, 295.

4. Slim Keith with Annette Tapert, *Slim: Memories of a Rich and Imperfect
   Life* (New York: Simon & Schuster, 1990), 95.

5. Keith, *Slim*, 100.

6. Keith, *Slim*, 101–103.

7. Keith, *Slim*, 124.

8. Lauren Bacall, *By Myself* (New York: Alfred A. Knopf, 1978), 65.

9. Bacall, *By Myself*, 66–67.

10. "The Home Front," *Harper's Bazaar*, May 1943, 38.

11. "The Sewing Box," *Harper's Bazaar*, February 1943, 34.
12. "New Slip, New Lipstick," *Harper's Bazaar*, March 1943, 81.
13. "A Fresh Start," *Harper's Bazaar*, April 1943, 62.
14. Bacall, *By Myself*, 67.
15. Bacall, *By Myself*, 67.
16. Quoted in Caroline Evans, *The Mechanical Smile: Modernism and the First Fashion Shows in France and America, 1900–1929* (New Haven: Yale University Press, 2013), 126.
17. Quoted in Evans, *The Mechanical Smile*, 126.
18. Snow, *The World of Carmel Snow*, 52–53.
19. Gross, *Model*, 36.
20. Gross, *Model*, 38.
21. Snow, *The World of Carmel Snow*, 50.
22. Dahl-Wolfe, *A Photographer's Scrapbook*, xi.
23. Snow, *The World of Carmel Snow*, 88.
24. Snow, *The World of Carmel Snow*, 88.
25. Snow, *The World of Carmel Snow*, 88.
26. Martin Munkácsi, "Think While You Shoot," *Harper's Bazaar*, November 1935, 92–93, 152.
27. Rowlands, *A Dash of Daring*, 166.
28. Ballard, *In My Fashion*, 302.
29. Katharine Hamill, "2,196 Families Are Living in the Williamsburg and Harlem River Housing Projects," *Harper's Bazaar*, August 1939, 100–103, 132.
30. Mae Morrissy, "Your Obedient Servant," *Harper's Bazaar*, January 1944, 57.
31. "Paris Working Girl," *Harper's Bazaar*, June 1946, 156.
32. "I Had My First Baby When I Was Forty," *Harper's Bazaar*, January 1942, 90.
33. Snow, *The World of Carmel Snow*, 102.
34. Dillon Wallace, "The History of Kodachrome," Aperture: A Kodak Digitizing Blog, https://kodakdigitizing.com/blogs/news/the-history-of-kodachrome, accessed May 30, 2023.
35. Quoted in Rowlands, *A Dash of Daring*, 208.
36. Rowlands, *A Dash of Daring*, 208.
37. *High Heels and Ground Glass*, produced by Deborah Irmas and Barbara Kasten (New York: Filmmakers Library, 1993).

38. Dahl-Wolfe, *A Photographer's Scrapbook*, xii.

39. "Edward Weston," National Inventors Hall of Fame, https://www.invent.org/inductees/edward-weston, accessed May 30, 2023.

40. Dahl-Wolfe, *A Photographer's Scrapbook*, 39.

41. Dahl-Wolfe, *A Photographer's Scrapbook*, 85.

42. Snow, *The World of Carmel Snow*, 100.

43. Dahl-Wolfe, *A Photographer's Scrapbook*, 21.

44. Dahl-Wolfe, *A Photographer's Scrapbook*, 1.

45. *High Heels and Ground Glass*, produced by Irmas and Kasten.

46. Dahl-Wolfe, *A Photographer's Scrapbook*, 5.

47. Dahl-Wolfe, *A Photographer's Scrapbook*, 7.

48. Dahl-Wolfe, *A Photographer's Scrapbook*, 106.

49. Dahl-Wolfe, *A Photographer's Scrapbook*, 105.

50. Dahl-Wolfe, *A Photographer's Scrapbook*, 106.

51. Dahl-Wolfe, *A Photographer's Scrapbook*, 13.

52. Dahl-Wolfe, *A Photographer's Scrapbook*, 19.

53. Dahl-Wolfe, *A Photographer's Scrapbook*, 14.

54. Cecil Beaton, *The Glass of Fashion: A Personal History of Fifty Years of Changing Tastes & the People Who Have Inspired Them* (New York: Rizzoli, 2014), 371.

55. Quoted in Lisa Immordino Vreeland, *Diana Vreeland: The Eye Has to Travel* (New York: Abrams, 2011), 73.

56. Eleanor Dwight, *Diana Vreeland* (New York: William Morrow, 2002), 13.

57. Diana Vreeland, *D.V.*, 10–11.

58. Schiaparelli, *Shocking Life*, 17.

59. Diana Vreeland, "Why Don't You," *Harper's Bazaar*, August 1936, 65.

60. Diana Vreeland, "Why Don't You," *Harper's Bazaar*, July 1937, 58.

61. Diana Vreeland, "Why Don't You," *Harper's Bazaar*, November 1937, 165.

62. Diana Vreeland, "Why Don't You," *Harper's Bazaar*, January 1937, 89.

63. S. J. Perelman, "Frou-Frou, or the Future of Vertigo," *New Yorker*, April 16, 1938, 54.

64. Diana Vreeland, "Why Don't You," *Harper's Bazaar*, November 1936, 90.

65. Quoted in Lisa Immordino Vreeland, *Diana Vreeland*, 51.

66. Diana Vreeland, *D.V.*, 89.

67. Rowlands, *A Dash of Daring*, 247.

68. Diana Vreeland, *D.V.*, 108–109.

69. "Sun Red and Sun Yellow," *Harper's Bazaar*, June 1946, 100.

70. Dwight, *Diana Vreeland*, 86

71. Amy Fine Collins, "The Cult of Diana," *Vanity Fair*, November 1993, https://www.vanityfair.com/culture/1993/11/diana-vreeland-199311.

72. Ballard, *In My Fashion*, 290.

73. Stephen Mooallem, "The 1940s," *Harper's Bazaar*, April 2017, 232.

74. Amy Fine Collins, "The Cult of Diana."

75. Amy Fine Collins, "The Cult of Diana."

76. Quoted in Lisa Immordino Vreeland, *Diana Vreeland*, 73.

77. Lisa Immordino Vreeland, "The Secrets of Diana Vreeland," Harpers Bazaar.com, August 17, 2012, https://www.harpersbazaar.com/culture/features/a893/diana-vreelands-secrets-0912/.

78. Beaton, *The Glass of Fashion*, 366.

79. Diana Vreeland, *D.V.*, 164.

80. Pope, "The Fashion Capital Moves," 92.

81. "Advocates Designing for Personalities," *WWD*, November 14, 1940, 40.

82. Diana Vreeland, *D.V.*, 1.

83. Vicki Goldberg, "Louise Dahl-Wolfe," in *Louise Dahl-Wolfe: A Retrospective* (New York: Harry N. Abrams, 2000), 22.

84. Dahl-Wolfe, *A Photographer's Scrapbook*, 39.

85. Dahl-Wolfe, *A Photographer's Scrapbook*, back cover.

86. Ballard, *In My Fashion*, 293.

87. Dorothy Hay Thompson, "The Secret of Exercise," *Harper's Bazaar*, April 1948, 137.

88. Quoted in Rowlands, *A Dash of Daring*, 336.

89. Goldberg, "Louise Dahl-Wolfe," 23.

90. Goldberg, "Louise Dahl-Wolfe," 23.

91. Sally Eauclaire, *Louise Dahl-Wolfe: A Retrospective Exhibition* (Washington, DC: The National Museum of Women in the Arts, 1987), 13.

92. Goldberg, "Louise Dahl-Wolfe," 22.

93. "The Editor's Guest Book," *Harper's Bazaar*, June 1941, 24.

94. Diana Vreeland, *D.V.*, 110.

95. Ballard, *In My Fashion*, 290.

96. "Flight to the Valley of the Sun," *Harper's Bazaar*, January 1942, 39.

97. Table of Contents, *Harper's Bazaar*, January 1942, 33.

98. Quoted in Goldberg, "Louise Dahl-Wolfe," 30.

99. "Lauren Bacall in the Evening Sweater," *Harper's Bazaar*, April 1945, 86–87.

100. Sally Kirkland, "Sportswear for Everywhere," in *All-American: A Sportswear Tradition* exhibition catalogue (New York: Fashion Institute of Technology, 1985), 38–39.

101. "Clothing Designers Overjoyed at Liberation of Paris, Doubt City Will Dominate Fashion," *New York Times*, August 24, 1944, 16.

102. "French Ready to Export Gowns," 13.

103. Alice Hughes, "Here's a Fantastic Fact!" *Cosmopolitan*, September 1945, 53.

9: Sportswear Is Universal

1. "Designer Honored by Fashion Critics," *New York Times*, January 23, 1942, 10.

2. Snow, *The World of Carmel Snow*, 148.

3. Rowlands, *A Dash of Daring*, 306.

4. Lee Carson, "Preview of Paris Collections," *Harper's Bazaar*, October 1944, 66–67.

5. Lee Miller, "Liberation of Paris," *Vogue*, October 15, 1944, 95.

6. Taylor, "Paris Couture, 1940–1944," 135.

7. "First Hat from Free Paris," *Vogue*, November 1, 1944, 118.

8. "Mrs. Harry L. Hopkins and Diana," *Harper's Bazaar*, September 1942, 63.

9. Rowlands, *A Dash of Daring*, 292.

10. "Calling 100,000," *Harper's Bazaar*, June 1942, 54.

11. Amy Fine Collins, "The Lady, the List, the Legacy."

12. Frank Castigliola, "Broken Circle: The Isolation of Franklin D. Roosevelt in World War II," *Diplomatic History* 32, no. 5 (November 2008), 701.

13. Susan Geib, "How Elizabeth Arden Lured Urban One-Percenters to the Maine Woods," *DownEast*, June 2020, https://downeast.com/history /elizabeth-arden-belgrade-lakes/.

14. Rowlands, *A Dash of Daring*, 300.

15. Rowlands, *A Dash of Daring*, 301.

16. Rowlands, *A Dash of Daring*, 301.

17. Snow, *The World of Carmel Snow*, 145.

18. Snow, *The World of Carmel Snow*, 146–47.

19. Rowlands, *A Dash of Daring*, 304–5.

20. Snow, *The World of Carmel Snow*, 148.

21. Rowlands, *A Dash of Daring*, 306.

22. Snow, *The World of Carmel Snow*, 148.

23. B. J. Perkins, "Glimpses of Paris," *WWD*, December 4, 1944, 2.

24. Rowlands, *A Dash of Daring*, 307.

25. Snow, *The World of Carmel Snow*, 150–51.

26. Snow, *The World of Carmel Snow*, 151.

27. "American Red Cross Western Front," *Harper's Bazaar*, April 1945, 74–77.

28. Victoria Chappelle, "Dearest I Love You," *Harper's Bazaar*, May 1945, 56–59.

29. "Believe It: Lee Miller Cables from Germany," *Vogue*, June 1, 1945, 103–5.

30. Chase and Chase, *Always in Vogue*, 354.

31. Snow, *The World of Carmel Snow*, 148.

32. Ballard, *In My Fashion*, 196.

33. Meryle Secrest, *Elsa Schiaparelli: A Biography* (London: Fig Tree, 2014), 249–50.

34. Ballard, *In My Fashion*, 188, 199.

35. Ballard, *In My Fashion*, 202.

36. Taylor, "Paris Couture, 1940–1944," 133.

37. Rowlands, *A Dash of Daring*, 306.

38. "Paris: Sidelights on What Paris Reads, Wears, Does," *Vogue*, December 1, 1944, 140.

39. Carmel Snow, speech to the Fashion Group, April 18, 1945, Fashion Group International records, New York Public Library.

40. Quoted in Yuniya Kawamura, *The Japanese Revolution in Paris Fashion* (Oxford: Berg, 2004), 46.

41. Dominique Veillon, *Fashion Under the Occupation*, trans. Miriam Kochan (Oxford: Berg, 2002), 42.

42. Snow, *The World of Carmel Snow*, 151.

43. "New Styles from Paris & New York," *Life*, August 16, 1943, 42.

44. Taylor, "Paris Couture, 1940–1944," 140.

45. Virginia Pope, "Paris Collections," *New York Times*, November 12, 1944, SM34.

46. Mildred Smolze, speech to the Fashion Group, October 25, 1944, Fashion Group International records, New York Public Library.

47. Sophie Kurkdjian, "From Paris Haute Couture to New York: Maintaining the French Domination of Fashion Across the Atlantic, 1939–1946, Through Women's Fashion Magazines," in *Paris Fashion and World*

War Two: Global Diffusion and Nazi Control, ed. Lou Taylor and Marie McLoughlin (New York: Bloomsbury, 2020), 130.

48. Ballard, *In My Fashion*, 201–2.

49. Snow, speech to the Fashion Group, April 18, 1945.

50. Snow, speech to the Fashion Group, April 18, 1945.

51. Veillon, *Fashion Under the Occupation*, 101.

52. Taylor, "Paris Couture, 1940–1944," 131.

53. Rhonda K. Garelick, *Mademoiselle: Coco Chanel and the Pulse of History* (New York: Random House, 2014), 351.

54. "Paris: Lelong Speaks for the Paris Couture," *Vogue*, November 15, 1944, 74.

55. Veillon, *Fashion Under the Occupation*, 85.

56. Veillon, *Fashion Under the Occupation*, 21–22.

57. Veillon, *Fashion Under the Occupation*, 85.

58. Quoted in Kawamura, *The Japanese Revolution in Paris Fashion*, 45–46.

59. Blum, *Shocking!*, 225.

60. Taylor, "Paris Couture, 1940–1944," 129.

61. Taylor, "Paris Couture, 1940–1944," 135.

62. Kawamura, *The Japanese Revolution in Paris Fashion*, 46.

63. Winifred Ovitte, "Thrill of Paris in the Air," *WWD*, August 11, 1944, 1.

64. Quoted in "Paris Not to Dim Style Center Here," *New York Times*, September 2, 1944, 14.

65. "Looking Back at Paris Fashions," *Vogue*, January 1, 1945, 71–72.

66. Carmel Snow, "Notes from Paris," *Harper's Bazaar*, May 1946, 124.

67. Snow, speech to the Fashion Group, April 18, 1945.

68. Rowlands, *A Dash of Daring*, 325.

69. Ballard, *In My Fashion*, 204.

70. Ballard, *In My Fashion*, 173.

71. Ballard, *In My Fashion*, 228.

72. Taylor, "Paris Couture 1940–1944," 140.

73. Taylor, "Paris Couture 1940–1944," 136.

74. Snow, speech to the Fashion Group, April 18, 1945.

75. Snow, speech to the Fashion Group, April 18, 1945.

76. Taylor, "Paris Couture, 1940–1944," 137.

77. Snow, *The World of Carmel Snow*, 158.

78. Ballard, *In My Fashion*, 235–36.

79. Ballard, *In My Fashion*, 236–37.

80. Quoted in Rowlands, *A Dash of Daring*, 365.

81. "The House of Dior," *Life*, March 24, 1947, 65.

82. Rowlands, *A Dash of Daring*, 363.

83. Quoted in Rowlands, *A Dash of Daring*, 369.

84. Carmel Snow, speech to the Fashion Group, April 1947, Fashion Group International records, New York Public Library.

85. "Watch This Skirt Length," *Harper's Bazaar*, November 1941, 41.

86. Snow, *The World of Carmel Snow*, 158–59; Snow, "Notes from Paris."

87. Elliott, "The American Look."

88. "Fashion: The Undressed Look," *Time*, August 13, 1956, https://content .time.com/time/subscriber/article/0,33009,865474-1,00.html.

89. Long, "On and Off the Avenue: Feminine Fashions," *New Yorker*, April 19, 1947, 82.

90. Long, "On and Off the Avenue: Feminine Fashions," *New Yorker*, June 7, 1947, 84.

91. "Southwest Women Protest Skirts Are Too Far South," *WWD*, August 18, 1947, 4.

92. "Dior," *Life*, March 1, 1948, 85.

93. "'We the People' Will Air Views on Skirts," *WWD*, August 25, 1947, 36.

94. "Dior," *Life*, 85.

95. "Fashion Counter Revolution," *Time*, September 15, 1947, 88.

96. R. Donovan, "That Friend of Your Wife's Called Dior," *Collier's*, June 10, 1955, 34.

97. Friedan, "The Gal Who Defied Dior," 32–33, 97–98.

98. Quoted in Dickinson, "A Dress for Everyone."

99. Smolze, speech to the Fashion Group.

100. Smolze, speech to the Fashion Group.

101. Smolze, speech to the Fashion Group.

102. "1944 Outline of Fashion," *Vogue*, January 15, 1944, 96.

103. Snow, speech to the Fashion Group, April 18, 1945.

104. Snow, *The World of Carmel Snow*, 153.

105. "In the American Grain," *Harper's Bazaar*, October 1944, 89, 120.

106. Milbank, *New York Fashion*, 175.

107. J. W. Cohn, "Variety of High-Style Apparel at Saks-5th Astounds French," *WWD*, March 13, 1947.

108. Milbank, *New York Fashion*, 175.

109. Quoted in Richard Martin, *American Ingenuity: Sportswear, 1930s–1970s* (New York: Metropolitan Museum of Art, 1998), 59.

110. Madge Garland, "U.S.A.," *Harper's Bazaar* London, November 1945, 43.

111. Barbara Gould, "Beauty in the American Tradition" (advertisement), *Harper's Bazaar*, July 1946, 103.

112. American Girl Shoe Company, "Beauty in a Walking Mode" (advertisement), *Good Housekeeping*, September 1945, 199.

113. Freedom-Valvoline Oil Company, "The Girl, Her Car" (advertisement), *Time*, September 15, 1947, 49.

114. "The American Look Is a Proud Thing," *Look*, March 15, 1949, 71, 73.

115. Grace Grether, "Lambert Reports on European Fashions," *Salt Lake Tribune*, December 6, 1949, 17.

116. "American Modern," *Vogue*, February 1, 1946, 148–49.

117. "American First Editions," *Harper's Bazaar*, June 1945, 44.

118. B. H. Wragge, "American Modern" (advertisement), *Vogue*, September 15, 1946, 34.

119. Bernadine Taub, "'Sportswear' Now Is Universal Fashion: Maxwell," *WWD*, April 29, 1959, 29.

120. "Europe's Clothes," *Life*, October 18, 1943, 49.

121. Nicola White, *Reconstructing Italian Fashion: America and the Development of the Italian Fashion Industry* (Oxford: Berg, 2000), 5.

122. Claire Wilcox, ed., *The Golden Age of Couture: Paris and London 1947–1957* (London: V&A Publishing, 2009).

123. "Saint Laurent Rive Gauche," Musée Yves Saint Laurent, https://museeysl paris.com/en/biography/saint-laurent-rive-gauche, accessed December 4, 2023.

124. "Yves Saint Laurent's Rive Gauche Revolution," Museum at FIT, March 3, 2015.

125. "Fashion: Yves in New York," *Time*, September 27, 1968, 63.

126. Alice Rawsthorn, *Yves Saint Laurent: A Biography* (New York: Doubleday, 1996), 107.

127. Rawsthorn, *Yves Saint Laurent*, 90–91.

128. "Yves Saint Laurent's Rive Gauche Revolution," Museum at FIT.

10: The Battle of Versailles

1. *Eleanor*, directed by Moses Berkson.

2. Elaine Woo, "G. Van der Kemp, 89; Led Restoration of Versailles," *Los Angeles Times*, January 18, 2012, https://www.latimes.com/archives/la -xpm-2002-jan-18-me-vanderkemp18-story.html.

3. Paul Lewis, "Gerald Van der Kemp, 89, Versailles' Restorer," *New York Times*, January 15, 2002, A19.

4. Woo, "G. Van der Kemp, 89."

5. Robin Givhan, *The Battle of Versailles: The Night American Fashion Stumbled into the Spotlight and Made History* (New York: Flatiron Books, 2015), 82.

6. Nina S. Hyde, "At Home . . . In Versailles and Preparing for the Carters," *Washington Post*, January 5, 1978, https://www.washingtonpost.com/archive/lifestyle/1978/01/05/at-home-in-versailles-and-preparing-for-the-carters/a7ad1144-c244-4f82-bbac-aeeeabe1dc07/.

7. Woo, "G. Van der Kemp, 89."

8. Hyde, "At Home . . . In Versailles."

9. Dominick Dunne, "Memento Mori," *Vanity Fair*, March 1991, https://archive.vanityfair.com/article/1991/3/memento-mori.

10. Woo, "G. Van der Kemp, 89."

11. "Versailles," *WWD*, October 16, 1973, 4.

12. Nancy Collins, "Halston to Join Franco-American Fashion Summit," *WWD*, August 9, 1973, 19.

13. Marie Antoinette Esterhazy, "The Battle of Versailles," *WWD*, November 26, 1973, 1.

14. John Tiffany, interview by Nancy MacDonell, August 2, 2023, Brooklyn, NY.

15. Tiffany, interview by MacDonell, August 2, 2023.

16. Myra MacPherson, "Governors' Wives Discover 'America in Style' at White House," *New York Times*, March 1, 1968, 42.

17. Eric Wilson, "The Long Fall of the House of Blass," *New York Times*, December 25, 2008, E1.

18. Rawsthorn, *Yves Saint Laurent*, 133.

19. "The King Is Dead," *WWD*, March 27, 1972, 4–5.

20. Barbara Hulanicki, *From A to Biba* (London: W. H. Allen, 1983), 60–61.

21. Jean Baer, *The Single Girl Goes to Town* (New York: Macmillan, 1968), 139.

22. "Halston Today," *WWD*, December 3, 1968, 1, 26.

23. "Vogue's Own Boutique," *Vogue*, February 1, 1970, 213.

24. Grace Mirabella, *In and Out of Vogue* (New York: Doubleday, 1995), 150.

25. Ed Cripps, "Party Animals: The Rothschild Surrealist Ball," *The Rake*, May 2023, https://therake.com/stories/icons/party-animals-the-rothschild-surrealist-ball/.

26. Tiffany, interview by MacDonell, August 2, 2023.

27. Milbank, *New York Fashion*, 191.

28. Judith Cummings, "Anne Klein Dead; Designer Was 51," *New York Times*, March 20, 1974, 64.

29. Ruth La Ferla, "The Bill Blass Legacy: Simplicity with a Kick," *New York Times*, June 14, 2002, B10.

30. Milbank, *New York Fashion*, 291.

31. Nancy Collins, "Halston to Join," 19.

32. Givhan, *The Battle of Versailles*, 107.

33. "Versailles," *WWD*, 4.

34. "Eye," *WWD*, September 18, 1973, 22.

35. "Versailles," *WWD*, 4.

36. "Versailles," *WWD*, 4.

37. Enid Nemy, "Fashion at Versailles: French Were Good, Americans Great," *New York Times*, November 30, 1973, 26.

38. Givhan, *The Battle of Versailles*, 190.

39. Naomi Gordon, "The Battle of Versailles: The True Story Behind the Fashion Extravaganza as Seen in Netflix's *Halston*," HarpersBazaar.com, May 25, 2021, https://www.harpersbazaar.com/uk/fashion/fashion-news/a36475199/battle-of-versailles-true-story-netflix-halston/.

40. Tiffany, interview by MacDonell, August 2, 2023.

41. Givhan, *The Battle of Versailles*, 127.

42. Givhan, *The Battle of Versailles*, 188.

43. Givhan, *The Battle of Versailles*, 189.

44. Givhan, *The Battle of Versailles*, 188.

45. Roslyn Sulcas, "Zizi Jeanmaire, French Star of Ballet, Cabaret, and Film, Dies at 96," *New York Times*, July 22, 2020, A21.

46. Givhan, *The Battle of Versailles*, 186.

47. Givhan, *The Battle of Versailles*, 193.

48. Monique, "Fashion Kings Merge in a Surge of Elegance," *Chicago Tribune*, December 1, 1973, 38.

49. "Observations," *Vogue*, February 1974, 87.

50. Pat Shelton, "Elite Sip Champagne to Save Versailles Palace," *Los Angeles Times*, November 30, 1973, 22.

51. Monique, "Fashion Kings Merge," 38.

52. Givhan, *The Battle of Versailles*, 201.

53. Nemy, "Fashion at Versailles," 26.

54. Shelton, "Elite Sip Champagne," 22.

55. Eugenia Sheppard, "Yanks Pull Off Fashion Heist," *Los Angeles Times*, December 2, 1973, 65.

56. Rowlands, *A Dash of Daring*, 460.

57. Jacki Lyden, "The Ebony Fashion Fair: Changing History on the Catwalk," NPR, February 15, 2014, https://www.npr.org/2014/02/15 /276987206/the-ebony-fashion-fair-changing-history-on-the-catwalk.

58. Givhan, *The Battle of Versailles*, 207.

59. Givhan, *The Battle of Versailles*, 206–13.

60. Shelton, "Elite Sip Champagne," 22.

61. Nemy, "Fashion at Versailles," 26.

62. Givhan, *The Battle of Versailles*, 215.

63. "Versailles: Americans Came, They Sewed, They Conquered," *WWD*, November 30, 1973, 1, 6.

64. Nemy, "Fashion at Versailles," 26.

65. Sheppard, "Yanks Pull Off Fashion Heist," 65.

66. "Global Fashion Industry Statistics," Fashion United, https://fashionunited .com/global-fashion-industry-statistics, accessed December 5, 2023.

67. Katie Van Syckle, "Return to Form: Fashion Journalists on Going Back to the Runway," *New York Times*, July 19, 2021, https://www.nytimes .com/2021/07/19/insider/fashion-shows-return.html.

68. "Costume Institute Two-Part Exhibition to Focus on American Fashion" (press release), Metropolitan Museum of Art, September 7, 2021, https://www.metmuseum.org/press/exhibitions/2021/costume-institute -in-america.

Afterword

1. Mirabella, *In and Out of Vogue*, 43.

2. Rowlands, *A Dash of Daring*, 478.

3. Rowlands, *A Dash of Daring*, 472.

4. Truman Capote, "A Tree of Night," *Harper's Bazaar*, October 1945, 110, 176, 178, 180, 182, 184, 187–88.

5. Rowlands, *A Dash of Daring*, 477–78.

6. Mirabella, *In and Out of Vogue*, 73.

7. Rowlands, *A Dash of Daring*, 476.

8. Rowlands, *A Dash of Daring*, 485.

9. Snow, *The World of Carmel Snow*, 3.

10. Rowlands, *A Dash of Daring*, 502.

11. Janet Flanner, "Carmel Snow," *Harper's Bazaar*, July 1961, 46.

12. Cathy Horyn, "Before There Was Vreeland," *New York Times*, December 4, 2005, Section 7, 46.

13. Rowlands, *A Dash of Daring*, 360.

14. Blum, *Shocking!*, 224–25.

15. Blum, *Shocking!*, 225.

16. Blum, *Shocking!*, 254.

17. Berch, *Radical by Design*, 92.

18. Berch, *Radical by Design*, 100.

19. Elizabeth Hawes, *Why Women Cry, or Wenches with Wrenches* (New York: Reynal & Hitchcock, 1943), 179.

20. Hawes, *Why Women Cry*, 160.

21. Berch, *Radical by Design*, 126.

22. Berch, *Radical by Design*, 129.

23. "Talk of the Town: Fashion Show," *New Yorker*, October 30, 1948, 18–19.

24. Berch, *Radical by Design*, 175–76.

25. Bernadine Morris, "Retrospective Showing for Two 'Modern Artists of Dress,'" *New York Times*, April 6, 1967, 34.

26. "Sportswear & Leisure Living: In Retrospect," *WWD*, March 29, 1967, 52–53.

27. "Elizabeth Hawes, Dress Designer, Is Dead at 66," *New York Times*, September 7, 1971.

28. Kirkland, "McCardell," 295.

29. Yohannan and Nolf, *Claire McCardell*, 123.

30. Yohannan and Nolf, *Claire McCardell*, 123, 126.

31. McCardell, *What Shall I Wear?*, 63.

32. Kirkland, "McCardell," 295.

33. Yohannan and Nolf, *Claire McCardell*, 135.

34. Eugenia Sheppard, "Inside Fashion: A Daniel Boone on Seventh Avenue," *WWD*, August 13, 1968, 8.

35. "Humphreys Tops Key Shifts in Lord & Taylor Echelons," *WWD*, February 23, 1970. 8.

36. "Marjorie Griswold," obituary, *The Item of Millburn and Short Hills*, February 28, 1991, 12.

37. "Dorothy Shaver Is Dead at 66; Headed Lord & Taylor Since '45," *New York Times*, June 29, 1959, 1, 29.

38. "Dorothy Shaver Services Are Set for Today," *WWD*, June 30, 1959, 1, 49.

39. Long, "On and Off the Avenue: Feminine Fashions," *New Yorker*, October 25, 1969, 163.

40. Kennedy Fraser, *Ornament and Silence: Essays on Women's Lives from Edith Wharton to Germaine Greer* (New York: Penguin, 1998), 235.

41. Fraser, *Ornament and Silence*, 236.

42. Richard Severo, "Joseph Mitchell, Chronicler of the Unsung and Unconventional, Dies at 87," *New York Times*, May 25, 1996, 12.

43. "Lois Long Is Dead," *New York Times*, July 31, 1974, 36.

44. Gill, *Here at* The New Yorker, 206.

45. Bernadine Morris, "Virginia Pope, 92, Fashion Editor of The Times 22 Years, Is Dead," *New York Times*, January 17, 1978, 36.

46. Mirabella, *In and Out of Vogue*, 130.

47. Dwight, *Diana Vreeland*, 153.

48. Dwight, *Diana Vreeland*, 184.

49. Dwight, *Diana Vreeland*, 159.

50. Dwight, *Diana Vreeland*, 280, 284.

51. Dahl-Wolfe, *A Photographer's Scrapbook*, 145.

52. Ginia Bellafante, "What Louise Dahl-Wolfe's Eye Created in a Lens," *New York Times*, June 6, 2000, B11.

53. Bellafante, "What Louise Dahl-Wolfe's Eye Created," B11.

54. John Tiffany, *Eleanor Lambert: Still Here* (New York: Pointed Leaf, 2011), 303.

SELECTED BIBLIOGRAPHY

Arnold, Rebecca. *The American Look: Fashion, Sportswear and the Image of Women in 1930s and 1940s New York*. London: I. B. Tauris, 2009.

Bacall, Lauren. *By Myself*. New York: Alfred A. Knopf, 1978.

Ballard, Bettina. *In My Fashion*. New York: David McKay, 1960.

Beaton, Cecil. *The Glass of Fashion: A Personal History of Changing Tastes & the People Who Have Inspired Them*. New York: Rizzoli, 2014.

Bender, Marylin. *The Beautiful People*. New York: Coward-McCann, 1967.

Berch, Bettina. *Radical by Design: The Life and Style of Elizabeth Hawes, Fashion Designer, Union Organizer, Best-Selling Author*. New York: E. P. Dutton, 1988.

Berkson, Bill. *Since When: A Memoir in Pieces*. Minneapolis: Coffee House Press, 2018.

Berkson, Moses, dir. *Eleanor: Godmother of American Fashion*. Documentary film, 2013.

Blum, Dilys. *Shocking! The Art and Fashion of Elsa Schiaparelli*. Philadelphia: Philadelphia Museum of Art, 2003.

Buckland, Sandra Stansbery. "Promoting American Designers, 1940–1944: Building Our Own House." In *Twentieth-Century American Fashion*, edited by Linda Welters and Patricia A. Cunningham. Oxford: Berg, 2007.

Burke, Carolyn. *Lee Miller: A Life*. New York: Alfred A. Knopf, 2005.

Cantwell, Mary. *Manhattan, When I Was Young*. New York: Penguin Books, 1996.

Chase, Edna Woolman, and Ilka Chase. *Always in Vogue*. Garden City, NY: Doubleday, 1954.

Chase, Ilka. *Past Imperfect*. Garden City, NY: Blue Ribbon Books, 1945.

Christiansen, Rupert. *City of Light: The Making of Modern Paris*. New York: Basic Books, 2018.

Collins, Amy Fine. *The International Best-Dressed List: The Official Story*. New York: Rizzoli, 2019.

Dahl-Wolfe, Louise. *A Photographer's Scrapbook*. New York: St. Martin's/Marek, 1984.

Daves, Jessica. *Ready-Made Miracle: The Story of American Fashion for the Millions*. New York: G. P. Putnam's Sons, 1967.

DeJean, Joan. *The Essence of Style: How the French Invented High Fashion, Fine Food, Chic Cafés, Style, Sophistication, and Glamour*. New York: Free Press, 2006.

——. *How Paris Became Paris: The Invention of the Modern City*. New York: Bloomsbury, 2015.

Dwight, Eleanor. *Diana Vreeland*. New York: William Morrow, 2002.

Eells, George. *Ginger, Loretta and Irene Who?* New York: G. P. Putnam's Sons, 1976.

Fitz-Gibbon, Bernice. *Macy's, Gimbels, and Me: How to Earn $90,000 a Year in Retail Advertising*. New York: Simon & Schuster, 1967.

Fraser, Kennedy. *The Fashionable Mind: Reflections on Fashion, 1970–1981*. Boston: David R. Godine, 1985.

——. *Ornament and Silence: Essays on Women's Lives from Edith Wharton to Germaine Greer*. New York: Penguin, 1998.

Garelick, Rhonda K. *Mademoiselle: Coco Chanel and the Pulse of History*. New York: Random House, 2014.

Givhan, Robin. *The Battle of Versailles: The Night American Fashion Stumbled into the Spotlight and Made History*. New York: Flatiron Books, 2015.

Gross, Elaine, and Fred Rottman. *Halston: An American Original*. New York: HarperCollins, 1999.

Gross, Michael. *Model: The Ugly Business of Beautiful Women*. New York: Perennial, 2003.

Hawes, Elizabeth. *Fashion Is Spinach*. New York: Random House, 1938.

——. *It's Still Spinach*. Boston: Little, Brown, 1954.

———. *Why Women Cry, or Wenches with Wrenches.* New York: Reynal & Hitchcock, 1943.

Kawamura, Yuniya. *The Japanese Revolution in Paris Fashion.* Oxford: Berg, 2006.

Keith, Slim, with Annette Tapert. *Slim: Memories of a Rich and Imperfect Life.* New York: Simon & Schuster, 1990.

Kirkland, Sally. "McCardell." In *American Fashion: The Life and Lines of Adrian, Mainbocher, McCardell, Norell, and Trigère*, edited by Sarah Tomerlin Lee. New York: Quadrangle, 1975.

———. "Sportswear for Everywhere." In *All-American: A Sportswear Tradition.* New York: Fashion Institute of Technology, 1985.

Levin, Phyllis Lee. *The Wheels of Fashion.* Garden City, NY: Doubleday, 1965.

Martin, Richard. *American Ingenuity: Sportswear, 1930s–1970s.* New York: Metropolitan Museum of Art, 1998.

McCardell, Claire. *What Shall I Wear? The What, Where, When, and How Much of Fashion.* New York: Abrams Image, 2022.

Mears, Patricia. *American Beauty: Aesthetics and Innovation in Fashion.* New Haven: Yale University Press, 2009.

Milbank, Caroline Rennolds. *New York Fashion: The Evolution of American Style.* New York: Harry N. Abrams, 1996.

Mirabella, Grace, with Judith Warner. *In and Out of Vogue: A Memoir.* New York: Doubleday, 1995.

O'Brien, Scott. *Kay Francis: I Can't Wait to Be Forgotten: Her Life on Film and Stage.* Albany, GA: Bear Manor Media, 2007.

Oglesby, Catharine. *Fashion Careers, American Style.* New York: Funk & Wagnalls, 1935.

Rawsthorn, Alice. *Yves Saint Laurent: A Biography.* New York: Doubleday, 1996.

Rowlands, Penelope. *A Dash of Daring: Carmel Snow and Her Life in Fashion, Art, and Letters.* New York: Atria Books, 2005.

Saunders, Edith. *The Age of Worth.* Bloomington: University of Indiana Press, 1955.

Schiaparelli, Elsa. *Shocking Life: The Autobiography of Elsa Schiaparelli.* London: V&A Publishing, 2007.

Secrest, Meryle. *Elsa Schiaparelli: A Biography.* London: Fig Tree, 2014.

Seebohm, Caroline. *The Man Who Was Vogue: The Life and Times of Condé Nast*. New York: Viking Press, 1982.

Snow, Carmel, with Mary Louise Aswell. *The World of Carmel Snow*. New York: McGraw-Hill, 1962.

Steele, Valerie. *Paris Fashion: A Cultural History*. Oxford: Berg, 1999.

———. *Women of Fashion: Twentieth-Century Designers*. New York: Rizzoli, 1991.

Steele, Valerie, ed. *Paris, Capital of Fashion*. London: Bloomsbury Visual Arts, 2019.

Summers, Julie. *Dressed for War: The Story of* Vogue *Editor Audrey Withers, from the Blitz to the Swinging Sixties*. London: Simon & Schuster, 2020.

Taylor, Lou. "Paris Couture, 1940–1944." In *Chic Thrills: A Fashion Reader*, edited by Juliet Ash and Elizabeth Wilson. Berkeley: University of California Press, 1993.

Veillon, Dominique. *Fashion Under the Occupation*. Translated by Miriam Kochan. Oxford: Berg, 2002.

Vreeland, Diana. *D.V.* Edited by George Plimpton and Christopher Hemphill. New York: Alfred A. Knopf, 1984.

Vreeland, Lisa Immordino. *Diana Vreeland: The Eye Has to Travel*. New York: Abrams, 2011.

Weber, Caroline. *Queen of Fashion: What Marie Antoinette Wore to the Revolution*. New York: Picador, 2007.

Wharton, Edith. *The Age of Innocence*. New York: Charles Scribner & Sons, 1968.

Whitaker, Jan. *Service and Style: How the American Department Store Fashioned the Middle Class*. New York: St. Martin's Press, 2006.

White, Nicola. *Reconstructing Italian Fashion: America and the Development of the Italian Fashion Industry*. Oxford: Berg, 2000.

Williams, Beryl. *Fashion Is Our Business*. Philadelphia: J. B. Lippincott, 1945.

Yohannan, Kohle, and Nancy Nolf. *Claire McCardell: Redefining Modernism*. New York: Harry N. Abrams, 1998.

Zeitz, Joshua. *Flapper: A Madcap Story of Sex, Style, Celebrity, and the Women Who Made America Modern*. New York: Crown Publishers, 2006.

INDEX

ABOUT THE AUTHOR

Tamara Beckwith

Nancy MacDonell is a fashion journalist and fashion historian. She writes the column "Fashion with a Past" for *The Wall Street Journal*, in which she explores the historic roots of current fashion trends. Her writing has appeared in *The New York Times, Elle, Vogue,* and many other publications. She is the author of five books, including *The Classic Ten: The True Story of the Little Black Dress and Nine Other Fashion Favorites*. Nancy is an adjunct lecturer in fashion history at the Fashion Institute of Technology. She was born in Montréal and lives in Brooklyn with her family.